HISTORY BY ERA

Prosperity, Depression, and War: 1920–1945

VOLUME 7

Other titles in the American History by Era series:

AMERICAN HISTORY BY ERA

Prosperity, Depression, and War: 1920–1945

VOLUME 7

Laura K. Egendorf, *Book Editor*

Daniel Leone, *President*
Bonnie Szumski, *Publisher*
Scott Barbour, *Managing Editor*

GREENHAVEN
PRESS ®

THOMSON

™

GALE

San Diego • Detroit • New York • San Francisco • Cleveland
New Haven, Conn. • Waterville, Maine • London • Munich

© 2003 by Greenhaven Press. Greenhaven Press is an imprint of The Gale Group, Inc., a division of Thomson Learning, Inc.

Greenhaven® and Thomson Learning™ are trademarks used herein under license.

For more information, contact
Greenhaven Press
27500 Drake Rd.
Farmington Hills, MI 48331-3535
Or you can visit our Internet site at http://www.gale.com

Cover credit: © CORBIS

Library of Congress, 22, 36, 53, 63, 108, 114, 132, 147, 153, 177
National Archives, 219, 228
U.S. Navy, 261

Cover inset photo credits (from left): Planet Art; Corel; Digital Stock; Corel; Library of Congress; Library of Congress; Digital Stock; Painet/Garry Rissman

LIBRARY OF CONGRESS CATALOGING-IN-PUBLICATION DATA

Prosperity, depression, and war: 1920–1945 / Laura K. Egendorf, book editor.
   p. cm. — (American history by era; vol. 7)
   Includes bibliographical references and index.
   ISBN 0-7377-1144-2 (alk. paper) — ISBN 0-7377-1143-4 (pbk. : alk. paper)
   1. United States—History—1919–1933. 2. United States—History—1933–1945.
I. Egendorf, Laura K., 1973– . II. Series.
E784 .P76 2003
973.91—dc21   2002069332

Printed in the United States of America

CONTENTS

to the rise of racist societies such as the Ku Klux Klan that worked to get restrictive immigration laws passed.

sized personal experiences and the merits of democracy while disdaining popular American values such as the obsessions with happiness and automobiles.

Chapter 3: 1929–1933: Depression and Unrest

Chapter 4: 1934–1939: The Turbulence Continues

Chapter 5: 1940–1945: America at War

During the sixteenth century, events occurred in North America that would change the course of American history. In 1512, Spanish explorer Juan Ponce de León led the first European expedition to Florida. French navigator Jean Ribault established the first French colony in America at Fort Caroline in 1564. Over a decade later, in 1579, English pirate Francis Drake landed near San Francisco and claimed the country for England.

These three seemingly random events happened in different decades, occurred in various regions of America, and involved three different European nations. However, each discrete occurrence was part of a larger movement for European dominance over the New World. During the sixteenth century, Spain, France, and England vied for control of what was later to become the United States. Each nation was to leave behind a legacy that would shape the political structure, language, culture, and customs of the American people.

Examining such seemingly disparate events in tandem can help to emphasize the connections between them and generate an appreciation for the larger global forces of which they were a part. Greenhaven Press's American History by Era series provides students with a unique tool for examining American history in a way that allows them to see such connections. This series divides American history—from the time that the first people arrived in the New World from Asia to the September 11, 2001, terrorist attacks—into nine discrete periods. Each volume then presents a collection of both primary and secondary documents that describe the major events of the period in chronological order. This structure provides students with a snapshot of events occurring simultaneously in all parts of America. The reader can then gain an appreciation for the political, social, and cultural movements and trends that shaped the nation. Students reading about the adventures of individual European explorers, for instance, are invited to consider how such expeditions compared in purpose and consequence to earlier and later expeditions. Rather than simply learning that Ponce de León was the first Spaniard to try to colonize Florida, for example, students can begin to understand his expedition in a larger context. Indeed, Ponce's voyage was an extension of Spain's desire to conquer the Caribbean and Mexico, and his expedition was to inspire other Spanish explorers to head north from Hispaniola and New Spain in search of rich empires to conquer.

Another benefit of studying eras is that students can view a "snapshot" of America at any given moment of time and see the various social, cultural, and political events that occurred simultaneously. For example, during the period between 1920 and 1945, Charles Lindbergh became the first to make a solo transatlantic flight, Babe Ruth broke the record for the most home runs in one season, and the United States dropped the atomic bomb on Hiroshima. Random events occurring in post–Cold War America included the torching of the Branch Davidian compound in Waco, Texas, the emergence of the World Wide Web, and the 2000 presidential election debacle in which ballot miscounts in Florida held up election results for weeks.

Each volume in this series offers features to enhance students' understanding of the era of American history under discussion. An introductory essay provides an overview of the period, supplying essential context for the readings that follow. An annotated table of contents highlights the main point of each selection. A more in-depth introduction precedes each document, placing it in its particular historical context and offering biographical information about the author. A thorough chronology and index allow students to quickly reference specific events and dates. Finally, a bibliography opens up additional avenues of research. These features help to make the American History by Era series an extremely valuable tool for students researching the political upheavals, wars, cultural movements, scientific and technological advancements, and other events that mark the unfolding of American history.

I n 1925, President Calvin Coolidge famously declared, "The business of America is business." However, when examining the history of the United States from 1920 to 1945, it may be more accurate to say that the business of America was America. In that quarter-century—which spanned from America's emergence from World War I (which was then known as the Great War) to the Allies' triumph over Germany, Japan, and Italy in World War II—the United States turned inward as Americans began to examine what values and characteristics best defined the nation and its citizens. In some respects, this self-examination had positive effects, as in the memorable literature by authors such as F. Scott Fitzgerald and the unity the nation displayed in World War II. However, the obsession with defining the "true" America also led to violence and bigotry.

America's isolationism began shortly after the end of World War I. Although the United States had not entered the fray until April 6, 1917, nearly three years after the war had begun, it suffered 320,518 casualties, including 116,516 fatalities. The U.S. Senate refused to ratify the Treaty of Versailles, which set the terms for Germany's surrender, and instead negotiated a separate treaty. The senate also rejected President Woodrow Wilson's urging that the United States enter the League of Nations, an international alliance that had been established in 1920 to ensure the continuance of peace. Although the league operated until 1946, its effectiveness was undermined by the United States' refusal to participate fully.

THE 1920S: FEAR OF THE UNKNOWN

In their book *The American Pageant*, Thomas A. Bailey and David M. Kennedy observe, "Bloodied by the war and disillusioned by the peace, Americans turned inward in the 1920s."[1] What many Americans saw as they turned inward was something they considered a serious threat to national security: the influx of communism into American society.

American interest in communism began in 1917 during the Russian Revolution. First, socialist Alexander Kerensky led the overthrow of the czarist regime that March; Kerensky's short-lived rule ended in November when Communist revolutionaries Nikolai Lenin and Leon Trotsky supplanted him. The Bolsheviks intrigued American radicals, especially immigrants who belonged to the Socialist Party. Bolshevik propaganda, such as the *Communist International*, began arriving in the United States in 1919, further raising American interest. By 1919 approximately seventy thousand people belonged to the two major American Communist parties, the Communist Labor Party and the Communist Party. The latter party had sixty thousand members, of whom 90 percent were immigrants. Thus, it was not surprising that when the anti-Communist movement took hold in America shortly after World War I, immigrants were the primary targets in what was known as the "Red Scare."

The Palmer raids of 1919 and 1920—named after their leader, Attorney General A. Mitchell Palmer—were the first indication that the United States was perhaps not as welcoming of its huddled masses as the plaque on the Statue of Liberty might indicate. Palmer's distaste for Socialist and Communist sympathizers was likely due to the bombing of his house in June 1919, presumably by radicals. The first raid was held on November 7, 1919, while the second occurred on January 2, 1920. More than six thousand suspected radicals, primarily eastern European immigrants who belonged (or were believed to belong) to the Communist and Communist Labor Parties, were rounded up in the raids. In many cases, those who had been arrested had no involvement with communism but were nonetheless jailed without being permitted access to attorneys. Most of the arrested were freed, although others were deported.

The fear of immigrants, particularly those who appeared to reject American values such as democracy, led to the Sacco-Vanzetti trial. On May 5, 1920, Nicola Sacco and Bartolomeo Vanzetti were arrested in Massachusetts on charges of attempted robbery and murder. Despite the fact that neither man had a previous criminal record, no discernable motive, and well-supported alibis, they were considered likely suspects because they were Italian immigrants who had dodged the draft and were linked with leading radicals. In his 1927 examination of the trial, Felix Frankfurter—a lawyer and professor who would later be appointed to the Supreme Court—wrote, "The prosecutor systematically played on the feelings of the jury by exploiting the unpatriotic and despised beliefs of Sacco and Vanzetti."[2] Even though it was highly unlikely that the two men committed the crime, they were convicted on July 14, 1921, and sentenced to death. Although Sacco and Vanzetti had considerable support among progressives and radicals, additional evidence to support their innocence, and the acknowledgment by a government-appointed committee that judicial misconduct had occurred during their trial, the sentences were not overturned. The two men were executed on August 23, 1927.

In addition to persecuting immigrants living in America, the United States barred many people from entering the nation. Seeking to end the influx of immigrants from southern and eastern Europe, Congress passed two immigration laws in the 1920s. The Emergency Quota Act of 1921 decreed that an annual maximum of 357,000 immigrants could enter the United States, and it set quotas for the number of immigrants that could be accepted from any particular nation. The Immigration Act of 1924 reduced the total number of immigrants to 164,000. As a result, immigration from northern and western Europe fell from an annual average of 177,000 in 1914 to 141,000 after 1924, a very modest reduction in comparison to immigration from the rest of Europe. Immigration from other parts of Europe plummeted from 685,500 in 1914 to 21,847 a decade later. These quotas did not apply to Canadians or Latin Americans. Japanese were completely barred from immigrating.

ANTI-SEMITISM AND THE KU KLUX KLAN

A subset of European immigrants living in America who faced particular prejudice in the 1920s was Jews. Jews faced discrimination in the workplace and restrictions on where they could live and associations they could join. Quotas limited the number of Jewish students who could enroll in prestigious colleges. The most influential American anti-Semite was industrialist Henry Ford. In 1919 he purchased a newspaper, the *Dearborn Independent*, that published editorials and articles which blamed Jews for World War I and the national debt and alleged the existence of a worldwide Jewish conspiracy. The *Independent* also reprinted *Protocols of the Elders of Zion*, a forgery that claimed to detail the Jewish plan to control the world. In 1927, Ford would apologize for his actions and shut down the *Independent*, but he would later express admiration for Adolf Hitler, whose policies resulted in the extermination of 6 million European Jews.

While Henry Ford used the press to espouse his views, others chose to take extralegal actions against those who were not considered properly "American." In particular, the Ku Klux Klan grew extraordinarily popular in the 1920s. The Klan, whose members were primarily white Protestant males, had formed during the Reconstruction. The organization sought to destroy the Republican governments that had developed in southern states following the Civil War and had guaranteed the political and civil rights of freed slaves. The Klan objected to these new rights and engaged in acts of violence to prevent former slaves and their white supporters from voting. In the Klan's eyes, the only true Americans were white and Protestant. By the end of World War I, the Klan included immigrants, Jews, and Catholics among its enemies.

By 1924, Klan membership had reached 5 million. Its members burned crosses, held parades (including one held in Washington, D.C., in 1925 that drew thirty thousand Klan members), and performed a number of violent acts in order to publicize their beliefs. People who were believed to transgress the Klan's moral code—namely, those who were members of, or associated with, races and creeds that the Klan considered un-American— were beaten, sometimes fatally, lynched, tarred and feathered, and whipped. However, by decade's end the Klan had lost much of its power and popularity as the general population became sickened by the Klan's violence; congressional investigation of embezzlement by Klan officials further damaged whatever influence the organization might have still had.

1920S LITERATURE AND MUSIC

The isolationist tendency of the 1920s was not restricted to Klan members and opponents of immigration. Some of the most detailed examinations of American culture and the way it stood apart from the rest of the world can be found in the literature of the 1920s. Among the authors who addressed the issue of what it meant to be an American were F. Scott Fitzgerald, Sinclair Lewis, Ernest Hemingway, and the authors of the Harlem Renaissance.

Fitzgerald embodied the "Roaring Twenties." He was young, handsome, successful, and wed to the clever and pretty (but deeply troubled) Zelda Sayre. His books dealt with the lives of similarly young and rich characters. In his landmark novel, *The Great Gatsby*, Fitzgerald examines the American trope of "rags to riches" and its often-tragic consequences.

As most readers know, *The Great Gatsby* is the story of how the lower-class James Gatz transforms himself into the wealthy Jay Gatsby in order to win the heart of Daisy, his former girlfriend who is now wed to the rich and brutish Tom Buchanan. However, by novel's end Daisy has remained with Tom, and Gatsby, along with several other characters that entered the Buchanans' world, is dead. The novel's narrator, Nick Carraway, survives but is disappointed by the shallow lives of his former friends. *The Great Gatsby* examines why the American dream of success cannot always be realized. In his article, "Scott Fitzgerald's Criticism of America," Marius Bewley writes: "*The Great Gatsby* embodies a criticism of American experience . . . more radical than anything in [Henry] James's own assessment of the deficiencies of his country. The theme of *Gatsby* is the withering of the American dream."[3] During this time of isolationism, America was fixated on itself, and authors like Fitzgerald pointed out that this fixation with being an American did not always lead to happiness.

While Fitzgerald painted a tragic and romantic look at the American success story, Sinclair Lewis took a more satirical approach. During the 1920s, Americans were steadily moving away from the country and into the city and suburbs. Lewis's novels *Babbitt* and *Main Street* mocked the prejudices and closed-mindedness of middle-class businessmen and small town matrons. In his essay "Lewis's Satire—A Negative Emphasis," Daniel R. Brown writes: "Most of Lewis's assaults were upon standardization, religious provinciality, narrow-mindedness, and hypocrisy."[4] Lewis's works describe the common features of suburban America, from expensive shops to influential churches to zealous chambers of commerce. In his view, the move away from rural life had led to an America that, while considerably wealthier, had become increasingly materialistic, monotonous, and lacking any real values. His books showed that an isolationist America, closed off from ideas that did not mesh with the middle-class paradigm, was not the best setting for intellectual flowering.

Ernest Hemingway was more interested in the experiences of Americans living in Europe, both during and after World War I. At the same time, he also expressed his concern about the influx of immigrants into the United States in the novel *The Sun Also Rises*. In her essay "(Re)Teaching Hemingway: Anti-Semitism as a Thematic Device in *The Sun Also Rises*," Gay Wilentz writes: "[The] novel is a response to what Hemingway saw as a breakdown of values. . . . It is truly a cultural document illustrating mainstream Americans' irrational fears of a multi-cultural, industrial society."[5]

The literary world of the 1920s was a high point for African American writers as well. The collective works of these authors are part of what is known as the Harlem Renaissance, named for the New York City neighborhood. These writers, many of whom would write well into the 1940s, found themselves in an America in which the African American middle class was expanding. There was also a growing demand for racial equality. Sean Dennis Cashman suggests that the works of the Harlem Renaissance "expressed the conflict of values in society between old and new, countryside and town, following World War I and artists' alienation from small town bourgeois society."[6] For these authors, isolationism was taken one step further than their white counterparts took it, as major works of the Harlem Renaissance often centered on a world that had little interaction with whites. The major authors and works included James Weldon Johnson, a leader of the National Association for the Advancement of Colored People, who published books of spirituals, sermons, and a poetry anthology; Alain Locke, whose 1925 work *The New Negro: An Interpretation* consisted of stories, poems, articles, and essays, and whose writing was optimistic about the future of African Americans; Claude McKay, who published *Harlem Shadow*, a collection of poetry, in 1922 and the novel *Home to Harlem* in 1928; and Langston Hughes, whose poems borrowed from jazz and black folk music rhythms and whose works included *Weary Blues* and *The Ways of White Folks*. Prominent female writers of the Harlem Renaissance included Zora Neale Hurston, whose works, including *Their Eyes Were Watching God*, depicted African Americans living apart from white society and Jessie Fauset, who wrote about the lives of middle-class African Americans in novels such as *Chinaberry Tree*.

The African American contribution to 1920s' culture went beyond literature, however. One of the decade's monikers is the

"Jazz Age," after the uniquely American music that provided the soundtrack for the decade. Jazz was a variation of ragtime that emphasized improvisation and spontaneity. In its own way, jazz was an isolationist force, as it rebelled against Old World formality and conventional European instrumentation. J.A. Rogers wrote of the music: "The true spirit of jazz is a joyous revolt from convention."[7] Radio and phonograph records helped the music of artists such as W.C. Handy, Louis Armstrong, Bessie Smith, and Duke Ellington spread from the South to the rest of the nation, particularly Chicago, Kansas City, and New York City. Jazz orchestras, whose leaders included Paul Whiteman and Sam Stewart, were also popular.

THE BUSINESS OF AMERICA IS BUSINESS

In their way, American authors, musicians, and anti-immigration organizations sought to explain what it meant to be an American. However, what truly defined the American way of life in the 1920s was the endless drive for prosperity. Although there was a significant recession in 1920 and 1921, and smaller doldrums in 1924 and 1927, the 1920s was overall a picture of rosy economic health.

According to Lynn Dumenil, author of *The Modern Temper*, "The twenties . . . embodies much of what constitutes consumer culture: [such as] the cornucopia of material goods."[8] What Americans wanted to spend their money on were items that would allow them to see and hear more of their fellow citizens. Between 1919 and 1929, the number of passenger cars in the nation nearly quadrupled, from 6,771,000 to 23,121,000. By the end of the decade, more than $842 million was spent on radios. With radio, people could hear news from around the nation, the latest in popular music, and college football games. In a sense, cars and radios made a sprawling nation smaller. With Americans able to travel across the country with relative speed and ease, or listen to sports events taking place a dozen states away, there was even less reason to be interested in the goings-on of the rest of the world.

Not surprisingly, a boom in industrial productivity accompanied this increase in consumer spending. Between 1920 and 1930, industrial production increased 64 percent. Assembly lines, which Ford had popularized at his automobile factories, helped make this rapid increase in production possible. Indeed, business was the centerpiece of American life, as the earlier quote by Coolidge indicated. In those heady days, people believed that there were almost no problems that could not be solved with American capitalism—to doubt American business was to doubt America.

Another sign of economic good times was that everyone invested in the stock market, or so it seemed. According to William K. Klingaman, "It seemed almost unpatriotic *not* to invest in the market."[9] Participation in the stock market was not limited to men; by 1929, women made up 20 percent of all investors. Between March 1, 1928, and March 1, 1929, more than one billion shares were traded. Only five years earlier, 280 million shares had been traded.

However, not everyone benefited from America's seemingly permanent wealth. Dumenil writes, "Family income, race, and ethnicity mediated between working-class people and consumer culture and made their participation in it ambiguous and complex."[10] Even assuming that they could find steady work, unskilled workers—especially women, immigrants, and African Americans—were unable to earn incomes that were large enough to purchase cars and other more costly consumer goods. By October 1929, no matter how hard Americans worked, the prosperity could not be maintained. In a matter of days, the stock market tumbled and ended America's ostensible economic invincibility.

THE BOTTOM FALLS OUT

One reason why the market crashed was that it was too easy to buy stocks. In Stud Terkel's *Hard Times*, a collection of reminiscences about the Great Depression, industrialist Arthur A. Robeson remembered: "Today, if you want to buy $100 worth of stock, you have to put up $80 and the broker will put up $20. In those days, you could put up $8 or $10. That was really responsible for the collapse."[11] Other reasons that have been cited include a trade imbalance, weak corporate and banking structures, and the government's lack of useful economic knowledge.

October 1929 was, at that time, the worst month ever for the New York Stock Exchange; the Dow Jones fell thirty-one points on October 29, hitting a new low for the year. In a matter of days, the prosperity of the 1920s had vanished. The market lost $50 billion that month, including $15 billion on October 29 alone. Within five months unemployment more than doubled, from 1.5 million to 3.2 million. The sharp decline of the U.S.

A crowd gathers outside the New York Stock Exchange following the October 29, 1929, crash.

economy continued into the early 1930s. By the spring of 1932, 12 million Americans were unemployed. Businesses and banks collapsed like the proverbial house of cards; a total of 3,646 banks and 54,640 businesses failed in 1930 and 1931. America's identity and its prosperity had been intertwined since the end of World War I, but with the onset of the Great Depression, that symbiosis came to an end.

The man on whom the responsibility of ending the depression fell was Herbert Hoover, who had been inaugurated president in January 1929 after defeating Democratic candidate Al Smith in the 1928 election. Hoover wanted to encourage business activity, so he sought tax reductions and an expansion in exports. He also authorized $700 million in public works projects. After initial reluctance, Hoover approved the Reconstruction Finance Corporation, which provided emergency loans to railroads, banks, life insurance companies, farm mortgage associations, and building and loan associations. However, Hoover also signed the Hawley-Smoot Tariff in 1930. The act was intended to strengthen American industries by placing a high tariff on imports; in other words, the United States attempted economic isolationism. The policy backfired, leading to an even worse—and now worldwide—depression because European factories could no longer afford to export, and Europe did not have enough consumers to purchase all its own goods.

With unemployment worsening, American distrust of outsiders, especially Mexican immigrants, increased. According to T.H. Watkins, "Unemployment among Anglo workers could be blamed on the presence of a labor force willing to work cheap and under conditions 'real' American workers would not tolerate—the Mexican Americans."[12] Numerous white workers turned to discrimination and intimidation, which led to the departure of thousands of immigrants.

With his policies failing to put a dent in the Great Depression, Herbert Hoover found himself a one-term president. As Albert U. Romasco explained, "By mid-1932, [Hoover] was the figure hindering the nation in its search for new ways to master the problem which had eluded all his exertions."[13] He was defeated in the 1932 presidential election by Democratic candidate Franklin Delano Roosevelt, a cousin of former president Theodore Roosevelt and the governor of New York.

THE NEW DEAL BEGINS

Roosevelt's immediate focus was the American economy. In a series of laws and programs passed with astonishing speed, FDR aimed to return the nation to its former economic strength. His domestic relief package was known as the New Deal. Legislation enacted within the first one hundred days of his inauguration included the Emergency Banking Relief Act; the Civilian Conservation Corps, which by 1942 provided 3 million jobs for men between the ages of eighteen and twenty-five; the Agricultural Adjustment Act; the establishment of the Federal Emergency Relief Administration; the creation of the Tennessee Valley Authority, which established flood control, built dams, and generated and sold electricity; the Federal Securities Act; the creation of the Securities and Exchange Commission; and the establishment of the National Industrial Recovery Act and the Federal Deposit Insurance Corporation.

The New Deal did not end after three months. In late 1933, Roosevelt established the Civil Works Administration. Although it would only last until March 31, 1934, the CWA employed more than 1 million people. The men who participated built and repaired roads, schools, parks, airports, and hospitals, while the women were employed in tasks such as nursing, housekeeping, sewing, and secretarial work. The National Youth Administration, founded in July 1935, provided employment on public works projects, vocational guidance, and job training and placement for sixteen- to twenty-five-year-olds who had graduated from or dropped out of high school. It also offered part-time employment for high school and college students. Congress approved the Social Security Act in August 1935, guaranteeing an income for retirees and widows.

The New Deal programs did not meet with universal support. Some people, like journalist H.L. Mencken, argued that the New Deal had failed to increase the incomes of the poorest Americans and had not reduced the national debt. A leading critic was the Roman Catholic priest Charles Edward Coughlin, who delivered his views on Roosevelt's policy in weekly radio broadcasts. In one address, Coughlin suggested tax reforms to ease the burden of poor Americans and the replacement of the Federal Reserve Banking System with a government-owned Central Bank. He declared, "If the financial debauchery, resultant from the Federal Reserve credit inflation, is any criterion upon which to gauge the future, history has proven eloquently but sadly that it is impossible to cure ourselves or our multiple maladies by placing confidence in the quack panacea of Federal Reserve dictatorship."[14]

Although largely interested in economic policies, the president did not neglect culture in his New Deal programs. The Works Progress Administration's Federal Writers Project provided jobs for sixty-five hundred writers, reporters, scholars, and teachers. The WPA also founded the Federal Theater Project. Twelve thousand people in New York, Boston, Chicago, Los Angeles, and New Orleans were hired to produce and act in inexpensive plays, musicals, and operas. Among the discoveries of the FTP was a young writer, actor, and director named Orson Welles. However, the WPA was not the be-all and end-all of American literature and culture in the 1930s. Books by the popular writers of the 1920s continued to be well received, while new authors made their mark on the literary landscape. As had been the case a decade earlier, the greatest of America's writers remained fascinated with what it meant to live and survive in the United States. Two of these authors were John Steinbeck, whose novels *Of Mice and Men* and *The Grapes of Wrath* described the lives of people seeking employment and economic security in California, and William Faulkner, who focused on

the South in books such as *As I Lay Dying* and *Absalom, Absalom!*
Roosevelt's efforts benefited millions of Americans, but not
all. African Americans, particularly those who lived in the Deep
South, found themselves unable to participate in many of the
New Deal programs. African American women typically found
themselves hired to work on farms or as domestic laborers, jobs
ineligible for Social Security benefits. Despite the horrors of
lynching (277 such crimes took place between 1922 and 1934),
Congress failed to approve antilynching legislation several
times during the 1930s. However, African Americans did make
considerable strides in government, as Roosevelt hired more
African Americans than any other president. African American
delegates participated in the Democratic national convention
for the first time in 1936.

By 1937, many supporters of Roosevelt's policies believed
that the depression was over. Among the signs of an improved
economy were gains in personal income, employment, and industrial production. Between spring 1933 and fall 1937, unemployment fell from 12.8 million to 7.7 million, and the average
annual income for a factory worker rose from $1,086 to $1,376.
However, a recession at year's end dashed hopes that the depression would soon be a memory. The unemployment rolls increased by 4 million names.

STAYING OUT OF THE WORLD'S PROBLEMS

By increasingly turning inward during the 1930s, in part as a result of economic problems at home, Americans were remarkably unfazed by tumultuous events occurring elsewhere in the
world. From 1936 to 1939, Spain was embroiled in a civil war
that pitted the Loyalist government against the Fascists; the latter group, led by General Francisco Franco, was victorious. In
1931 Japan invaded China and seized Manchuria, while Italy
conquered Ethiopia in 1935. Most troubling was the fact that a
failed artist from Austria had become the most powerful man
in Germany. Adolf Hitler became chancellor of Germany in
1933, and it was soon clear that he intended to expand his
power well beyond the nation's borders. On March 7, 1936, German troops occupied the Rhineland, a region in western Germany that had been occupied by Allied troops after World
War I. Two years later Germany invaded Austria and announced that the nations were uniting. In September 1938,
France, Great Britain, and Germany signed the Munich Pact,

transferring the Sudetenland from Czechoslovakia to Germany; five months later, Germany took over the rest of Czechoslovakia. World War II would be less than six months away.

American politicians wanted to avoid the problems in Europe, Asia, and Africa. In 1935, Congress passed the first Neutrality Act. The act banned loans to belligerent nations while encouraging noninvolvement in foreign affairs. The second Neutrality Act was approved in 1937. In addition to banning loans to belligerent nations, it also forbade the selling of arms. Roosevelt expressed the sentiments of most Americans, who did not want to see their sons sent overseas, in a radio address when he declared, "The common sense, the intelligence of the people of America agree with my statement that 'America hates war. America hopes for peace. Therefore, America actively engages in the search for peace.'"[15]

ANOTHER WORLD WAR BEGINS

America was initially an uninvolved observer during World War II, with Roosevelt declaring the nation's neutrality on September 5, 1939. He had the support of his citizens; in a September 1939 poll, 70 percent of those surveyed favored neutrality. In contrast, Great Britain, France, New Zealand, and Australia declared war on Germany on September 3, with Canada following suit one week later.

The overall bent toward neutrality in America was manifested in a strong isolationist movement in 1940 and 1941. The most powerful of these organizations was the America First Committee (AFC), which at its peak had eight hundred thousand members. Although the AFC had some pro-Nazi and pro-Fascist members, most of its participants opposed American involvement in World War II because of distrust of Europeans, concern over the horrors of war, and the fear that intervention could lead to the spread of fascism, communism, and socialism. The AFC's most famous member was aviation hero Charles Lindbergh. Two weeks after Germany invaded Poland, Lindbergh gave a radio address in which he declared that the United States should not join the conflict. Believing the United States could not enter the war and win, he joined AFC in early 1941 and resigned from the army later that spring. However, when the United States decided to enter the war, Lindbergh decided to return to his military career. His request to reenlist was denied, but he did serve as a civilian adviser to the U.S. Army and Navy in the Pacific, even flying fifty combat missions, and was a test pilot for the Ford Motor Company and United Aircraft Corporation.

THROWING ASIDE THE ISOLATIONIST CLOAK

As events in Europe and elsewhere in the world worsened, America found it increasingly difficult to maintain its isolationist stance. On November 4, 1939, Roosevelt signed a revision of the Neutrality Act that lifted the arms embargo. Britain was the first country to benefit from the end of the embargo; by June 1940 it would be the only nation in western Europe that had not joined the Axis or surrendered to the Nazis. On December 17, 1940, Roosevelt proposed a "lend-lease" aid program, which would permit the United States to send supplies to Great Britain and any other nation facing Nazi aggression. The Lend-Lease Act became law on March 11, 1941. Other steps that indicated the United States would not remain neutral much longer included the passage of the first peacetime draft in American history in September 1940 and the nation's decision in July 1941 to cease trading with Japan following the latter country's occupation of French Indochina. In taking steps to aid European nations that were victims of Nazi aggression, the United States was drawn further into the conflict. For example, when American ships broadcast the locations of German boats to the British Royal Navy, Germany attacked several U.S. vessels. The deadliest of these attacks was the sinking of the USS *Reuben James* in the North Atlantic on October 28, 1941. More than one hundred crewmembers died in the attack.

The United States took its final steps into the war on December 7, 1941, after a surprise attack by the Japanese on the American naval facilities at Pearl Harbor in Hawaii. The attack destroyed or damaged 21 vessels, killed 2,388 people, and wounded another 2,000 troops. The next day, Congress declared war on Japan. Three days later, Germany and Italy declared war on the United States. Barely two years after Americans were overwhelmingly against entering the imbroglio, the most powerful nation in the world was throwing its full weight behind the Allied forces. It was a decision that would spark a wartime recovery of the struggling economy and unite an entire nation.

UNITING BEHIND THE WAR

World War II redefined what it meant to be an American—although some isolationists continued to speak out against U.S.

involvement, most Americans wholeheartedly supported the war effort. As Geoffrey Perrett asserted in his book *Days of Sadness, Years of Triumph: The American People 1939–1945*, "In the unity of wartime, a disparate people was fused into a community, and that community was cemented in victory."[16] Sixteen million American men were mobilized for military service; more than 10 million of them went overseas (407,318 of whom died). Even the wealthiest and most famous of men—Jimmy Stewart, Clark Gable, and Ted Williams among them—enlisted, many winning medals and commendations for their accomplishments. For those who could not join the military, there was scrap metal to be collected, Victory gardens to be planted, bonds to be purchased, blood to be donated. The jobs that had been filled by now-enlisted men went to women. During World War II, the number of working women in the United States rocketed from 12 million to 19 million. By the end of 1943, 5 million women were employed in the war industries, helping to build planes, ships, and weapons.

Hollywood played a major role in uniting America behind the war effort. In addition to producing feature-length films about World War II, the studios produced training and orientation films for military recruits. All these films were created with the help of the Office of War Information (OWI), which Roosevelt established as the umbrella organization for all government press and information services. The OWI had a particular vision for wartime films. As Thomas Doherty, author of *Projections of War: Hollywood, American Culture, and World War II*, explained, OWI "doted on collective villainy [and] preferred group heroism."[17] World War II films invariably featured a band of men from disparate cultures and backgrounds who came together to conquer their German, Japanese, and Italian enemies.

INTERNMENT CAMPS AND ANTI-SEMITISM

And yet, despite the apparent unity among all Americans, certain groups—in particular Jews and Japanese Americans—were considered suspect. From the beginning, America's isolationist tendencies had manifested themselves in racism and anti-Semitism. Anti-Semitism was a larger problem during World War II than it had been twenty years earlier. Fear of immigrants led to the passage of more restrictive laws in 1939 and 1941. One group that was especially affected by these new restrictions was European Jews, who, suffering under Nazi rule, wanted to emigrate to America. David S. Wyman, in his book *The Abandonment of the Jews: America and the Holocaust, 1941–1945*, cites anti-Semitism as a major factor in Americans' growing distaste for immigrants and refugees. He writes, "The plain truth is that many Americans were prejudiced against Jews and were unlikely to support measures to help them."[18]

Jews who had already immigrated to the United States were also affected by America's isolationist fears. Numerous Jews and synagogues, largely in the Northeast, were attacked during the war. Many people falsely claimed that American Jews were shirking their military responsibility and refusing to enlist, while poll results indicated that a majority of Americans felt that Jews had too much power. It was perhaps for those reasons that, despite knowledge of the Holocaust, the American government made no effort to rescue Europe's Jews until 1944.

However, the American population that suffered the most during World War II was Japanese Americans. The attack on Pearl Harbor sparked fears that Japanese Americans living on the West Coast were serving as spies for their mother country. In what was arguably the greatest violation of American civil liberties during wartime, Roosevelt signed Executive Order 9066 on February 19, 1942. The order authorized the evacuation of all Japanese Americans living on the West Coast and in Arizona. They were first sent to one of fifteen assembly camps, and then to one of ten relocation camps located in California, Arizona, Arkansas, Wyoming, Idaho, and Colorado. Between ten thousand and twenty-five thousand Japanese Americans lived in each camp, often under unhealthy conditions and with inadequate diets. Hiro Mizushima, a resident of one of the camps, remembered: "They called it a relocation camp, but it was a concentration camp. There was barbed wire. They told us the machine guns were to protect us, but the machine guns were pointing toward us."[19]

TRUMAN TAKES OVER: A NEW ROLE FOR AMERICA

Executive Order 9066 is considered by many people to be one of the more regrettable moments of Franklin Delano Roosevelt's presidency, which was the longest in American history. He was president when the war began, during the low points such as the losses in the Philippines in spring 1942, and during the triumphs of Italy's surrender, the successful invasion of Normandy, and the liberation of Paris. However, he did not live to see the Allied forces complete their triumph. Roosevelt, who had long been in ailing health, died of a cerebral hemorrhage on April 12, 1945, and was succeeded by his vice president Harry S. Truman. The fighting in Europe concluded within one month of Truman's inauguration; Hitler committed suicide in his bunker on April 30 and Germany surrendered one week later.

Three months after Germany's surrender, Truman was faced with one of the toughest decisions any president has ever had to make. The atomic bomb had been in development since 1939. By summer 1945, Truman and his advisers believed that Japan would not surrender and that the only way to end the war was to drop the bomb. The first bomb fell on Hiroshima on August 6; the second bomb targeted Nagasaki three days later. This decision made it clear how swiftly the United States had moved away from the isolationism and disinterest in military affairs that marked the two decades following World War I. As a result of America's dropping the atomic bomb, Japan surrendered unconditionally on August 14. World War II officially ended on September 2, 1945, when Japan signed final surrender terms on the American battleship *Missouri*.

The Allied victory solidified the United States' position as the most powerful democracy in the world. Isolation may have been possible before 1941, but the events of World War II proved that Americans would no longer be able to spend all their time looking inward. The introspection and obsession over American identity that had filled the lives of citizens in the 1920s and 1930s were replaced by the recognition that to be Americans meant opening the doors and seeing the world before them.

NOTES

1. Thomas A. Bailey and David M. Kennedy, *The American Pageant: A History of the Republic*. Vol. 2. Lexington, MA: D.C. Heath, 1994, p. 745.

2. Felix Frankfurter, *The Case of Sacco and Vanzetti: A Critical Analysis for Lawyers and Laymen*. Boston: Little, Brown, 1927, p. 46.

3. Marius Bewley, "Scott Fitzgerald's Criticism of America," *Sewanee Review*, April–June 1954, p. 223.

4. Daniel R. Brown, "Lewis's Satire—A Negative Emphasis," *Renascence*, Winter 1966, p. 63.

5. Gay Wilentz, "(Re)Teaching Hemingway: Anti-Semitism as a Thematic Device in *The Sun Also Rises*," *College English*, February 1990, p. 192.

6. Sean Dennis Cashman, *America in the Twenties and Thirties: The Olympian Age of Franklin Delano Roosevelt*. New York: New York University Press, 1989, pp. 278–79.

7. J.A. Rogers, "Jazz at Home," *Survey*, March 1, 1925, p. 665.

8. Lynn Dumenil, *The Modern Temper: American Culture and Society in the 1920s*. New York: Hill and Wang, 1995, p. 57.

9. William K. Klingaman, *1929: The Year of the Great Crash*. New York: Harper and Row, 1989, p. 60.

10. Dumenil, *The Modern Temper*, p. 78.

11. Arthur A. Robeson, quoted in Studs Terkel, *Hard Times: An Oral History of the Great Depression*. New York: Pantheon Books, 1970, p. 65.

12. T.H. Watkins, *The Great Depression: America in the 1930s*. Boston: Little, Brown, 1993, p. 69.

13. Albert U. Romasco, *The Poverty of Abundance: Hoover, the Nation, the Depression*. New York: Oxford University Press, 1965, p. 233.

14. Charles Coughlin, "Program Not a Panacea," radio broadcast, March 24, 1935.

15. Franklin D. Roosevelt, radio address, October 12, 1937.

16. Geoffrey Perrett, *Days of Sadness, Years of Triumph: The American People 1939–1945*. New York: Coward, McCann, and Geoghegan, 1973, p. 433.

17. Thomas Doherty, *Projections of War: Hollywood, American Culture, and World War II*. New York: Columbia University Press, 1993, p. 123.

18. David S. Wyman, *The Abandonment of the Jews: America and the Holocaust, 1941–1945*. New York: Pantheon Books, 1984, p. 9.

19. Hiro Mizushima, quoted in Deborah Gesensway and Mindy Roseman, *Beyond Words: Images from America's Concentration Camps*. Ithaca, NY: Cornell University Press, 1987, p. 84.

1920–1924: An Age of Political and Social Tumult

| CHAPTER 1 |

WOMEN'S SUFFRAGE AND ITS IMMEDIATE AFTERMATH

SARAH JANE DEUTSCH

In July 1848, the attendees of a women's rights convention in Seneca Falls, New York, decided that their primary goal should be to win the right to vote. For the next seven decades, women such as Susan B. Anthony, Elizabeth Cady Stanton, and Lucy Stone helped lead the campaign for women's suffrage. Between 1893 and 1918, fourteen states gave women the vote. The campaign culminated on August 18, 1920, with the ratification of the Nineteenth Amendment to the U.S. Constitution, which stated, "The right of citizens of the United States to vote shall not be denied or abridged by the United States or by any State on account of sex."

Sarah Jane Deutsch examines the effects of women's suffrage during the early 1920s in the following selection. In the first two years of suffrage, women were electing other women to public office, organizing political movements, and gaining civil liberties. However, by 1924, women were not voting as a united force and had found it difficult to win further political power. Deutsch is a women's studies professor at Clark University in Worcester, Massachusetts, and the author of *From Ballots to Breadlines: American Women, 1920–1940*, from which the following selection was excerpted.

Sarah Jane Deutsch, *From Ballots to Breadlines: American Women, 1920–1940*. New York: Oxford University Press, 1994. Copyright © 1994 by Oxford University Press. Reproduced by permission.

I t was August 1920, and Tennessee's legislature was debating the national woman suffrage amendment. Tennessee's ratification would put the number of states needed to ratify the 19th Amendment over the top (the Constitution required approval by three-fourths of the state legislatures) and women across the country would have the right to vote. "It's hot, muggy, nasty, and this last battle is desperate," wrote Carrie Chapman Catt, leader of the main national woman suffrage organization. Mrs. Catt had arrived in Tennessee in July with an overnight bag and stayed five weeks to ensure victory.

SUFFRAGE IS OBTAINED

Suffrage opponents threatened legislators with ruin if they voted for ratification, and suffragists like Catt haunted the railroad stations to make sure their male allies did not flee the town. According to one historian, it all came down to Harry Burn. He came from a rural district in east Tennessee where the political leaders opposed ratification. But he was the youngest member of the legislature, and his mother, a staunch suffragist, had written her son: "Hurrah! And vote for suffrage and don't keep them in doubt. . . . Don't forget to be a good boy and help Mrs. Catt put 'Rat' in Ratification." Thanks to Burn, the amendment carried, by a vote of 49 to 47. On August 26, 1920, the governor of Tennessee certified the state's ratification of the 19th Amendment. Catt declared, "We are no longer petitioners, we are not wards of the nation, but free and equal citizens."

After 70 years of ups and downs, of local victories but many defeats, suffragists had learned to work on a number of levels at once and to benefit from a loosely knit set of coalitions. They had campaigned door to door, organizing women into political parties precinct by precinct. They had dared to hold open-air meetings on street corners. They had organized vast parades. Some had chained themselves to the White House fence to protest fighting for democracy abroad when it was lacking at home. Others had lobbied senators and representatives in their chambers. Some had tried to bridge racial gulfs; others avoided them. Some had even argued for women's votes on racial and ethnic grounds, so that, with the help of native-born white women, native-born white voters could outnumber voters of color and immigrants. However, African-American women and Latinas had long fought for the vote as well. They occasionally could join organizations led by white women, but more often they had their own organizations. Suffragists came in every style, race, and ethnicity, and for this one moment, they came together in the largest women's movement up to that time.

And then, suddenly, it was over. What had the victory meant? By the end of the 1920s, this united power of American womanhood seemed scarcely visible. The promises of unity would not be met in succeeding decades. During the 1920s, the country moved from an era of intense, collective action by women on behalf of women to an era when women's groups had little visibility and limited validity in the eyes of most people. It was not clear whether gaining the vote had liberated women or whether liberation had changed its meaning.

TWO BASIC ARGUMENTS

Suffragists had argued for giving women the vote on a wide range of grounds, but there were two basic camps. One claimed that justice demanded that women, as humans equal to men, have equal rights. In 1892, Elizabeth Cady Stanton was a suffrage leader; her home state of New York assumed that as a married woman with children she had a husband voting for her interests. Mrs. Stanton disputed that idea in front of Congress. "The individuality of each human soul," she insisted, "the right of individual conscience and judgment; our republican idea of individual citizenship" all demanded that women "have the same rights as all other members [of the country], according to the fundamental principles of government."

By the second decade of [the twentieth] century, however, Stanton's argument was fading. Whereas Stanton and others had argued that women deserved the vote simply because, like men, they were fully adult citizens, other suffragists argued that women deserved the vote precisely because they were *not* like men. Men had led us into war and corrupt government; women would nurture us into a more peaceful, ordered existence. Women would vote political machines out of office, would further refine the social welfare agencies they had already helped establish in many cities, and would eradicate the traffic in liquor and prostitution. Some people called the argument that women's votes would benefit society expedient, claiming that suffragists used such an argument because it would not threaten prevailing views of womanhood and the differences between women and men.

With these arguments dominant, Americans had high expectations of woman suffrage. The world, they were convinced, would be a different place once women had the vote. After 1920, politicians began to respond more carefully to women's grievances.

POLITICAL AND LEGISLATIVE VICTORIES

For a time, it seemed safest to do so. Yoncalla, Oregon, woke up after the election of 1920 to a "feminist revolution," according to one journalist. In this town of 323 residents, men outnumbered women by almost two to one, but the *Literary Digest* reported that the women had "risen in their wrath, stirred by the alleged inefficiency of the municipal officials, and swept every masculine office-holder out of his job." The women of the town had worked in absolute secrecy, not even telling their brothers and husbands. Only the town's women were in on the secret, and they prevailed at the polls. Mrs. Mary Burt, a university graduate, was the new mayor. She had lived in Yoncalla for 40 years and had long been active in the community. Also elected to the town government was Mrs. Laswell, wife of the ousted mayor. The only thing Mr. Laswell and his assistants could find to tell the press was that they were "much surprised."

At the other end of the country, in Washington, D.C., a spate of legislative and other victories also greeted women. The

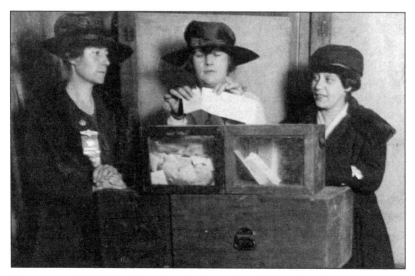

Women cast their ballots for the first time following the passage of the Nineteenth Amendment.

women's peace movement succeeded in getting the United States to host and participate in an international disarmament conference in 1921. The Cable Act of 1922 gave married women independent citizenship; no longer would women who married foreigners lose their United States citizenship. And the Women's Bureau of the federal government, created during the war to look after the interests of women workers, became a permanent part of the Department of Labor in 1920.

Women streamed into public office in the 1920s, the largest single increase in women's officeholding to that date, leveling off only after 1930. The Democrats and Republicans began to mandate equal representation of men and women on party committees. Altogether, these achievements covering peace, politics, labor, health care, and the home seemed to indicate a wide acceptance of women's significance in the public arena.

AN INEFFECTIVE USE OF POWER

Yet by 1924 popular magazines were running articles (written by men) with such titles as "Is Woman Suffrage a Failure?" and "Women's Ineffective Use of the Vote." There were signs, even early on, that not all was going according to plan. The only woman in Congress in 1921, Alice Robertson, was an anti-suffragist. Women vastly increased their numbers in office, but the meaning of that increase must be set in a wider context. In 1924, there were 84 women legislators in 30 states. Five years later there were 200, an increase of almost 250 percent. But while there were 200 women in office, there were 10,000 men. The numbers were similar at other levels of government. In New Jersey, for example, only 19 of 788 county officeholders were women. At the federal level, there were just 10 women in Congress in 1926; that year only two women were reelected to Congress in their own right, and only one was elected without the benefit of having completed a dead family member's term. The gains women sought could obviously not rely on strength at the top.

Political parties were reluctant to nominate women for offices that mattered. After arguing for so long that they were above politics, that they were interested in human welfare, not part of self-serving party political machines, women would have to prove to the men controlling political parties that they knew how to play the game. They had to prove that they could be loyal to the party and not just to principles. They had to prove that they represented a separate constituency, a group of voters they could mobilize to support them.

But women did not vote as a block. The fragments that had come together for the suffrage fight once more went their separate ways. As the 1920s wore on without the appearance of a solid block of women voters, an increasing number of delegations of women came to party conventions, only to have the party leaders pay less and less attention to them. At the 1924 Democratic convention, there were 180 women delegates and 239 women alternates. Eleanor Roosevelt, long active in politics and social welfare, headed a subcommittee to gather suggestions from women's organizations for planks on social welfare. But, as she recalled in her autobiography, *This Is My Story*, at the convention itself the women "stood outside the door of all important meetings and waited." Their turn never seemed to come.

THE TROUBLED HARDING ADMINISTRATION

FON W. BOARDMAN JR.

In November 1920, Republican presidential candidate Warren G. Harding defeated Democratic candidate James M. Cox by 7 million popular votes. In the following selection, Fon W. Boardman Jr. details the major events of the Harding presidency, which ended after only two and a half years with Harding's death on August 2, 1923. Boardman writes that Harding's presidency was marked by few legislative accomplishments in both domestic and international affairs. His administration became more widely known for the scandals caused by the friends and supporters he had granted political appointments. The most famous of these scandals was Teapot Dome, which involved the questionable leasing of federal land to oilmen. Boardman is the author of more than a dozen books, including *The Thirties: America and the Great Depression* and *America and the Jazz Age: A History of the 1920s*, the source of the following essay.

I n November, 1920, American voters had a new opportunity to choose the general direction in which they wanted to go. The Democratic party, somewhat unenthusiastically, had to uphold President [Woodrow] Wilson's policies and try to demonstrate that the country still wanted to join the League of

Nations.[1] With Wilson too ill to be considered for a third term, the Democrats nominated Governor James M. Cox of Ohio and, for his running mate, Franklin D. Roosevelt of New York, who had been the able Assistant Secretary of the Navy during the war. The Republicans nominated an undistinguished senator from Ohio, Warren G. Harding, after the two leading contenders, Leonard Wood and Frank O. Lowden, had deadlocked the convention. To run for Vice President with Harding the Republicans chose Governor Calvin Coolidge of Massachusetts. His chief claim to consideration was that he had broken the Boston police strike in 1919 and at the time had proclaimed: "There is no right to strike against the public safety by anybody, anywhere, any time." As later study showed, Coolidge did his best to do nothing about the strike until it was politically safe for him to step in.

HARDING'S TRIUMPH

Harding was a handsome man who looked like a President and who reminded older voters nostalgically of President William McKinley. He struck the right note with the public when he asserted:

> America's first need is not heroics, but healing; not nostrums, but normalcy; not revolution, but restoration . . . not surgery, but serenity.

On Election Day the voters decided that "normalcy" was just what they wanted. They gave Harding 16,152,000 popular votes to 9,147,000 for Cox and 404 electoral votes to 127. All of the dissatisfactions of recent years that stemmed from [the first World War], from the dispute over the [Treaty of Versailles], and from the high moral pitch at which Wilson had tried to keep the nation made a Republican victory certain. If Harding promised nothing very positive, he at least promised to leave people alone to pursue their own desires.

Warren G. Harding was a kind, well-intentioned man, loyal to his friends, and somewhat aware of his own shortcomings in relation to the American Presidency. Born in 1865, he gradually worked his way up in business and politics until he was a United States senator and proprietor of a prosperous newspa-

1. The League of Nations, which existed from 1920 to 1946, was an international alliance established to preserve peace. The United States never became a member, although it did send diplomats to league meetings.

per in Marion, Ohio. He had an ambitious wife and an inability to say no to his friends and supporters. As a public speaker he was glib and could talk for two hours without saying anything. H.L. Mencken remarked that Harding's English "reminds me of a string of wet sponges." His faults as well as his virtues helped carry him to the White House and disaster.

HARDING'S ACCOMPLISHMENTS

The legislative accomplishments of Harding's short administration were few and of dubious value—with one exception. That was the establishment in 1921 of the Budget Bureau, with provision for the President to submit a budget to Congress each year and for a controller general to supervise government accounting. For the first time a practical business system was introduced into the national finances. After his inauguration Harding called for new and higher tariff rates which Congress approved as an "emergency" measure. A more permanent law, the Fordney-McCumber Act, became effective in 1922 and set the highest import duties in the nation's history. At a time when the world needed more and easier trading rules, this tariff helped reduce America's imports and exports alike.

For a variety of reasons, but basically because of the antiforeign feeling that seemed so widespread, there was at this time a demand for restrictions on immigration into the United States. For decades the people of Europe had been pouring into the country, which in their eyes was "the promised land" where the streets were paved with gold. Some Americans were proud of their country's role as "the melting pot," where all kinds of persons could live together in peace. Now sentiment was changing. For many years the immigrants had largely been from Great Britain and western Europe, people who were most easily assimilated into the dominant English-speaking culture of the country. In recent years, however, the bulk of the immigrants had come from eastern and southern Europe. In the first ten years of the twentieth century nearly nine million persons were admitted, mostly from Russia, Poland, Austria-Hungary, the Balkans, and Italy. Their languages and customs were more difficult to assimilate or change. Also, while the nineteenth-century immigrants had spread over a good deal of the country (many of them being farmers), the new immigrants largely remained in the big cities, forming Jewish, Polish, or Italian enclaves that had minimum contact with others.

In the decade 1911–20 immigration dropped to 5,735,811 because of the war, but many considered this still far too large a number of strangers to be absorbed. Organized labor had been against unrestricted immigration right along, because it supplied cheap labor. Industry, on the other hand, had wanted the constant flow of new factory hands in order to keep wages down, but now did not feel it was as necessary as before. The superpatriots and the racists turned out pseudoscientific writings seeking to prove that the "superior" Anglo-Saxon race was being overwhelmed by "inferior" racial stock. The result was a temporary "emergency" law passed in the first year of the Harding administration and setting up a quota system which limited immigration each year to 3 per cent of the number of each nationality group that was living in the United States in 1910. In 1924 the Johnson-Reed Act replaced the 1921 law. It established a quota of 2 per cent of the nationals of any country residing in the United States in 1890, and it prohibited all immigration from Japan. Thus it went even further than the earlier act in favoring the immigration of people from western and northern Europe over those from the rest of the continent. Despite the new laws, 4,107,209 persons came into the country during the 1920s.

Harding appointed Andrew Mellon, one of the six wealthiest men in the country, Secretary of the Treasury, a post he continued to hold through Coolidge's Presidency and into the Hoover administration. Mellon recommended income tax reductions for both business and individuals, but when the plan was examined closely it was seen to favor those with large incomes. His first proposals, for example, would not have cut the tax for anyone with an income of less than $66,000 a year. To make up for the reductions, he proposed taxes that would have been burdens on those with lower incomes. Raising the penny postcard to two cents was one idea. Mellon's proposals were considerably modified by Congress, but several times during the decade taxes were cut. Even so, Mellon was able to reduce the national debt by $8,000,000,000, or about a third.

Harding's kindness of heart was shown in an incident near the end of 1921. Eugene V. Debs, the leader of the Socialist party, was finishing two years of a ten-year jail sentence for allegedly obstructing the conduct of the war. He had been outspoken against America's part in it. President Wilson had refused to pardon him, but Harding did so and made sure it was effective in time for Debs to spend Christmas with his family.

In spite of Harding's popularity, the Republicans suffered losses in the midterm Congressional elections of 1922. The losses were worse than they appeared, because some conservative Republicans were replaced by progressives and by representatives of the dissatisfied farmers whose wartime prosperity was gone.

FOREIGN POLICY DURING THE HARDING ADMINISTRATION

In international affairs, Harding's record was somewhat better. Under the League of Nations a Permanent Court of International Justice was created and began to function early in 1922. About a year later the President, at the urging of Secretary of State Charles Evans Hughes, asked the Senate to approve American adherence to the World Court.[2] The Senate, still under the influence of those who opposed anything that seemed like "Wilsonism," refused to act. Nearly three years later, when Coolidge had succeeded to the Presidency, the Senate voted for adherence, but with reservations that made the action futile.

In November, 1921, at the invitation of the United States, the Washington Naval Conference assembled in the capital. Eight European and Asiatic nations were represented and the delegates were astounded when Secretary of State Hughes immediately made concrete proposals for the scrapping of some of the largest battleships in the world and for a ten-year naval holiday during which time no more capital ships would be built. Great Britain, hitherto the strongest naval power in the world, accepted parity with the United States, and Japan agreed to a somewhat lower allotment. Thus was established the 5-5-3 ratio. Great Britain and the United States agreed not to strengthen the fortifications of their various island possessions between Singapore and Hawaii. A four-power treaty among Great Britain, France, Japan, and the United States bound these nations to respect one another's rights in the Pacific. Secretary Hughes concluded his remarkable leadership of the conference by arranging a nine-power treaty involving all the nations present that guaranteed China's sovereignty and territorial integrity and committed everyone to the "open door" policy. Al-

---

2. The World Court was an international tribunal established by the League of Nations. The International Court of Justice replaced it in 1945.

though eventually the work of the conference dissolved in the turmoil of World War II, it did, for a while, slow down the international arms race.

DEATH AND SCANDALS

By early 1923 Harding's health had deteriorated. Even worse for a man who wanted the voters to love him, he knew his reputation was declining. He was becoming aware that the friends he had brought with him to Washington and appointed to Federal office were letting him down. Scandals were starting to come out in the open. In an attempt to get away from his troubles and frustrations and perhaps with the hope of rebuilding his popularity by showing himself to the people, Harding determined on a train trip across the continent and a boat trip up the coast to Alaska. In June the expedition set forth but it was an unhappy trip for everyone. Harding was distraught and wanted to play bridge almost every moment, as though to take his mind off his troubles. In Seattle on the way back from Alaska he became ill, presumably from eating tainted food. In San Francisco the doctors decided the President was suffering from a heart attack. On the evening of August 2, while Mrs. Harding was reading to him, he died.

So ended the short, unhappy administration of a well-meaning man in a job too big for either his mental or moral capacity. When Harding became President in March, 1921, he brought with him to Washington a number of friends and supporters whom he appointed to various offices and who became known as the Ohio Gang. None of them had any particular qualifications for public office but the naive President believed they would all do their best for him. He named a former sheriff of an Ohio county director of the mint. His brother-in-law, a one-time missionary to Burma, was appointed superintendent of Federal prisons after Harding removed the office from the civil service list. The man he chose to head the Veterans' Bureau was a chance acquaintance, Charles R. Forbes, and he was the first whose betrayal of trust became public. Investigation revealed that in less than two years Forbes's various swindles had cost the country $200,000,000. He had sold great quantities of bedding, bandages, drugs, and other supplies as surplus at a time when war veterans in the hospitals needed them, and had shared in the proceeds. He was tried and convicted.

The headquarters of the Ohio Gang became known as "the

little green house on K Street." It was presided over by Jess Smith, who held no public office but was a general handyman for the Attorney General, Harry M. Daugherty. Here bootleg liquor seized under the Volstead Act by government agents was diverted to the President's friends; appointments to office, pardons, and immunity from prosecution were sold. When these activities became too obvious even for the easygoing atmosphere of the Harding regime, Jess Smith committed suicide, about a month before the disheartened President set out on his last trip.

The worst of the Harding administration scandals did not come to light until after his death. One of the scoundrels in high office was Attorney General [Harry M.] Daugherty, another Ohioan, who had for years been Harding's political mentor and had managed his campaign for the Presidency. Under his regime the Federal Bureau of Investigation became a tool for blackmail and for harassing anyone who threatened the administration in any way. Daugherty was also involved in a scandal connected with the office of the Alien Property Custodian. Despite the Attorney General's unsavory reputation, President Coolidge did not request his resignation until 1924. Eventually, in 1927, Daugherty was tried twice for fraud but both times the juries failed to reach a verdict.

The scandal that has gone down in history as Teapot Dome made the corrupt practices of the Ohio Gang look like the work of amateurs. The story begins with Harding's appointment of Albert B. Fall of New Mexico, the living likeness of a slightly shady, old-time western rancher, as Secretary of the Interior. Fall knew that in California and Wyoming two large areas of land belonging to the Federal government—and believed to contain large oil deposits—had been set aside for future or emergency needs of the United States Navy. Fall had little trouble convincing the incompetent Secretary of the Navy, Edwin Denby, and President Harding that these reserves should be transferred from the Navy Department to the Department of the Interior. In April 1922, Fall secretly leased the Teapot Dome reserve in Wyoming to Harry F. Sinclair, a prominent oilman, without any competitive bidding. In the course of the year he similarly leased the Elk Hills Reserve in California to another oilman, Edwin M. Doheny, who was also his friend. Rumors concerning the deals caused the Senate to investigate and gradually the main facts were uncovered. Fall had great difficulty explaining a "loan" of $100,000 that had come to him from Doheny in cash in a black satchel, and how his run-down ranch had suddenly begun to prosper. There had been loans from Sinclair, too, through a Canadian corporation. Fall resigned and he, Doheny, and Sinclair were all indicted. They were acquitted of conspiracy; and although Doheny was acquitted of bribery, Fall was found guilty of receiving a bribe from him. Sinclair eventually spent three months in jail, not for any crime in connection with the oil deals, but for contempt of the Senate and for hiring detectives to shadow jurors at his trial.

By the time all the investigations and trials were over it was 1930. Harding—who might have been impeached had he lived—had been dead for seven years and the nation in the meantime had elected two more Republican Presidents. In spite of all the talk, the newspaper headlines, and the trials, the voters did not work up enough moral indignation to throw out the party and the politicians under whom all this had happened.

A Speakeasy Owner Remembers Prohibition

Charles Berns, as told to John Kobler

Prohibition is a legal ban on the manufacturing and selling of alcoholic beverages. Although prohibition movements had existed throughout the history of the United States, the campaign did not become a national force until the 1870s. By 1916, twenty-three states had adopted anti-saloon laws that closed saloons and barred the manufacture of alcoholic beverages. In December 1917, Congress presented the states with a proposed Eighteenth Amendment to the Constitution, one that would prohibit "the manufacture, sale, or transportation of intoxicating liquors." The amendment was ratified in January 1919, and Prohibition became a national law on January 16, 1920. Prohibition was ultimately a failure, largely because people continued to drink, albeit illegally. Gangsters rose to power as distributors of alcohol, and countless people became ill or died from drinking poorly made bootleg liquor. Less than fifteen years after its ratification, Prohibition was overturned by the Twenty-First Amendment, which was ratified in December 1933.

Charles Berns, who died in 1971, owned several speakeasies (illegal saloons) in New York City during Prohibition. In the following account told to author John Kobler, he explains how he and his partners were able to keep their businesses open and thriving during the 1920s. Berns details his experiences with local gangsters, police, and federal agents. Kobler is the author of several books on the 1920s and 1930s, including *Capone: The Life*

Charles Berns, as told to John Kobler, *Ardent Spirits: The Rise and Fall of Prohibition*. New York: G.P. Putnam's Sons, 1978. Copyright © 1978 by G.P. Putnam's Sons. Reproduced by permission of Ms. Rita Stein.

and World of Al Capone and *Ardent Spirits: The Rise and Fall of Prohibition*, from which the following account has been excerpted.

I n 1919, when I was eighteen, I went to the New York University School of Commerce to study accounting. Jack Kriendler was a distant cousin—our families had immigrated from Austria and we lived near each other on the Lower East Side—and he attended Fordham. In the evenings we both worked as salesmen for Jack's uncle, Sam Brenner, who owned a shoe store on the corner of Essex and Rivington streets. He also owned a saloon across the way, and we made ourselves generally useful there as well. For instance, there came a time when the government slapped an additional tax on whiskey of 25 cents a barrel. So whenever the tax collector was due to drop around, Jack and I would cart away a few barrels and hide them at home until the danger passed.

A NEW ENTERPRISE

The year I graduated, 1922, Jack and a classmate named Eddie Irving bought a controlling interest in a type of place near the campus known as a "Village [Greenwich Village) tea room." They called it the Redhead. In addition to food they sold liquor in one-ounce flasks, miniatures, which the customers could drink right there if they wished or take home. They asked me to keep the books. They couldn't afford to pay me a salary. So they made me a partner. Our only idea behind the enterprise at the start was to earn enough money to continue our education, I having decided to practice law instead of accountancy and Jack to become a pharmacist. The way things developed, neither of us realized his ambition.

The Redhead served good, solid, simple food—Jack had a natural culinary gift—and the best liquor we could find. We dealt with two neighborhood bootleggers who would deliver the merchandise to Jack's home on East Fourth Street. When we needed fresh supplies, Jack's kid brothers, Mac and Pete, would wheel it over, a few bottles at a time. Who was going to suspect a couple of kids that age? We never did discover the original source of our liquor, but it was always authentic imported stuff.

We attracted a small but choice crowd, young people mostly from the schools and colleges, and an occasional tourist. We were a success. But even before we started, we had been approached by a group of Village gangsters who declared themselves in. Being innocent college boys, we refused to discuss the matter. A couple of weeks later they came around again. They told us unless we paid for certain protective services, they would wreck the joint. We remained unimpressed. A few nights later, as Jack and I were walking home, a couple of them jumped us. We gave a pretty good account of ourselves, and they took quite a licking. The next time I wasn't so lucky. Jack survived in one piece; but my attacker had a razor, and I wound up in St. Vincent's Hospital with a dozen stitches in my throat. A third fight took place a month later, but again we managed to drive them off.

WORKING WITH THE POLICE

Meanwhile, we had become acquainted with the district police captain through friends in the James Heron Association. This was a very powerful Lower East Side Democratic organization. These friends let the captain know that Jack and Charlie were decent people who ran an orderly place, no bookmaking, no gambling, no hookers. He came to see us. "Why didn't you let me know about these things that have been happening to you?" he asked. Jack said: "We didn't understand how serious it was." "I'll see what we can do," he said. And nobody ever bothered us again the whole time we operated in the Village.

Every speakeasy had to make some arrangements with the cops to survive. In our case it wasn't exactly a shakedown, nothing on a regular basis, more like an act of friendship. We would slip the captain a $50 bill from time to time and a box of cigars to the cops on the beat. They could always count on us for free meals and drinks, and at Christmastime, of course, we had a gift for everybody.

In 1925 we sold the Redhead (we had bought out Eddie Irving meanwhile) and opened a place we called the Fronton at 88 Washington Place, a basement nightclub this time with dancing and entertainment. Our star attraction was Al Segal, a great jazz pianist, who later coached performers like Ethel Merman. At the Redhead the door was always open. People just wandered in, paid a 50-cent cover charge on weekend nights and drank their miniature flasks. But the Fronton was a bigger, riskier operation. We felt we had to know our customers. So we kept the front door locked and looked people over carefully through a peephole before we admitted them.

The Fronton prospered, too, and it wasn't long before we heard from our gangster friends again. But we got an unusual break, thanks to a boyhood chum of mine. His name was Jimmy Kerrigan. His father once ran a saloon on Fiftieth Street and Broadway before the Capitol Theater was built there. I peddled newspapers in the area at the age of thirteen, and that's how my path crossed Jimmy's. Well, Jimmy grew up to be a revenue agent, which may explain why we never had any trouble with the feds back at the Redhead.

The minute I got the word from those hoodlums that they were planning to visit us on a certain night I got in touch with Jimmy. He arrived in a car with five of his fellow agents, parked across the street and waited. When the gangsters showed, the agents swarmed all over them. They held a long conversation out there on the sidewalk, and that's the last we ever heard from that particular group.

Two Disasters and a Move

First a flood, then a flash fire hit the Fronton, and it taught us the importance of having friends in the fire department, as well as the police. Chief Purdy headed the fire brigade nearest us. Off duty he liked to drop in for a few snorts with the missus, and we never charged him anything. One spring day it rained so hard the sewers backed up. Our main room being below street level, the water started rushing up through the toilet bowls and flooding the place. Chief Purdy answered our distress call with powerful pumps and pumped us dry.

Not long after, the flash fire broke out. We never found out how it started. This time Chief Purdy and his men arrived with axes and started to wreck the premises. "Think of all the money you're going to get from the insurance," he said. "My God!" I told him. "We're not insured!" He felt terrible. "Never mind," he said, "we'll fix it all up." And they did, too.

The construction of the Sixth Avenue subway forced us to abandon the Fronton in 1926, and we moved uptown into a brownstone house with an iron gate at 42 West Forty-ninth Street. The main reason we chose it was that the Italian bootlegger who owned it and wasn't doing too well because he couldn't speak much English agreed to guarantee our mortgage payments if we would buy all our stock from him. We found both him and his liquor reliable. In fact, if we overbought, he would always take back a few cases. We quickly established a reputation for our French and Italian cooking and our cellar.

Soon after we opened, a police captain from the Forty-seventh Street station came to pay his respects and explain that to protect himself, he had to make a friendly arrest——that is, to put it on the record that we sold liquor. "Now you just leave a couple of pints out in the open," he told us. "We'll have a man come by and pick them up. But don't worry. You'll go free on bail, and that'll be the end of the matter." Which is exactly how it worked out.

A certain group of federal agents presented a more serious problem. They were young men of good families, socialites, who saw a means of making some extra easy money by joining the Prohibition Unit. To put it crudely, they were shakedown artists. The way we handled them, a number of us speakeasy operators in the neighborhood created a sort of informal association. John Perona of the Bath Club, who later founded El Morocco, was the main negotiator who spoke for us all. When one of those agents tried to make a case against us, we'd tell him: "You know John Perona. Call him. He'll tell you we're all right and he'll take care of everything." Then we'd square it with John. It cost us about a thousand a year, not including free meals and drinks.

Our Forty-ninth Street place changed its name every year in order to avoid continuity in the IRS records——the Iron Gate, the Grotto, 42, Jack & Charlie's, the Puncheon Club. One evening a Yale student named Ben Quinn came in, took a quick look around and cried, "My God, this is my old home! I grew up here!" He was right. The house had passed through several hands since his father sold it. Ben became a regular visitor, and the place was sometimes called "Ben Quinn's kitchen."

EXPERIENCING A RAID

In spite of all the payoffs we did have one serious raid. It was ordered personally by Mabel Walker Willebrandt.* Two things put her on our trail. First, the rumor that we were the only New York speakeasy in continuous operation that had never been bothered by the city police or the feds. Secondly, a valued customer, a Southern gentleman, who didn't trust his local brew, telephoned to ask us to send him some of our whiskey. The employee who took the call stupidly sent it through the mail with

*The Harding-appointed Assistant Attorney General in charge of prohibition enforcement.

the return address on the package. The post office spotted it, reported it to the prohibition authorities and made Mrs. Willebrandt doubly determined to get us, selling liquor through the mail being an additional offense.

It was a long-drawn-out case, but thanks to our able counselor-at-law we reached a compromise. We pleaded guilty to possession of liquor and paid a fine. Ironically, the raid turned out to be the best advertising we ever got. It made us. Because the confiscated liquor was analyzed by federal chemists, who declared it to be of the finest quality. The press cheered. H.L. Mencken wrote, as nearly as I can remember: "Why raid a place that is serving good liquor and not poisoning anybody?"

Although we owned the building on Forty-ninth Street, we only leased the ground, and in 1929 the lease ran out. By then the Rockefellers, who had bought up or leased a lot of land in the Forties and Fifties, including our location, were planning to construct Rockefeller Center. So we had to move again. We didn't want to leave the neighborhood, not after the good relations we had established there with various prohibition agents. We considered several houses in West Fifty-third and West Fifty-fourth, but there were Rockefellers living on both those streets, and they didn't like speakeasies. Nobody exactly liked to have a speakeasy as a neighbor, but some people were more broad-minded than others. We finally settled for the brownstone we've occupied ever since at 21 West Fifty-second.

The last night on Forty-ninth Street, which was not long before a wrecking crew started to tear down the building, we threw a private farewell party for some of our favorite customers. Bea Lillie, for example. And Bob Benchley. We gave every guest a crowbar or spade and let them go to work breaking down the walls and digging up the floor. Then we all loaded the bottles, crockery, furnishings and so forth onto carts and wheeled them three blocks north to our new address.

We weren't there very long before three hoodlums paid us a visit. They represented Jack "Legs" Diamond [Of all the gang overlords, possibly the most barbarous. The nickname derived from his fleet-footedness as an adolescent thief. It amused him, a kidnapper, as well as bootlegger, hijacker, extortioner and dope dealer, to burn the bare soles of his captives' feet with matches. He killed, or ordered to be killed, dozens of competitors. He himself was shot up so often that the underworld dubbed him "the Clay Pigeon."] It was like the old days in the

Prohibition agents pour bootleg whiskey down a sewer. Despite their efforts, alcohol remained readily available during Prohibition.

Village again. Diamond wanted a piece of our business. The doorman threw the hoodlums out. We were lucky. Before Diamond had a chance to strike back at us, he was shot to death.

GUARDING AGAINST RAIDS

We continued on friendly terms with the prohibition agents. We also became quite friendly with some of the assistant U.S. attorneys, who would drop in for an occasional drink or when they needed a good bottle as a gift would ask us to help them out. But you could never be sure. You could never relax completely. Some new officials might be appointed to the New York district or the agents you took care of might be reassigned elsewhere, and the first thing you knew you got raided.

We had this engineer we trusted, and he installed a series of contraptions for us that worked on different mechanical or electrical impulses. For example, the shelves behind the bar rested on tongue blocks. In case of a raid the bartender could press a button that released the blocks, letting the shelves fall backward and dropping the bottles down a chute. As they fell, they hit against angle irons projecting from the sides of the chute and smashed. At the bottom were rocks and a pile of sand through which the liquor seeped, leaving not a drop of evidence. In addition, when the button was pressed, an alarm bell went off warning everybody to drink up fast. We once put too many bottles on the shelves and they collapsed under the weight. Another time a bartender pressed the button by mistake. But we had only one serious raid. The agents searched the building for twenty-four hours. They never found a single contraption.

The most important was the secret door to our wine cellar. [Here Berns led the author down to the subterranean depths of the building. We paused before an alcove, its white walls bare, and he produced a long, thin steel rod.] Unless you know exactly where to look, all you can see are solid walls, no visible cracks of any kind. But there's this tiny aperture here. You'd have to have an eagle eye. [He shoved the rod through.] When I push this a little further in, you'll hear a noise. That's the tongue lock being released on the other side. It takes very little pressure on my part, even though with the steel frame support the thing weighs over a ton. It works like a trigger on a gun. Listen. [I heard a sharp, metallic click, and the wall swung back on silent hinges, revealing bin upon bin of bottles cradled on their sides.] This is the only entrance or exit. No other way in or out. If the mechanism broke, we'd have to dig through the concrete and pull out the whole lock. But that never happened. And no agent ever discovered the cache either. We still keep the contraption because people like to come down here and see the way things were in the old days.

Anti-Immigrant Feelings in the Early 1920s

Robert K. Murray

When World War I ended, American distrust for immigrants, particularly those seen as dangerous because of their anarchic or socialist political views, was at a fever pitch. The years of 1919 and 1920 were known as the "Red Scare." Several thousand aliens were rounded up for deportation during that time, a great number of them during raids initiated by Attorney General Alexander Mitchell Palmer.

In the following selection, Robert K. Murray details how the Red Scare influenced public attitudes toward immigrants throughout the 1920s. According to Murray, the Red Scare helped boost the popularity of "patriotic societies" that distributed antiradical literature and blamed the nation's ills on socialism and immigrants. These societies spurred the passage of restrictive immigration laws. Murray writes that this antipathy toward immigrants was directly expressed by the Sacco-Vanzetti trial, in which Italian immigrants and anarchists Nicola Sacco and Bartolomeo Vanzetti were convicted of a robbery and murder they most likely did not commit. Murray is professor emeritus of American history at Pennsylvania State University in State College and the author of *Red Scare: A Study in National Hysteria, 1919–1920*, the source of the following essay.

Robert K. Murray, *Red Scare: A Study in National Hysteria, 1919–1920*. Minneapolis: University of Minnesota Press, 1955. Copyright © 1955 by University of Minnesota Press. Reproduced by permission.

T he decline of anti-Red hysteria and the return of public stability by late 1920 technically marked the end of the Great Red Scare. Gone were the bombings, the government raids, the mass deportations, the shocking displays of mob violence.

THE INFLUENCE OF THE RED SCARE

However, the underlying fear of radicalism and the proclivity for intolerance which the Red Scare had engendered remained long after these various events were forgotten and hysteria had passed from the scene. In fact, the antiradical emotionalism emanating from the Scare affected both governmental and private thinking for almost a decade to come and left its unmistakable imprint upon many phases of American life. Continued insistence upon ideological conformity, suspicion of organized labor, public intolerance toward aliens, and a hatred for Soviet Russia were but a few of the more important legacies left by the Red Scare. Moreover, the decline in liberal thought, the general apathy toward reform, and the intense spirit of nationalism which so characterized the 1920s were, partially at least, outgrowths of the Scare period.

A more detailed analysis than is possible here would probably show that the Red Scare was a much more vital conditioning factor for the "Roaring Twenties" than has generally been supposed. True, it is common knowledge that the Red Scare ushered in the twenties and served as a sort of bridge between war and peace. But its influence did not stop there. Even a cursory examination of the Scare's ramifications reveals that while the phenomenon did not basically change the pattern of modern American history, it did greatly affect certain subsequent developments, and, indeed, to some extent even colors public opinion today. If for no other reason than the latter, the Red Scare has a timely significance which is worthy of considerable attention.

The aftermath period following the Red Scare hysteria has no well-defined limits nor does it lend itself easily to critical or accurate examination. Generally speaking, there was a high degree of Scare-inspired psychology at work on public opinion down to 1924–25. In the broader view, the whole pattern of thought and action common to the 1920s was in part at least traceable to the Red Scare.

Here, however, we are most interested in those developments which related most directly to the Scare phenomenon, for the receding tide of anti-Red hysteria did cast up some distinctive pebbles on the beach of normalcy. The first was the continuing crusade for 100 per cent Americanism.

"TRUE PATRIOTS" VERSUS IMMIGRANTS

Still rooted in the belief that true patriotism could be instilled by slogans and parades, this campaign mushroomed as a result of the Red Scare. For example, the American Defense Society, National Security League, and National Civic Federation were soon joined by other such agencies as the Better America Federation (1920), Allied Patriotic Societies (1923), National Patriotic Council (1924) , and Unified States Patriotic Society (1925). Using the Red Scare as their point of departure, these organizations, amply aided by the American Legion and the Ku Klux Klan, persisted in distributing much antiradical literature during the entire decade and as late as 1928 maintained the nation was still riddled with bolshevism. They claimed the churches, schools, colleges, and labor unions were all badly infected, and they kept such prominent individuals as Rev. S. Parkes Cadman, Clarence Darrow, and Dean Roscoe Pound[1] in the parlor Red category. Such irresponsible charges served to sustain a degree of public intolerance by retaining the word "Bolshevik" [a radical socialist or supporter of Communism] as a scare word and the easiest means of eliminating all opposition. As before, wise schoolteachers, college professors, and clergymen remained clear of controversial subjects; a whispered "He's a Bolshevist" was still an effective weapon to use against a man in 1929.

During the twenties these patriotic societies kept alive some public intolerance not only by the means cited above, but also by supplying anti-Red speakers, often dressed as Uncle Sam, to fraternal meetings, business luncheons, women's clubs, schools, and the like. At the same time, they lobbied for the enactment of peacetime sedition legislation, anti-strike laws, and other sorts of repressive measures. In particular, the American Legion and the Ku Klux Klan, the latter having an estimated membership of 4,500,000 in 1924, propagandized the need for the "Americanization" of school texts, loyalty oaths for teachers, and more stringent immigration legislation.

1. S. Parkes Cadman was a preacher and president of the Federal Council of Churches. Clarence Darrow was a defense lawyer whose clients included Eugene V. Debs, Nathan Leopold and Richard Loeb, and John T. Scopes. Roscoe Pound was a jurist and writer whose work is believed to have inspired the New Deal, Franklin D. Roosevelt's plan to end the depression. Many business leaders felt the New Deal veered on socialism.

This problem of immigration legislation and the public attitude toward aliens in general reflected the most obvious effect of the continuing patriotic crusade. Through it, the belief was perpetuated that most aliens were susceptible to radical philosophies and therefore represented an element which particularly endangered the nation. As a result the American Federation of Labor (AFL), the general press, and a host of other institutions, agencies, and prominent citizens had long since joined the patriotic societies in demanding more stringent immigration laws for this as well as for other reasons. As far as the specific factor of radicalism was concerned, General Leonard Wood . . . summed up opinion fairly well when he exclaimed, "We do not want to be a dumping ground for radicals, agitators, Reds, who do not understand our ideals."

Such constant agitation was not lost on Congress and with the opening of the decade new immigration measures were rapidly taken under consideration. While an analysis of the congressional debates shows that most congressmen emphasized that unrestricted immigration would increase domestic unemployment, depress native labor standards, and destroy traditional blood lines, the argument that American institutions had to be protected somehow from immigrant "Reds" and all others who were likely to be unsympathetic to the existing order was not ignored. Such a belief ultimately found expression in both the Emergency Immigration Act of 1921 and the permanent statute of 1924 which discriminated especially against prospective immigrants from southern and southeastern Europe, the origin of the newer, more radical, less educated, and less assimilable groups. The National Origins Quota System which followed was but a further expression and adaptation of this discriminatory attitude toward "unorthodox" aliens.

SACCO AND VANZETTI

Even more directly expressive of this continued anti-alien feeling was the case of Nicola Sacco and Bartolomeo Vanzetti, the *cause célèbre* of the 1920s. These men, both Italian aliens and avowed anarchists, were arrested in May 1920 for the robbery and murder of a shoe company paymaster in South Braintree, Massachusetts. Although at their trial the state was unable to prove conclusively that the two Italians were responsible for the crime, they were found guilty under what appeared to be highly prejudicial circumstances and were sentenced to death in July 1921 by Judge Webster Thayer of Worcester.

The execution date, however, was continually postponed as a result of widespread protests both at home and abroad concerning the validity of the decision. For six years Sacco and Vanzetti remained in prison awaiting death while bitter controversy raged over their trial. Meanwhile, such eminent figures as Anatole France, George Bernard Shaw, H.G. Wells, John Galsworthy, and Albert Einstein[2] appealed for a complete review of their case. Simultaneously, radical elements throughout the world seized upon their plight and made "Sacco and Vanzetti" a rallying cry against American capitalism, claiming the two men were being railroaded to their deaths merely because they were radical aliens and not because of any crime.

But, in the long run, Massachusetts's justice was not to be denied. After a series of refusals for a rehearing and the investigation of an advisory committee appointed by Governor Alvan T. Fuller, the execution date was finally set for August 22, 1927. As this date approached and clamor throughout the world increased, the American press, which itself up to this point had been divided on the issue, now sharply reverted to an intense nationalism and staunchly defended the decision in the belief that the whole fabric of American law and justice was undergoing a radical foreign attack.

Sacco and Vanzetti went to their deaths with "This is our career, and our triumph" being the last words they gave to the world. Quite naturally, they were regarded as martyrs by their many sympathizers. These latter continued to claim that the word "anarchist" rather than any criminal act had sent them to the electric chair, and the whole incident was denounced as a prime example of American disdain for justice and prejudice against the foreigner. Feeling ran so high in some areas of the world that upon receipt of the news of their execution, American embassies were stoned, diplomatic officials were assaulted, and the American flag was defamed. Indeed, in most parts of the world, the prestige of American justice dropped so sharply that the damage done to the reputation of American freedom was a long time repairing. It was a costly price to pay for the lives of two men.

Such was the legacy of Sacco and Vanzetti—and of the Red Scare.

2. Anatole France was a French author and Nobel Prize winner. John Galsworthy was a British novelist and playwright and Nobel Prize winner.

THE KU KLUX KLAN EXPANDS THROUGHOUT THE NATION

ARNOLD S. RICE

The Ku Klux Klan is a secret organization that developed in the southern United States after the Civil War. Its members, who were primarily white Protestant males, sought to destroy the Republic Reconstructionist governments that had developed in the 1860s and 1870s. These governments—led by newly freed slaves, white Republicans, and Northerners who had moved to the South—guaranteed the political and civil rights of freed slaves. The Klan objected to the new power granted to freed slaves and engaged in acts of violence to keep them and white Republicans from voting. The Klan particularly targeted African Americans, whom they considered inferior. The Klan's politics expanded in the 1920s to include antipathy for Catholics, Jews, and immigrants.

Arnold S. Rice details how the Klan's popularity spread far beyond the south during the 1920s. By 1924 the organization had made significant inroads on the West Coast and in the Midwest. It was able to attract millions of members by appealing to local businessmen, prominent citizens, and the many Americans who were uncomfortable with immigrants, African Americans, and the looser morals of the decade. Rice is a history professor at Kean University in Union, New Jersey, and the author

Arnold S. Rice, *The Ku Klux Klan in American Politics*. Washington, DC: Public Affairs Press, 1962. Copyright © 1962 by Public Affairs Press. Reproduced by permission.

of *The Ku Klux Klan in American Politics*, the source of the following selection.

I t is a serious mistake to think that the Ku Klux Klan of the 1920's was a powerful force only in the Deep South. To be sure, the order was founded in Georgia, and then spread rather quickly to the neighboring states of Alabama and Florida. However, the Klan reached its first peak of success, after a Congressional investigation [which had been prompted by journalist disclosures of Klan crimes] in October 1921, in the vast area to the west of the lower Mississippi River, in Texas, Oklahoma, and Arkansas. Then the organization took firm root on the Pacific coast, first in California and later in Oregon. And by 1924 the fraternity reached extraordinary success in the Middle West generally and fantastic success in the states of Indiana and Ohio particularly.

One of the most astute of the many contemporary students of the Klan, Stanley Frost, calculated that the order at its height of activity had about 4,000,000 members distributed as follows: Indiana, 500,000; Ohio, 450,000; Texas, 415,000; California, New York, Oklahoma, Oregon 200,000 each; Alabama, Arkansas, Florida, Georgia, Illinois, Kansas, Kentucky, Louisiana, Maryland, Michigan, Mississippi, Missouri, New Jersey, Tennessee, Washington, and West Virginia, between 50,000 and 200,000 each.

EXPLAINING THE KLAN'S POPULARITY

One might wonder at the large number of Klansmen in states having so few Negroes, Catholics, Jews, or foreign-born—states lacking, therefore, in all those things against which the Klan railed and upon which it thrived. The secret is that in the 1920's the bulk of the people in the states of the western reaches of the lower Mississippi Valley, the Pacific coast, and the Middle West were the descendants—both physical and spiritual—of that old American stock from which the anti-Catholic and nativistic movements of the preceding century drew their chief support.

The Klan was in the main a village and small town phenomenon. Neither the city, as a potpourri of many racial, religious, and ethnic groups, nor the country, as an isolated area with far-spread inhabitants, lent itself to the effective launching and developing of a local chapter. The appreciable Klan following in many of the large cities and much of the countryside all over the

United States during the 1920's must not be discounted. But the secret fraternity drew its millions primarily from the villages and towns which had been left rather undisturbed by the immigration, industrialization, and liberal thought of modern America.

Eligible for membership in the Invisible Empire, Knights of the Ku Klux Klan was any white, native-born, Christian, American male, who (in order to debar Catholics) owed "no allegiance of any nature or degree to any foreign government, nation, institution, sect, ruler, person. . . ."

Among those millions of individuals who could, and did, join the order, one contemporary observer, Robert L. Duffus, found six classes: (1) the organizers and promoters; (2) businessmen; (3) politicians; (4) preachers and pious laymen; (5) incorrigible "joiners" and lovers of "horseplay"; and (6) bootleggers who joined for protection. Using this classification as the basis for a discussion of the caliber of men who associated themselves with the Klan—and this classification will have to serve for lack of another by a contemporary more knowledgeable and objective—it becomes immediately apparent that Klansmen belonged to a variety of socio-economic classes.

INFLUENCING THE LOCAL COMMUNITY

Not always, but sometimes, the leaders of a community would join the local Klan chapter. In each new territory that the Kleagle [a member of the Klan] "worked," he made a practice, for obvious reasons, of approaching the prominent citizens first. Imperial Kligrapp H.K. Ramsey, writing of the Klan's Second Klonvokation, held in Kansas City, Missouri, in September 1924, declared that "Ministers of the Gospel, Attorneys (some representing our common judiciary), Educators, businessmen (a number of them millionaires and capitalists) . . . all sat together."

After the Kleagles had flattered and persuaded as many of the leading citizens of the community into joining the secret fraternity as they could, they then turned their attention to enlisting the middle class. The remark of Ramsey, as a member of the Klan's hierarchy, might well be taken with the proverbial grain of salt. Nevertheless, it is most important to note that practically all anti-Klan writers described the vast majority of Klansmen as members of America's respectable middle class. One journalist, for example, wrote that most Klansmen were "solid, respectable citizens, loving husbands and fathers, conscientious members of their churches"; another penned that most of the persons who joined the order were "good, solid, middle-class citizens, the 'backbone of the Nation.'"

After the Kleagles had enlisted as many of the middle class as they were able, they then directed their sales talk to the less desirable elements. Hustling agents "sought out the poor, the romantic, the short-witted, the bored, the vindictive, the big-oted, and the ambitious, and sold them their heart's desire." Stanley Frost, in his reportorial study of the Klan for *The Out-look*, commented that he had not learned of a single case in which a Kleagle refused an individual membership in the secret fraternity—"no matter how vicious or dangerous he might be"—if he had the necessary $10. Henry Peck Fry, who resigned from the Klan as a disillusioned Kleagle, branded his former colleagues for "selling memberships as they would sell insurance or stock."

It was this indiscriminate recruiting by Kleagles (resulting, naturally, from the fact that their incomes depended upon the number of men enlisted) that forced one W.M. Likins to sever

More than thirty thousand Ku Klux Klan members participated in this 1925 parade in Washington, D.C.

all contacts with his local Klan chapter. This individual joined the secret fraternity because he believed in its nationalistic and Protestant creed; he soon quit the organization because he found it to contain an element of "low characters, not educated or moral." Most chapters had their share of the community's dregs on their membership lists. In the South this element seemed to be an active minority in most localities, and a forceful majority in some.

THE SPIRIT OF THE 1920'S

There was something about the United States of the 1920's that influenced a surprisingly large number of Americans in their decision to join the order. The spirit of the times demands analysis.

The decade 1920–1930 was what it was largely because of the effects of World War I. During the armed struggle America mistrusted and mistreated aliens, deprived itself of food and fuel, and poured its money into the Liberty Loan[1] campaigns. But the war was over too quickly for the nation to spend fully its ultrapatriotic psychological feelings. In the decade following, America permitted itself to reject the League of Nations,[2] to curtail immigration, to deport aliens wholesale, and to accept the Klan with its motto of "one hundred per cent Americanism."

Another result of the war was the intensifying of racial antipathies. The bearing of arms and the freedom of contact with whites in France by Negro servicemen and the receiving of high wages by many Negroes of the South who moved to northern cities in order to work for war industries made the colored people of the nation feel a human dignity they had never before experienced. During the 1920's this served to increase hostility on the part of whites and to decrease the endurance of such hostility on the part of Negroes. The Klan was quick to capitalize on the feeling of those whites who believed they saw everywhere Negro "uppitiness."

A third effect of World War I was the violent death of the old American way of life—evangelical, didactic, prudish—and the sudden birth of a new. (No event serves as a nation's cultural watershed better than a war.) The 1920's meant "modernism." And "modernism," among other things, meant the waning of

---

1. Liberty Loans were five bonds issued by the U.S. government during World War I.
2. The League of Nations, which existed from 1920 to 1946, was an international alliance established to preserve peace. The United States never became a member, although it did send diplomats to league meetings.

church influence, particularly over the younger people; the breaking down of parental control; the discarding of the old-fashioned absolute moral code in favor of a freer or "looser" personal one, which manifested itself in such activities as purchasing and drinking contraband liquor, participating in ultra-frank conversations between the sexes, wearing skirts close to the knees, engaging in various extreme forms of dancing in smoke-filled road houses, and petting in parked cars. A host of Americans were unwilling, or unable, to adapt themselves to this post-war culture. In the Klan they saw a bulwark against the hated "modernism," an opportunity to salvage some of the customs and traditions of the old religio-moralistic order.

Although there was a spirit peculiar to the 1920's that influenced many into joining the secret fraternity, each individual had his own particular reason for donning the peaked hood and robe. Why certain leading citizens of a community were prompted to associate themselves with the Klan is not difficult to comprehend. Many businessmen most assuredly saw that by joining the Klan they could keep old and get new trade through their fraternal contacts; some physicians and lawyers must have realized that as the "best" of their community they would probably be the officers of the local chapter of the evergrowing order; numerous Protestant clergymen were undoubtedly won over by the organization's highly moral and religious ritual and code; large numbers of local politicians were ever mindful of the fact that each fellow Klansman would equal one vote they could count on.

Droves of middle-class Southerners eagerly paid the $10 initiation fee to the first Kleagle with whom they came in contact. Southern history has idealized the old Klan as a protector of the "peculiar way of life" below the Mason-Dixon line to the extent that to many inhabitants of that area the memory of the Reconstruction organization was something sacred. Besides, there was in the 1920's a new, vibrant interest in the old hooded order, for David W. Griffith's cinematic eulogy on the Klan, "The Birth of a Nation," has been thrilling the movie-going public since its first release in 1915. There was hardly a southern city that has not had the film for a return engagement. Thus when the twentieth century Klan was presented to the people as a memorial to the old organization, half the battle for recruitment in the South had been won.

THE RAPID RISE OF RADIO

GEORGE H. DOUGLAS

In the following selection, George H. Douglas writes on the rapid growth of the radio industry in the early 1920s. Between 1922 and 1924, sales for radio equipment rose by 600 percent. The industry took advantage of several forms of advertising such as billboards, sponsored radio programs, and window displays to expand its customer base. By the middle of the decade, radio had become a popular source of news and entertainment and a way for Americans to feel connected. Douglas is professor emeritus of English at the University of Illinois at Urbana-Champaign and the author of several books, including *The Early Days of Radio Broadcasting*, from which the following essay has been excerpted.

T he decade of the 1920s, as we remember from our schoolbooks, was a time of unparalleled growth in the American economy. When the twentieth century began, at least half of the wealth of the nation still derived from agricultural pursuits. World War I changed all that with stunning suddenness. During the 1920s, with the possible exception of a brief period in 1920–22 that was witness to a minor economic slump, manufacturing became the business of America. When the decade was over, the United States led all of the world in manufacturing of all sorts—automobiles, refrigerators, chemicals, dyes, clothing, tobacco, dynamos, road-building equipment, and, of course, radio. . . .

[Radio] rapidly became a giant—one of the great American

industries. The sales figures for radio equipment in the middle years of the 1920s tell the story:

1922	$ 60,000,000
1923	136,000,000
1924	358,000,000
1925	430,000,000
1926	506,000,000
1927	425,600,000
1928	650,550,000
1929	842,548,000

It is doubtful if any other manufacturing industry in the United States witnessed a growth of this rapidity at any point in our history. After three decades, the phonograph industry had managed to place 13,000,000 phonographs in homes. After a quarter of a century, the automobile industry in America had produced slightly more than 19,000,000 automobiles. In half a century, the telephone company had managed to boost the number of subscribers in the United States to 18,000,000—all this by 1928. In January 1922 there were a mere 60,000 radio sets in use in the United States, probably serving an audience of about 75,000 people. By 1928, however, 7,500,000 homes were equipped with radio sets, with a listening audience of nearly one-third of the population of the United States. The sales figures above show that from 1922 to 1929 there was an increase in sales volume of over 1,400 percent.

Obviously this unique growth was very largely tied to the proliferation of radio broadcasting stations in 1922 and thereafter. On the other hand, that is only one side of the story. The radio manufacturing and distributing industries geared up and met the challenge of the demand as soon as it appeared—even the Radio Corporation of America (RCA), which a few years earlier had laughed at the idea that individual citizens would want to have radio receiving sets in their homes. Looking back from the perspective of a much calmer and better organized electronics industry in the middle of the twentieth century, it is a great wonder how it all could have been accomplished.

AN EXPLOSION OF RADIO STORES

For some reason not altogether clear, the demand for radio was created as much on the retail level as anywhere else. When the great radio boom of 1922 began it seemed as though everybody wanted to get in on the sale of radio equipment. Radio stores popped up everywhere. Department stores all found it necessary to establish a radio department or section, and, as we are already aware, many of them established broadcasting stations right on their premises, sometimes right in the radio sales department itself. But that's only the beginning of the story. During the chaotic days of 1922 and 1923, everybody wanted to sell radio sets, no matter what his original line of business. Florist shops, drug stores, furniture stores, grocery stores, general stores, candy stores, even undertakers and plumbers clamored for franchises. Nearly everybody in any kind of retailing business tried to get in on the act. And because there were so many manufacturers selling their wares, almost anybody who wanted a franchise was able to get one from this manufacturer or that.

Whoever had radio sets for sale in the period between 1922 and 1924 could almost be assured that he would sell out his stock. One could wander down a street in a small town almost anywhere in Middle America and see signs advertising radio equipment. Ofttimes a general store or florist shop would have a radio loudspeaker placed outside blasting away, acting as an advertisement for the equipment on sale inside. It could be that the golden age of radio broadcasting would not arrive until the 1930s, but the 1920s was the golden age of radio technology and gadgetry; the public could not seem to get enough of this marvelous and still magical device.

The large manufacturing companies almost immediately assembled enormous sales forces to distribute their products. By 1923 RCA had 200 distributors of jobbers selling to 15,000 dealers. The jobber became the fulcrum of the sales operation in most of the big companies like RCA, Crosley and Atwater Kent, although other manufacturers—Stromberg-Carlson and Freshman for example—used direct manufacturer-to-dealer distribution.

METHODS OF ADVERTISING

In spite of the demand that seemed to be springing up so naturally in the early years of the radio boom, the radio manufacturing industry took nothing for granted, and adopted its own aggressive selling techniques to reach out to the general public.

Probably the most widely used advertising technique in the first few years was free newspaper publicity. Since the novelty of radio appealed to everybody, and the newspapers had not yet been threatened by this new medium, most were more than willing to cooperate in featuring news stories about radio broadcasting in the many fan magazines, such as *QST, Radio News* and *Wireless Age*. By 1924 there were nearly thirty such fan magazines with a combined circulation of over 1,000,000 copies. Advertising in such publications was a surefire way of reaching the hot-blooded radio enthusiast.

Another good way of reaching the enthusiastic amateur was through catalogues, price lists, slick paper brochures, newsletters and house organs. Specialized information of this kind was candy to multitudes who enjoyed being initiates in the arcane art of radio, given every opportunity to assemble the various parts and circuits readily becoming available.

By the middle twenties, every known medium of advertising had been used to sell home radio receivers: direct mail, billboards, newspapers, magazines, trade organs, sales brochures, window displays. Not to be forgotten as a sales tool is radio broadcasting itself. As the restrictions against radio advertising were slowly lifted, receiver manufacturers took to the airwaves and advertised their wares by sponsoring radio programs, some of them highly successful in the twenties. RCA, Atwater Kent, Philco and Crosley all sponsored programs with the perfectly evident and sensible idea of selling their equipment.

Atwater Kent created and sponsored some of the best programming of the decade. The famous "Atwater Kent Radio Hour" made its debut on New York's WEAF on January 22, 1925. Kent also sponsored the "Atwater Kent Radio Artists," and, perhaps most important of all as a trendsetter in excellence, the "WEAF Grand Opera Company," which took to the air late in 1925. These Sunday evening broadcasts became an immediate and smashing success and were channeled to a group of stations (although the NBC network had not yet been established). So it is a splendid truth of history that the radio manufacturers were not interested only in selling sets; they had a vested interest in the quality of broadcasting that reached the general public.

The selling of radio in the 1920s was a herculean effort by any standard of evaluation. On the other hand, when we consider the reluctance of giants like RCA, GE and AT&T to get into the field of broadcasting at the dawn of the decade, there is a certain sense in which we have to admit that the radio sold itself to the American public. This great little contraption was ideally suited to the American continent—a land of great physical distances and frequent isolation. During the 1920s there were literally millions of citizens who got their first radio only a shade after they received electrical power, and when they did so it was because of a felt need for communication with the centers of power, culture and affluence, often thousands of miles away.

When David Sarnoff originally made his prediction about the possible sale of hundreds of thousands of radio music boxes, he was doubtless thinking that these boxes would have widespread appeal because they would be pleasing sources of home entertainment. And they have been, of course. On the other hand, radio became much more—a household utility, yes, but a lifeline that held a nation and society together.

1925–1928: Prosperity and Change

CHAPTER 2

THE SCOPES TRIAL: FUNDAMENTALISM VERSUS MODERNISM

FREDERICK LEWIS ALLEN

Protestants in the 1920s were largely divided into two camps: Modernists, who were open to scientific and skeptical thoughts, and Fundamentalists, who believed in a strict interpretation of the Bible and sought to ban the teaching of evolution. These opposing views on the relationship between science and religion were brought to the forefront in Dayton, Tennessee, in the summer of 1925. The Fundamentalist-dominated Tennessee legislature had passed a bill forbidding the teaching of evolution. In what some believe was an attempt to use the new law to gain notoriety for his hometown, twenty-four-year-old teacher John T. Scopes allowed himself to be caught teaching evolution; his arrest led to what came to be known as the Scopes trial, one of the most famous trials in American history.

Frederick Lewis Allen describes the Scopes trial—one of the most publicized events of the 1920s—in the following article. Along with the local townspeople who filled the courtroom, the trial was also attended by dozens of reporters, cameramen, and telegraph operators, all of whom ensured that every detail of the trial was reported worldwide. Allen concludes that while the Fundamentalist position triumphed in the trial, the movement gradually lost its power. Allen was a social historian, an editor at several magazines, including *Atlantic Monthly*, *The Century*, and *Harper's*, and the author of *Only Yesterday: An Informal History of the 1920s*, the source of the following essay.

Frederick Lewis Allen, *Only Yesterday: An Informal History of the 1920s*. New York: John Wiley and Sons, 1997. Copyright © 1997 by John Wiley and Sons. Reproduced by permission.

The word science [became] a shibboleth [in the 1920s]. To preface a statement with "Science teaches us" was enough to silence argument. If a sales manager wanted to put over a promotion scheme or a clergyman to recommend a charity, they both hastened to say that it was scientific.

Modernists and Fundamentalists

The effect of the prestige of science upon churchmen was well summed up by [preacher and author] Dr. Harry Emerson Fosdick at the end of the decade:

"The men of faith might claim for their positions ancient tradition, practical usefulness, and spiritual desirability, but one query could prick all such bubbles: Is it scientific? That question has searched religion for contraband goods, stripped it of old superstitions, forced it to change its categories of thought and methods of work, and in general has so cowed and scared religion that many modern-minded believers . . . instinctively throw up their hands at the mere whisper of it. . . . When a prominent scientist comes out strongly for religion, all the churches thank Heaven and take courage as though it were the highest possible compliment to God to have [British astronomer Sir Arthur] Eddington believe in Him. Science has become the arbiter of this generation's thought, until to call even a prophet and a seer scientific is to cap the climax of praise."

So powerful was the invasion of scientific ideas and of the scientific habit of reliance upon proved acts that the Protestant churches—which numbered in their membership five out of every eight adult church members in the United States—were broken into two warring camps. Those who believed in the letter of the Bible and refused to accept any teaching, even of science, which seemed to conflict with it, began in 1921 to call themselves Fundamentalists. The Modernists (or Liberals), on the other hand, tried to reconcile their beliefs with scientific thought: to throw overboard what was out of date, to retain what was essential and intellectually respectable, and generally to mediate between Christianity and the skeptical spirit of the age.

The position of the Fundamentalists seemed almost hopeless. The tide of all rational thought in a rational age seemed to be running against them. But they were numerous, and at least there was no doubt about where they stood. Particularly in the South they controlled the big Protestant denominations. And they fought strenuously. They forced the liberal Doctor Fosdick out of the pulpit of a Presbyterian church and back into his own Baptist fold, and even caused him to be tried for heresy (though there was no churchman in America more influential than he). They introduced into the legislatures of nearly half the states of the Union bills designed to forbid the teaching of the doctrine of evolution; in Texas, Louisiana, Arkansas, and South Carolina they pushed such bills through one house of the legislature only to fail in the other; and in Tennessee, Oklahoma, and Mississippi they actually succeeded in writing their anachronistic wishes into law.

The Modernists had the *Zeitgeist* on their side, but they were not united. Their interpretations of God—as the first cause, as absolute energy, as idealized reality, as a righteous will working in creation, as the ideal and goal toward which all that is highest and best is moving—were confusingly various and ambiguous. Some of these interpretations offered little to satisfy the worshiper: one New England clergyman said that when he thought of God he thought of "a sort of oblong blur." And the Modernists threw overboard so many doctrines in which the bulk of American Protestants had grown up believing (such as the Virgin birth, the resurrection of the body, and the Atonement) that they seemed to many to have no religious cargo left except a nebulous faith, a general benevolence, and a disposition to assure everyone that he was really just as religious as they. Gone for them, as Walter Lippmann said, was "that deep, compulsive, organic faith in an external fact which is the essence of religion for all but that very small minority who can live within themselves in mystical communion or by the power of their understanding." The Modernists, furthermore, had not only Fundamentalism to battle with, but another adversary, the skeptic nourished on outlines of science; and the sermons of more than one Modernist leader gave the impression that Modernism, trying to meet the skeptic's arguments without resorting to the argument from authority, was being forced against its will to whittle down its creed to almost nothing at all.

THE BACKGROUND OF THE SCOPES TRIAL

All through the decade the three-sided conflict reverberated. It reached its climax in the Scopes case in the summer of 1925.

The Tennessee legislature, dominated by Fundamentalists, passed a bill providing that "it shall be unlawful for any teacher in any of the universities, normals and all other public schools of the State, which are supported in whole or in part by the public school funds of the State, to teach any theory that denies the story of the Divine creation of man as taught in the Bible, and to teach instead that man has descended from a lower order of animals."

This law had no sooner been placed upon the books than a little group of men in the sleepy town of Dayton, Tennessee, decided to put it to the test. George Rappelyea, a mining engineer, was drinking lemon phosphates in Robinson's drug store with John Thomas Scopes, a likeable young man of twenty-four who taught biology at the Central High School, and two or three others. Rappelyea proposed that Scopes should allow himself to be caught red-handed in the act of teaching the theory of evolution to an innocent child, and Scopes—half serious, half in joke—agreed. Their motives were apparently mixed; it was characteristic of the times that (according to so friendly a narrator of the incident as Arthur Garfield Hays) Rappelyea declared that their action would put Dayton on the map. At all events, the illegal deed was shortly perpetrated and Scopes was arrested. William Jennings Bryan forthwith volunteered his services to the prosecution; Rappelyea wired the Civil Liberties Union in New York and secured for Scopes the legal assistance of Clarence Darrow, Dudley Field Malone, and Arthur Garfield Hays; the trial was set for July, 1925, and Dayton suddenly discovered that it was to be put on the map with a vengeance.

There was something to be said for the right of the people to decide what should be taught in their tax-supported schools, even if what they decided upon was ridiculous. But the issue of the Scopes case, as the great mass of newspaper readers saw it, was nothing so abstruse as the rights of taxpayers versus academic freedom. In the eyes of the public, the trial was a battle between Fundamentalism on the one hand and twentieth-century skepticism (assisted by Modernism) on the other. The champions of both causes were headliners. Bryan had been three times a candidate for the Presidency, had been Secretary of State, and was a famous orator; he was the perfect embodiment of old-fashioned American idealism—friendly, naïve, provincial. Darrow, a radical, a friend of the underdog, an agnostic, had recently jumped into the limelight of publicity through his defense of Leopold and Loeb.[1] Even [boxing promoter] Tex Rickard

1. In 1924, Nathan Leopold and Richard Loeb were put on trial for the murder of schoolboy Bobby Franks. Their lawyer, Clarence Darrow, convinced the jury that the pair had suffered from temporary insanity, thereby saving them from the death penalty.

could hardly have staged a more promising contest than a battle between these two men over such an emotional issue.

DAYTON'S ATMOSPHERE

It was a strange trial. Into the quiet town of Dayton flocked gaunt Tennessee farmers and their families in mule-drawn wagons and ramshackle Fords; quiet, godly people in overalls and gingham and black, ready to defend their faith against the "foreigners," yet curious to know what this new-fangled evolutionary theory might be. Revivalists of every sort flocked there, too, held their meetings on the outskirts of the town under the light of flares, and tacked up signs on the trees about the courthouse—"Read Your Bible Daily for One Week," and "Be Sure Your Sins Will Find You Out," and at the very courthouse gate:

THE KINGDOM OF GOD

The sweetheart love of Jesus Christ and Paradise Street is at hand. Do you want to be a sweet angel? Forty days of prayer. Itemize your sins and iniquities for eternal life. If you come clean, God will talk back to you in voice.

Yet the atmosphere of Dayton was not simply that of rural piety. Hot-dog venders and lemonade venders set up their stalls along the streets as if it were circus day. Booksellers hawked volumes on biology. Over a hundred newspapermen poured into the town. The Western Union installed twenty-two telegraph operators in a room off a grocery store. In the courtroom itself, as the trial impended, reporters and cameramen crowded alongside grim-faced Tennessee countrymen; there was a buzz of talk, a shuffle of feet, a ticking of telegraph instruments, an air of suspense like that of a first-night performance at the theater. Judge, defendant, and counsel were stripped to their shirt sleeves—Bryan in a pongee shirt turned in at the neck, Darrow with lavender suspenders, Judge [John T.] Raulston with galluses of a more sober judicial hue—yet fashion was not wholly absent: the news was flashed over the wires to the whole country that the judge's daughters, as they entered the courtroom with him, wore rolled stockings like any metropolitan flapper's. Court was opened with a pious prayer—and motion-picture operators climbed upon tables and chairs to photograph the leading participants in the trial from every possible angle. The evidence ranged all the way from the admission of fourteen-year-old Howard Morgan that Scopes had told him about evolution and that it hadn't hurt him any, to the estimate of a zoölogist that life had begun something like six hundred million years ago (an assertion which caused gasps and titters of disbelief from the rustics in the audience). And meanwhile two million words were being telegraphed out of Dayton, the trial was being broadcast by the *Chicago Tribune*'s station WGN, the Dreamland Circus at Coney Island offered "Zip" to the Scopes defense as a "missing link," cable companies were reporting enormous increases in transatlantic cable tolls, and news agencies in London were being besieged with requests for more copy from Switzerland, Italy, Germany, Russia, China, and Japan. Ballyhoo had come to Dayton.

DARROW VERSUS BRYAN

It was a bitter trial. Attorney-General [A.T.] Stewart of Tennessee cried out against the insidious doctrine which was "undermining the faith of Tennessee's children and robbing them of their chance of eternal life." Bryan charged Darrow with having only one purpose, "to slur at the Bible." Darrow spoke of Bryan's "fool religion." Yet again and again the scene verged on farce. The climax—both of bitterness and of farce—came on the afternoon of July 20th, when on the spur of the moment Hays asked that the defense be permitted to put Bryan on the stand as an expert on the Bible, and Bryan consented.

So great was the crowd that afternoon that the judge had decided to move the court outdoors, to a platform built against the courthouse under the maple trees. Benches were set out before it. The reporters sat on the benches, on the ground, anywhere, and scribbled their stories. On the outskirts of the seated crowd a throng stood in the hot sunlight which streamed down through the trees. And on the platform sat the shirt-sleeved Clarence Darrow, a Bible on his knee, and put the Fundamentalist champion through one of the strangest examinations which ever took place in a court of law.

He asked Bryan about Jonah and the whale, Joshua and the sun, where Cain got his wife, the date of the Flood, the significance of the Tower of Babel. Bryan affirmed his belief that the world was created in 4004 B.C. and the Flood occurred in or about 2348 B.C.; that Eve was literally made out of Adam's rib; that the Tower of Babel was responsible for the diversity of languages in the world; and that a "big fish" had swallowed Jonah.

When Darrow asked him if he had ever discovered where Cain got his wife, Bryan answered: "No, sir; I leave the agnostics to hunt for her." When Darrow inquired, "Do you say you do not believe that there were any civilizations on this earth that reach back beyond five thousand years?" Bryan stoutly replied, "I am not satisfied by any evidence I have seen." Tempers were getting frazzled by the strain and the heat; once Darrow declared that his purpose in examining Bryan was "to show up Fundamentalism . . . to prevent bigots and ignoramuses from controlling the educational system of the United States," and Bryan jumped up, his face purple, and shook his fist at Darrow, crying, "To protect the word of God against the greatest atheist and agnostic in the United States."

It was a savage encounter, and a tragic one for the ex-Secretary of State. He was defending what he held most dear. He was making—though he did not know it—his last appearance before the great American public which had once done him honor (he died scarcely a week later). And he was being covered with humiliation. The sort of religious faith which he represented could not take the witness stand and face reason as a prosecutor.

On the morning of July 21st Judge Raulston mercifully refused to let the ordeal of Bryan continue and expunged the testimony of the previous afternoon. Scopes's lawyers had been unable to get any of their scientific evidence before the jury, and now they saw that their only chance of making the sort of defense they had planned for lay in giving up the case and bringing it before the Tennessee Supreme Court on appeal. Scopes was promptly found guilty and fined one hundred dollars. The State Supreme Court later upheld the anti-evolution law but freed Scopes on a technicality, thus preventing further appeal.

Theoretically, Fundamentalism had won, for the law stood. Yet really Fundamentalism had lost. Legislators might go on passing anti-evolution laws, and in the hinterlands the pious might still keep their religion locked in a science-proof compartment of their minds; but civilized opinion everywhere had regarded the Dayton trial with amazement and amusement, and the slow drift away from Fundamentalist certainty continued.

THE LIFE OF A FLAPPER

BRUCE BLIVEN

In the 1920s, young women began to break away from the traditional fashions and behavior of their predecessors. "Flappers" wore short dresses and makeup, smoked, and drank. In the following article, Bruce Bliven describes the clothes and attitudes of a flapper named Jane. According to Bliven, Jane and her contemporaries were looking to be treated as equal to men. Most important, these young women wanted to be appreciated for their qualities and accomplishments. Bliven was a writer and editor for the *New Republic*.

J ane's a flapper. That is a quaint, old-fashioned term, but I hope you remember its meaning. As you can tell by her appellation, Jane is 19. If she were 29, she would be Dorothy; 39, Doris; 49, Elaine; 59, Jane again—and so on around. This Jane, being 19, is a flapper, though she urgently denies that she is a member of the younger generation. The younger generation, she will tell you, is aged 15 to 17; and she professes to be decidedly shocked at the things they do and say. That is a fact which would interest her minister, if he knew it—poor man, he knows so little! For he regards Jane as a perfectly horrible example of wild youth—paint, cigarettes, cocktails, petting parties—oooh! Yet if the younger generation shocks her as she says, query: how wild is Jane?

Before we come to this exciting question, let us take a look at the young person as she strolls across the lawn of her parents' suburban home, having just put the car away after driving sixty

Bruce Bliven, "Flapper Jane," *New Republic*, September 9, 1925.

miles in two hours. She is, for one thing, a very pretty girl. Beauty is the fashion in 1925. She is frankly, heavily made up, not to imitate nature, but for an altogether artificial effect—pallor mortis, poisonously scarlet lips, richly ringed eyes—the latter looking not so much debauched (which is the intention) as diabetic. Her walk duplicates the swagger supposed by innocent America to go with the female half of a Paris Apache dance. And there are, finally, her clothes.

These were estimated the other day by some statistician to weigh two pounds. Probably a libel; I doubt they come within half a pound of such bulk. Jane isn't wearing much, this summer. If you'd like to know exactly, it is: one dress, one step-in, two stockings, two shoes.

A step-in, if you are 99 and 44/100ths percent ignorant, is underwear—one piece, light, exceedingly brief but roomy. Her dress, as you can't possibly help knowing if you have even one good eye, and get around at all outside the Old People's Home, is also brief. It is cut low where it might be high, and vice versa. The skirt comes just an inch below her knees, overlapping by a faint fraction her rolled and twisted stockings. The idea is that when she walks in a bit of a breeze, you shall now and then observe the knee (which is not rouged—that's just newspaper talk) but always in an accidental, Venus-surprised-at-the-bath sort of way. This is a bit of coyness which hardly fits in with Jane's general character.

Jane's haircut is also abbreviated. She wears of course the very newest thing in bobs, even closer than last year's shingle. It leaves her just about no hair at all in the back, and 20 percent more than that in the front—about as much as is being worn this season by a cellist (male); less than a pianist; and much, much less than a violinist. Because of this new style, one can confirm a rumor heard last year: Jane has ears.

The corset is as dead as the dodo's grandfather; no feeble publicity pipings by the manufacturers, or calling it a "clasp around" will enable it, as Jane says, to "do a Lazarus." The petticoat is even more defunct. Not even a snicker can be raised by telling Jane that once the nation was shattered to its foundations by the shadow-skirt. The brassiere has been abandoned, since 1924. While stockings are usually worn, they are not a sine-qua-nothing-doing. In hot weather Jane reserves the right to discard them, just as all the chorus girls did in 1923. As stockings are only a frantic, successful attempt to duplicate the color and texture of Jane's own sunburned slim legs, few but expert boulevardiers can tell the difference.

NOT JUST FOR FLAPPERS

These which I have described are Jane's clothes, but they are not merely a flapper uniform. They are The Style, Summer of 1925 Eastern Seaboard. These things and none other are being worn by all of Jane's sisters and her cousins and her aunts. They are being worn by ladies who are three times Jane's age, and look ten years older; by those twice her age who look a hundred years older. Their use is so universal that in our larger cities the baggage transfer companies one and all declare they are being forced into bankruptcy. Ladies who used to go away for the summer with six trunks can now pack twenty dainty costumes in a bag.

Not since 1820 has feminine apparel been so frankly abbreviated as at present; and never, on this side of the Atlantic, until you go back to the little summer frocks of Pocahontas. This year's styles have gone quite a long step toward genuine nudity. Nor is this merely the sensible half of the population dressing as everyone ought to, in hot weather. Last winter's styles weren't so dissimilar, except that they were covered up by fur coats and you got the full effect only indoors. And improper costumes never have their full force unless worn on the street. Next year's styles, from all one hears, will be, as they already are on the continent, even More So.

Our great mentor has failed us: you will see none of the really up-to-date styles in the movies. For old-fashioned, conservative and dowdy dressing, go and watch the latest production featuring [silent film stars] Bebe [Daniels], Gloria [Swanson] or Pola [Negri]. Under vigilant father [William H.] Hays [the president of the Motion Picture Producers and Distributors of America] the ensilvered screen daren't reveal a costume equal to scores on Fifth Avenue, Broadway—or Wall Street.

Wall Street, by the way, is the one spot in which the New Nakedness seems most appropriate.

Where men's simple passions have the lowest boiling point; where the lust for possession is most frankly, brazenly revealed and indeed dominates the whole diurnal round—in such a place there is a high appropriateness in the fact that the priestesses in the temple of Mammon, though their service be no more than file clerk or stenographer, should be thus Dionysiac in apparelling themselves for their daily tasks.

Where will it all end? do you ask, thumbing the page ahead in an effort to know the worst. Apologetically I reply that no one can say where it will end. Nudity has been the custom of many countries and over long periods of time. No one who has read history can be very firm in saying that It Never Can Happen Again. We may of course mutter, in feeble tones of hope, that our climate is not propitious.

FASHION AND MORALS

Few any more are so naive as not to realize that there are fashions in morals and that these have a limitless capacity for modification. Costume, of course, is A Moral. You can get a rough measure of our movement if you look at the history of the theatre and see how the tidemark of tolerance has risen. For instance:

> 1904—Performance of *Mrs. Warren's Profession* is halted by police.

> 1919—*Mrs. Warren* O. K. Town roused to frenzy by *Aphrodite*, in which one chorus girl is exposed for one minute in dim light and a union suit.

> 1923—Union suit O. K. Self-appointed censors have conniption fits over chorus girls naked from the waist up.

> 1925—Nudity from waist up taken for granted. Excitement caused by show in which girls wear only fig leaves.

Plotting the curve of tolerance and projecting it into the future, it is thus easy to see that complete nudity in the theatre will be reached on March 12, 1927. Just what will the appalling consequences be?

Perhaps about what they have been in the theatres of several European capitals, where such displays have long been familiar. Those who are interested in that sort of thing will go. Others will abstain.

At this point [evangelist] Billy Sunday, discussing this theme, would certainly drop into anecdotage. Were we to do the same, we might see Jane on the sun porch talking to a mixed group of her mother's week-end guests. "Jane," says one, "I hear you cut yourself in bathing."

"I'll say I did," comes crisply back. "Look!" She lifts her skirt three or four inches, revealing both brown knees, and above one of them a half-healed deep scratch. Proper murmurs of sympathy. From one quarter a chilly silence which draws our attention to the enpurpled countenance of a lady guest in the throes of what Eddie Cantor calls "the sex complex." Jane's knees have thrown her all a-twitter; and mistaking the character of her emotion she thinks it is justified indignation. She is glad to display it openly for the reproof thereby administered.

"Well, damn it," says Jane, in a subsequent private moment, "anybody who can't stand a knee or two, nowadays, might as well quit. And besides, she goes to the beaches and never turns a hair."

JANE'S POINT OF VIEW

Here is a real point. The recent history of the Great Disrobing Movement can be checked up in another way by looking at the bathing costumes which have been accepted without question at successive intervals. There are still a few beaches near New York City which insist on more clothes than anyone can safely swim in, and thereby help to drown several young women each year. But in most places—universally in the West—a girl is now compelled to wear no more than is a man. The enpurpled one, to be consistent, ought to have apoplexy every time she goes to the shore. But as Jane observes, she doesn't.

"Jane," say I, "I am a reporter representing American inquisitiveness. Why do all of you dress the way you do?"

"I don't know," says Jane. This reply means nothing: it is just the device by which the younger generation gains time to think. Almost at once she adds: "The old girls are doing it because youth is. Everybody wants to be young, now—though they want all us young people to be something else. Funny, isn't it?

"In a way," says Jane, "it's just honesty. Women have come down off the pedestal lately. They are tired of this mysterious-feminine-charm stuff. Maybe it goes with independence, earning your own living and voting and all that. There was always a bit of the harem in that coverup-your-arms-and-legs business, don't you think?

"Women still want to be loved," goes on Jane, warming to her theme, "but they want it on a 50-50 basis, which includes being admired for the qualities they really possess. Dragging in this strange-allurement stuff doesn't seem sporting. It's like cheating in games, or lying."

"Ask me, did the War start all this?" says Jane helpfully.
"The answer is, how do I know? How does anybody know?
"I read this book whaddaya-call-it by Rose Macaulay, and she
showed where they'd been excited about wild youth for three
generations anyhow—since 1870. I have a hunch maybe they've
always been excited.

"Somebody wrote in a magazine how the War had upset the
balance of the sexes in Europe and the girls over there were
wearing the new styles as part of the competition for husbands.
Sounds like the bunk to me. If you wanted to nail a man for life
I think you'd do better to go in for the old-fashioned line:
'March' me to the altar, esteemed sir, before you learn whether
I have limbs or not.'

"Of course, not so many girls are looking for a life mealticket
nowadays. Lots of them prefer to earn their own living and
omit the home-and-baby act. Well, anyhow, postpone it years
and years. They think a bachelor girl can and should do everything a bachelor man does.

"It's funny," says Jane, "that just when women's clothes are
getting scanty, men's should be going the other way. Look at the
Oxford trousers!—as though a man had been caught by the an-
kles in a flannel quicksand."

THE NEW GOALS OF WOMEN

Do the morals go with the clothes? Or the clothes with the
morals? Or are they independent? These are questions I have
not ventured to put to Jane, knowing that her answer would be
"so's your old man." Generally speaking, however, it is safe to
say that as regards the wildness of youth there is a good deal
more smoke than fire. Anyhow, the new Era of Undressing, as
already suggested, has spread far beyond the boundaries of
Jane's group. The fashion is followed by hordes of unquestion-
ably monogamous matrons, including many who join heartily
in the general ululations as to what young people are coming
to. Attempts to link the new freedom with prohibition, with the
automobile, the decline of Fundamentalism, are certainly without foundation. These may be accessory, and indeed almost certainly are, but only after the fact.

That fact is, as Jane says, that women to-day are shaking off
the shreds and patches of their age-old servitude. "Feminism"
has won a victory so nearly complete that we have even forgotten the fierce challenge which once inhered in the very word.

Women have highly resolved that they are just as good as men, and intend to be treated so. They don't mean to have any more unwanted children. They don't intend to be debarred from any profession or occupation which they choose to enter. They clearly mean (even though not all of them yet realize it) that in the great game of sexual selection they shall no longer be forced to play the role, simulated or real, of helpless quarry. If they want to wear their heads shaven, as a symbol of defiance against the former fate which for three millennia forced them to dress their heavy locks according to male decrees, they will have their way. If they should elect to go naked nothing is more certain than that naked they will go, while from the sidelines to which he has been relegated mere man is vouchsafed permission only to pipe a feeble Hurrah! Hurrah!

THE FUNDAMENTAL THEMES OF 1920S LITERATURE

WILLIAM GOLDHURST

Many famous writers established their fame in the 1920s, including F. Scott Fitzgerald, Ernest Hemingway, and Sinclair Lewis. Although these authors were unique, their works had several common themes. In the following essay, William Goldhurst examines the recurrent elements of 1920s literature. According to Goldhurst, these authors based their novels on personal experiences. Fitzgerald and his fellow writers were also united in their distaste for popular American values, such as the pursuit of happiness and worship of the automobile, and their interest in equality and democracy. Goldhurst was the author of *F. Scott Fitzgerald and His Contemporaries*, the source of the following critique.

There is no "key" to an understanding of the literature of the nineteen-twenties. Anyone attempting to reduce it to a single essential "formula" courts the error of oversimplification. Yet there are large areas in the works of [F. Scott] Fitzgerald and his contemporaries that reveal a fundamental agreement of interest and approach. These writers seem particularly in accord in their selection of themes and their attitudes toward literary technique.

Critics have noted the marked tendency toward technical innovation and experimentation during the twenties. The poetry

William Goldhurst, *F. Scott Fitzgerald and His Contemporaries*. Cleveland: World Publishing Company, 1963. Copyright © 1963 by World Publishing Company. Reproduced by permission.

of Hart Crane, E.E. Cummings, and T.S. Eliot suggests one manifestation of their artistic unorthodoxy. The drama of Eugene O'Neill suggests another. And the art of prose fiction constitutes still another—perhaps the most conspicuous area of improvisation and originality. Fitzgerald's *This Side of Paradise*, [Ernest] Hemingway's *In Our Time* and *The Sun Also Rises*, James Branch Cabell's *Jurgen*, [William] Faulkner's *The Sound and the Fury*, John Dos Passos' *Three Soldiers* and *Manhattan Transfer*—to cite only a few of the most important examples—suggest the variety and range of interest during the postwar decade in new forms of artistic expression.

EMPHASIZING THE PERSONAL

The writers of the period were united, moreover, in their approach to their sources of literary material: they stressed the importance of the immediate personal experience as a basis for art. Invention, of course, was still important; but the rendering of the actual, the concrete, the observed phenomena of life was given new emphasis. "It was, in fact, an age of indirect or direct 'transcription,'" writes Carlos Baker, "when the perfectly sound aesthetic theory was that the author must invent out of his own experience or run the risk of making hollow men out of his characters." The consistency with which the writers of the twenties and early thirties adopted this theory gives the literature they produced its intense documentary flavor and accounts for its many *romans à clef*.[1] The serious authors of the time felt that they had first to see for themselves before starting to work; they spared no effort to achieve a verisimilitude based on experienced, rather than imagined, reality. Sinclair Lewis did not hesitate to "research" a subject before committing it to novelistic form. Thomas Wolfe relied upon an amazingly profuse store of remembered events and conversations. Fitzgerald used his own experiences at Princeton, his acute observation of the campus, the classrooms, and the conversations of his classmates, in the preparation of *This Side of Paradise*. For *The Sun Also Rises* Ernest Hemingway drew on his recollections of "the way it was" in Pamplona during the summer festival of 1924. How closely Hemingway patterned his first novel on the actual events of that occasion may be seen in Harold Loeb's account, *The Way It Was* (Loeb was the model for [character] Robert Cohn), or in a

---

1. Novels in which some or all of the characters are based on real people

comment made by Donald Ogden Stewart: ". . . I didn't like the book, for the curious reason that it wasn't a 'novel.' Every damn thing in it was just 'reporting'—at least, up to the end of the fiesta." Stewart might well have underestimated the importance of Hemingway's imaginative presentation of his materials. But works such as Cummings' *Enormous Room* and Dos Passos' *Three Soldiers*—as well as those already mentioned—support the idea that the writers of the nineteen-twenties favored, to a greater extent than previous generations, a background of actual people and events to give their fiction substance and authenticity. Fitzgerald and his contemporaries reversed the doctrine of Shakespeare's Theseus and started, rather than ended, with "a local habitation and a name."

They drew their themes, in the same spirit, from the life around them. The writers of the twenties and early thirties were realists in this respect, too: each recorded with remarkable fidelity the issues and events—as well as the developing, ever-changing attitudes—of his time and place. There are, however, no simple patterns of agreement here. Fitzgerald, [Ring] Lardner, and Dos Passos, for example, all contributed treatments of the Younger Generation: but each one differs in its perspective. Fitzgerald was the chief historian of the emergent debutantes and playboys, and much of his early fiction is devoted to a romantic portrayal of their adventures. Lardner . . . made the same group targets of his satire. Dos Passos drew a picture of the flapper and her escort that emphasizes still another aspect of the subject: the girl is mildly insane and the boy is ignorant and self-interested. The reader discovers variety rather than uniformity in these treatments of a prominent theme of the twenties. Still, there is agreement in this instance—and in many others—in the writers' selection of subjects and materials to be treated in fiction.

SIMILAR VALUES AND ATTITUDES

Furthermore, many authors not only elected the same subjects, but shared similar attitudes toward them. They were particularly unified in their outspoken, sometimes vehement reaction against the popular aspirations and values of the American majority. "Never in history," remarked one of the most famous critics of the period, "did a literary generation so revile its country." Perhaps "revile" is too strong a word; but it is certain that many novelists and short-story writers turned out cynical interpretations of our habits and attitudes. We might consider, for example, fictional treatments of village life in the United States. President [Warren G.] Harding had expressed an opinion on the subject that may be taken as representative of the popular sentiment: "What is the greatest thing in life, my countrymen? Happiness. And there is more happiness in the American village than in any other place on earth." Sherwood Anderson did not agree, as is demonstrated by *Winesburg, Ohio* (1919); neither did Sinclair Lewis in *Main Street* (1920), Ring Lardner in "Haircut" (1925), Herbert Asbury in "Hatrack" (1925), or [Robert and Helen Lynd] in their documentary study, *Middletown* (1929).

A number of authors also turned their attention to the automobile, a commodity that had begun to assume significant proportions in the life of the average American citizen. Sinclair Lewis showed Babbitt's childish dependence on his motorcar for social status and self-esteem. Faulkner, in *Sartoris,* made the automobile a symbol of the returned veteran's reckless and futile quest for speed and excitement; indeed, for the hero of this Faulkner novel the motorcar is a means of escape from life in a peace-torn world. Other writers extended Faulkner's implication: in Lardner's "There Are Smiles," in Fitzgerald's *The Great Gatsby,* and in Dos Passos' *The Big Money,* the automobile is an instrument of death. Such treatments reflect not only the tremendous increase in production and purchase of automobiles during the twenties, but also the tendency toward machine worship in the public imagination of the time.

In other areas Fitzgerald, [H.L.] Mencken, and [Theodore] Dreiser protested Puritanism and "Comstockery." These same writers, along with Dos Passos and Hemingway, rejected the high-sounding slogans of World War I propaganda. On occasion writers even adopted the same imagery: Faulkner (in *Soldier's Pay*), Fitzgerald (in *The Great Gatsby*), and Hemingway (in *The Sun Also Rises*) all owed a profound debt to the sterile landscape of Eliot's *Waste Land,* one of the most influential depictions of twentieth-century society. These examples, which could easily be multiplied, illustrate the close communion of attitude shared by many of the major writers of the time; but they also suggest, as does the consistent emphasis upon experimental technique, the rebellious tendency of their fiction.

Rebellious they were, certainly, and critical of native mores, of which they were perceptive students. Many aspects of the "rebellion" have been recorded; yet the term is misleading if it creates an image of a spontaneous indictment of American institutions and customs. Taken as a whole, this body of fiction is emphatic in its iconoclasm and its vigorous assault on our weaknesses and illusions. But the same strain is evident in the works of earlier writers. In all periods of its relatively short history, in fact, American literature exhibits a rich vein of social satire and social criticism. Especially prominent since the Civil War, the theme of social criticism may be traced from the beginnings of our tradition to the present, from Hugh Brackenridge to Jack Kerouac. The fiction of the twenties differs, of course, in historical particulars; but it is still very much a traditional body of work in its preoccupations and its philosophy: it is part of the continuity of American letters rather than an isolated episode in its development.

THE KEY THEME OF 1920S LITERATURE

We might accurately call their fundamental theme Democracy in America, after [Alexis de] Tocqueville's keen and detached study of our society. The subject is dramatic and multifarious, and it was given particular relevance in the nineteen-twenties by the social and economic forces operating during the postwar era. At no other time in our history have the potential misfortunes of equalitarianism seemed so conspicuous and so close to realization. Brackenridge had observed some of these unwholesome tendencies during the first twenty years of the republic. In his conclusion to *Modern Chivalry* he states that the great moral of his book is "the evil of men seeking office for which they are not qualified." This assertion has familiar echoes to readers of H.L. Mencken, whose era provided abundant material for a similar "great moral" ("I am not fit for this office and should never have been here," confessed Warren Gamaliel Harding). Nineteenth-century writers as diverse as Nathaniel Hawthorne, Mark Twain, and Henry James had focused disillusioned eyes on the subject of the "American aristocracy"; the same theme occupies a prominent position in the works of Lardner, Mencken, Lewis, and Scott Fitzgerald.

In the eighteen-thirties Alexis de Tocqueville had mapped the contours of our culture that would engage native writers almost a century later. Tocqueville saw clearly the rationale of self-interest that dominated American business and the fluidity of movement that characterized our social structure:

It is strange to see with what feverish ardor the Americans pursue their own welfare and to watch the vague dread that constantly torments them lest they should not have chosen the shortest path which may lead to it. . . . A native of the United States clings to this world's goods as if he were certain never to die: and he is so hasty in grasping at all within reach that one would suppose he was constantly afraid of not living long enough to enjoy them. . . . If in addition to the taste for physical well-being a social condition be added in which neither laws nor customs retain any person in his place, there is a great additional stimulant to this restlessness of temper. Men change their track for fear of missing the shortest cut to happiness.

Tocqueville's comments on national pursuits and motives might easily be applied to the post–World War I period. The spirit of our commercial enterprise during those years of unprecedented prosperity was based in large measure upon the practice and principle of "grasping at all within reach" and a "clinging to this world's goods." The social aspirations of the aggressive middle class (in Tocqueville's telling phrase "the many men restless in the midst of abundance") were recorded time after time by the writers of the nineteen-twenties. These tendencies of democracy in America claimed the attention of Fitzgerald and his contemporaries, as they had attracted the notice of the astute European visitor to our shores almost a century earlier.

The writers of the twenties saw numerous possibilities for variation in these dominant motifs: they contained tragic implications, as in Dresser's *American Tragedy*; they provided material for comedy, invective, and satire—as in Lardner, Mencken, and Sinclair Lewis; they inspired the powerful sagas of social displacement by William Faulkner; they gave authority and universality to the fictional autobiographies of Thomas Wolfe; and they were the backdrop for the melancholy romances of Scott Fitzgerald.

JAZZ SWEEPS THE NATION

ETHAN MORDDEN

Jazz is a uniquely American musical style. Although it developed in the South, by the 1920s it had become popular throughout the United States, especially in Chicago. In the following essay, Ethan Mordden describes the "Jazz Age." According to Mordden, jazz is music that is impromptu and savage. Although sentimental music was also popular during the 1920s, composers began to include jazz in their works. However, people who wished to hear more authentic approaches to jazz turned to African American clubs and singers such as Bessie Smith. Mordden has written numerous fiction and nonfiction books, including *Make Believe: The Broadway Musical in the 1920s*, *The Hollywood Studios*, and *That Jazz!: An Idiosyncratic Social History of the American Twenties*, from which the following selection has been excerpted.

H ere's jazz . . . and right where it belongs, too, in a rubric for a criminal who's going to get off scot-free. What reverberation the word had then, jazz—the jive and juke of it, the insensate gambol, that sound and that dancing, rising up out of ragtime and nowhere to assert itself in the city of the big shoulders as a leitmotif for egotists. Sex and slang named it, from black patois (to jass: to copulate) into the dictionary; derelicts played it while classicists fumed; wastrels, above all, adored it—they were playing their song. [Pianist] Fats Waller defined it best: "Man, if you don't know what it is, don't mess with it."

Ethan Mordden, *That Jazz!: An Idiosyncratic Social History of the American Twenties*. New York: G.P. Putnam's Sons, 1978. Copyright © 1978 by G.P. Putnam's Sons. Reproduced by permission.

How Jazz Developed

Wise words. Pure jazz is a special item, made by elitists for elitists; "jazz" as popularly applied broadened out to include just about anything that one heard with a bass fiddle stalking below and a saxophone prancing above, the hot lick of musicians who hoisted "axes" (their word for their instruments) to pop tunes in clubs where patrons debunked Prohibition, spending jack and themselves. They were soloists, these musicians, gadflies of tone living a code as hit or miss as that of the gangsters. Drugged, alcoholic, down and out when they weren't on the bandstand, they respected only one truce, that of keeping to a steady tempo for the benefit of the dancers. No matter what the intention of a composer or lyricist—no matter how chaste or sophisticated—two seconds into any song they played, every song was jazz. That's how it was.

From the south it rolled up the Mississippi to Chicago, shrilling that law and order was a lie—and jazz, too, could lie: A nation of debunkers (and what did we debunk?—business, art, government, the past, the present, all) needed the music that debunked. Late at night, in the cities and towns one could hear the idle riffs of some combo fading away but still holding to it, impromptu, stalling for time till closing, hating daylight. Primitive man sought the essence of a thing in its word, and some cultures believed that to name a thing was to command it; the word "jazz" was magic in just this way. Today we say "Jazz Age" and invoke the whole era, from Teapot Dome[1] via [F. Scott Fitzgerald's] *The Great Gatsby* and The Sheik [a character played by Rudolph Valentino] to the market crash—but what *is* jazz? Folk art, American mode, the sound of gin singing . . . something, but something indigenous and savage and, like Chicago, the essence of a thing—the essence, perhaps, of us. To name it was to conjure up a store of associations; thus the Jazz Slayer, confession and exculpation at once, for if jazz demands surrender, how can the helpless compulsive be guilty? Roxie Hart, murderess of Chicago in [Maurine Dallas] Watkins's play, learns to jazz, and Roxie Hart is acquitted.

[Italian composer] Pietro Mascagni predicted that jazz would kill opera, and John Philip Sousa thought that it would eventually disappear, but Paul Whiteman, the bandleader who styled

---

1. A scandal during Warren G. Harding's presidency that involved the questionable leasing of federal lands

himself "the King of Jazz," called it "the folk music of the machine age," and of the three only Whiteman was proved correct. Jazz and [Henry] Ford, they were coevals. And they hated each other.

Jazz is apparently an outgrowth of the extemporized honky-tonk piano style through "creole" syncopation and solo virtuosity, loose, staccato, and anonymous, but its folk origin is of lesser import than its wild folk acceptance. Like Prohibition, it had been building up to a national explosion, through ragtime and the dance crazes of the 1910s, and when it finally arrived in the twenties, the speakeasy world was ready. They came together, bootleggers and jazzmen and the prominent advocates of the new morality—and all of these got along just fine, being of an unfastened character that Ford would not have understood. Jazz, it was said, made one lose control, but no: jazz was just something to hear while one lost the control that one was determined to lose anyway.

POWERFUL PERSONALITIES

Part of the swank of those days stems from the emphasis on wet personalities. Such noisy drys as [evangelist] Billy Sunday and [lawyer] Wayne Wheeler don't have the lure nowadays—and didn't, really, then—that [New York City mayor] Jimmy Walker, Texas Guinan, or Al Capone possess in the piecing together of the mystery of Prohibition. It is true that Sunday won a huge following from people as sold on bigotry and repression as he, but his name by itself lacks the reverberations of Walker and Capone. And who importunes the memory on behalf of the twenties more than Texas, the "Padlock Queen," Mary Louise Cecilia Guinan, the former movie cowgirl and then sucker-baiter from Waco?—Texas who ran a fleet of clubs in Manhattan, sailing one into infamous report as soon as the authorities docked another. "Three cheers for Prohibition," Texas once remarked. "Without it, where the hell would I be?"

Tender enough to give way to tears at Rudolph Valentino's funeral, Guinan was all the same as brassy as they come. It was her type of woman that replaced the wistful, truehearted maid of pastoral America and the old morality, the [educator and crusader for prohibition] Frances Willards, Louisa May Alcotts, and [soprano] Lillian Russells. When a jury found her not guilty of "maintaining a nuisance" at her Salon Royale on West Fifty-eighth Street, someone in the courtroom cried, "Give the little girl a great big hand," a phrase Texas herself was known to use on occasion.

It was not a naive era, and the jazz that held forth at Guinan's many haunts and at those of less familiar Guinans seconded the mores of the times. In *Processional*, a Theatre Guild attraction of 1925 billed as a "jazz symphony of American life," striking coal miners, radical organizers, Ku Kluxers, and just plain citizens were presented accompanied by a lithe combo, as if only jazz could set the tempo for contemporary drama—even one set in the open country of West Virginia. According to *Processional*, jazz had been received into the culture and was here to stay, jazz and its people. It was our problem and our consolation—in Vachel Lindsay's eyes, "our most Babylonian disease."

THE CHANGING STATE OF POPULAR MUSIC

And it was the key with which even serious composers thought they might unlock the secret doors of America. George Antheil, he who almost blew off the roof of Carnegie Hall with *Ballet Mécanique*, wrote an entire opera in 1929 in the doo-dah of jazz, *Transatlantic*, an absurd burlesque of business, money power, and politics. Of course it took place in New York, and of course its ecstatic finale tendered dawn on the Brooklyn Bridge, with the cast intoning a jazz hymn to the workday, though in fact the Czech lyricist-composer Ernst Křenek had already superseded Antheil's effort with the even more absurd opera *Jonny Strikes Up the Band*, which foretold the subversion of European art by a corrupt black American jazzman. This worthy was seen at the finale astride a globe of the world, jiving on a violin while red-white-and-blue-clad choristers acclaimed him and his blasphemous music.

Strangely, though the character of dissolution and cunning was evident to any jazz-hater who listened, America's pop music was undergoing a bizarrely sentimental stage in the twenties, trilling innocence and flirtation in both lyric and music. "(This is my) Lucky Day," sings a fellow who found his girl, courting her with "Tea for Two" and "(Kiss me, dear) What D'Ya Say?," then toddling off with her to "My Blue Heaven." Even the great [George] Gershwin, the nation's little Fauntleroy expounder of the new sound, aspired to great heights of sissy susceptibility. His gutsy "Nashville Nightingale" fell by the wayside, but scores of couples fell in love to the pristine "Somebody Loves Me," with its sweet, caressing blue note on "I wonder *who?*"

They were still tripping the waltz then, although such dance fads of the late twenties as the Charleston and the black bottom struck a livelier pose, and while the hoodoo of the black blues singers chimed in with a less naive strain, few people were in the audience when Bessie Smith launched into "Nobody in Town Can Bake a Sweet Jelly Roll Like Mine." Only in the seedier dumps of Chicago, each with its jazzy theme song ("The Sunset Café Stomp," "The Royal Garden Blues," and the more ambiguous "Twenty-ninth and Dearborn"), would one hear Bessie, and when the voices of the mainstream such as Kate Smith's did attempt to level with the "low down," it would be via something like "Red Hot Chicago," from the musical *Flying High*, backed up by the "poop-oop-a-doop!" of a vocal quartet and about as low-down as Calvin Coolidge's vest. Oh, the song does make some effort to address the low down on a personal level in its verse, pitched in the minor, but as soon as the chorus gets going, it's all vo-de-oh-do and the superficial self-congratulation of pop-tune sollipsism. "Blue singers," Kate warbles, "those heart wringers who sob ballads to the nation"—but how many of her listeners had heard the blues, the true blues? No matter: "Who furnishes the lot?" Kate continues, with oomph, "red-hot Chicago!" That was about as deeply into it as the brand-name American songs cared to go.

The smart city folk could always seek out the Negro quarter to absorb the aperçus of jazz; the sizable towns had their own private Chicagos just across the tracks, and there the white man made himself intelligent of the real McCoy. On Broadway's stages, lush revues celebrated the fetish of the black in terms that [songwriter] Stephen Foster would have kenned ("Pickin' Cotton," from one of George White's *Scandals* shows, opened with an evocation of "darkies," "lazy weather," and "Simon Legree," assuring its audience that "cotton pickin' is a kind of a spree"), but the in crowd slummed up to Harlem for the more apropos "Empty Bed Blues" or "You Been a Good Ole Wagon (Daddy, but you done broke down)."

That Bessie Smith—now *there* was a jazz slayer for you. She understood what it was all about; in her records, one hears a comprehension of era, even of incomprehensible Chicago during Prohibition. "Any bootlegger sure is a pal of mine," said she, and that does make more of a statement than "Pickin' Cotton" can. But the most complete statement of all these passes at the new lowdown was the lowdown itself, just jazz, manning the baton in the jurisdiction of pagan joyland. With [author] Bruce Barton and his messiah businessman on one side, and Billy Sunday and his Fundamentalist drys on the other, there had to be a midpoint, spitting pretty between the profane and the sacred, and of course that midpoint went right to extremes and blew jazz at them both.

JAZZ IS EVERYWHERE

But weren't the sacred and profane blowing their own jazz back? What were the media and their "presentations" if not a planned jazz? What was this punk superstition about immigrants and liquor and science if not instinctive jazz? "Even when she loses, she wins with her smile," opines a tennis player about a gorgeous model flashing a gorgeous grin in an ad for Colgate ribbon dental cream—isn't that jazz? "From beer to rum to skid row," shrieked the drys—now you have jazz! And what about our [President Calvin] Coolidge businessmen? Didn't they fall right in with the beat when [advertiser and writer Bruce] Barton purveyed a Christ who had apparently retired His opinion of the money-changers to fill the temple with commercial poesy? Look, they were all tooting their horns one way or another. In the ateliers of the highbrow, where debunking was croquet, everybody was subject to satire, and satire was the best jazz of all. Satire took the jazz out of those Roxie Harts who socked the System for sport, and out of the publicity machine and ballyhoo, and out of the younger generation and their new morality, and out of the money bosses and their corporate arrogations. Satire took the jazz out of jazz.

LINDBERGH REMEMBERS HIS FAMOUS FLIGHT

CHARLES A. LINDBERGH

Wilbur and Orville Wright made the first successful flight in 1903. Within twenty-four years, airplane technology had developed to the point where it was feasible to attempt a solo flight across the Atlantic Ocean. On May 20, 1927, aviator Charles A. Lindbergh departed from New York's Roosevelt Field in the *Spirit of St. Louis*, a single motor monoplane (an airplane with one pair of wings). Thirty-three-and-a-half hours later, he landed at Paris's Le Bourget airport, becoming the first person to fly solo across the Atlantic Ocean. Lindbergh's accomplishment made him an instant worldwide hero. In the following excerpt from his autobiography, *We*, Lindbergh details his flight and the reception he received in Paris and throughout Europe.

About 7:40 A.M. the motor was started and at 7:52 I took off on the flight for Paris.

The field was a little soft due to the rain during the night and the heavily loaded plane gathered speed very slowly. After passing the halfway mark, however, it was apparent that I would be able to clear the obstructions at the end. I passed over a tractor by about fifteen feet and a telephone line by about twenty, with a fair reserve of flying speed. I believe that the ship would have taken off from a hard field with at least five hundred pounds more weight.

I turned slightly to the right to avoid some high trees on a hill directly ahead, but by the time I had gone a few hundred yards I had sufficient altitude to clear all obstructions and throttled the engine down to 1750 R.P.M. I took up a compass course at once and soon reached Long Island Sound where the Curtiss Oriole with its photographer, which had been escorting me, turned back.

FROM NOVA SCOTIA TO NEWFOUNDLAND

The haze soon cleared and from Cape Cod through the southern half of Nova Scotia the weather and visibility were excellent. I was flying very low, sometimes as close as ten feet from the trees and water.

On the three hundred mile stretch of water between Cape Cod and Nova Scotia I passed within view of numerous fishing vessels.

The northern part of Nova Scotia contained a number of storm areas and several times I flew through cloudbursts.

As I neared the northern coast, snow appeared in patches on the ground and far to the eastward the coastline was covered with fog.

For many miles between Nova Scotia and Newfoundland the ocean was covered with caked ice but as I approached the coast the ice disappeared entirely and I saw several ships in this area.

I had taken up a course for St. Johns, which is south of the great Circle from New York to Paris, so that there would be no question of the fact that I had passed Newfoundland in case I was forced down in the north Atlantic.

I passed over numerous icebergs after leaving St. Johns, but saw no ships except near the coast.

FLYING AT NIGHT

Darkness set in about 8:15 New York time and a thin, low fog formed through which the white bergs showed up with surprising clearness. This fog became thicker and increased in height until within two hours I was just skimming the top of storm clouds at about ten thousand feet. Even at this altitude there was a thick haze through which only the stars directly overhead could be seen.

There was no moon and it was very dark. The tops of some of the storm clouds were several thousand feet above me and at one time, when I attempted to fly through one of the larger clouds, sleet started to collect on the plane and I was forced to turn around and get back into clear air immediately and then fly around any clouds which I could not get over.

The moon appeared on the horizon after about two hours of darkness; then the flying was much less complicated.

Dawn came at about 1 A.M. New York time and the temperature had risen until there was practically no remaining danger of sleet.

Shortly after sunrise the clouds became more broken although some of them were far above me and it was often necessary to fly through them, navigating by instruments only.

A FOGGY MORNING

As the sun became higher, holes appeared in the fog. Through one the open water was visible, and I dropped down until less than a hundred feet above the waves. There was a strong wind blowing from the northwest and the ocean was covered with white caps.

After a few miles of fairly clear weather the ceiling lowered to zero and for nearly two hours I flew entirely blind through the fog at an altitude of about 1500 feet. Then the fog raised and the water was visible again.

On several more occasions it was necessary to fly by instrument for short periods; then the fog broke up into patches. These patches took on forms of every description. Numerous shorelines appeared, with trees perfectly outlined against the horizon. In fact, the mirages were so natural that, had I not been in mid-Atlantic and known that no land existed along my route, I would have taken them to be actual islands.

As the fog cleared I dropped down closer to the water, sometimes flying within ten feet of the waves and seldom higher than two hundred.

There is a cushion of air close to the ground or water through which a plane flies with less effort than when at a higher altitude, and for hours at a time I took advantage of this factor.

Also, it was less difficult to determine the wind drift near the water. During the entire flight the wind was strong enough to produce white caps on the waves. When one of these formed, the foam would be blown off, showing the wind's direction and approximate velocity. This foam remained on the water long enough for me to obtain a general idea of my drift.

During the day I saw a number of porpoises and a few birds

but no ships, although I understand that two different boats reported me passing over.

Approaching Europe

The first indication of my approach to the European Coast was a small fishing boat which I first noticed a few miles ahead and slightly to the south of my course. There were several of these fishing boats grouped within a few miles of each other.

I flew over the first boat without seeing any signs of life. As I circled over the second, however, a man's face appeared, looking out of the cabin window.

I have carried on short conversations with people on the ground by flying low with throttled engine, shouting a question, and receiving the answer by some signal. When I saw this fisherman I decided to try to get him to point towards land. I had no sooner made the decision than the futility of the effort became apparent. In all likelihood he could not speak English, and even if he could he would undoubtedly be far too astounded to answer. However, I circled again and closing the throttle as the plane passed within a few feet of the boat I shouted, "Which way is Ireland?" Of course the attempt was useless, and I continued on my course.

Less than an hour later a rugged and semi-mountainous coastline appeared to the northeast. I was flying less than two hundred feet from the water when I sighted it. The shore was fairly distinct and not over ten or fifteen miles away. A light haze coupled with numerous local storm areas had prevented my seeing it from a long distance.

The coastline came down from the north, curved over towards the east. I had very little doubt that it was the southwestern end of Ireland but in order to make sure I changed my course towards the nearest point of land.

I located Cape Valentia and Dingle Bay, then resumed my compass course towards Paris.

After leaving Ireland I passed a number of steamers and was seldom out of sight of a ship.

The Final Stretch

In a little over two hours the coast of England appeared. My course passed over Southern England and a little south of Plymouth; then across the English Channel, striking France over Cherbourg.

The English farms were very impressive from the air in contrast to ours in America. They appeared extremely small and unusually neat and tidy with their stone and hedge fences.

I was flying at about a fifteen hundred foot altitude over England and as I crossed the Channel and passed over Cherbourg, France, I had probably seen more of that part of Europe than many native Europeans. The visibility was good and the country could be seen for miles around.

People who have taken their first flight often remark that no one knows what the locality he lives in is like until he has seen it from above. Countries take on different characteristics from the air.

The sun went down shortly after passing Cherbourg and soon the beacons along the Paris-London airway became visible.

I first saw the lights of Paris a little before ten P.M. or five P.M. New York time, and a few minutes later I was circling the Eiffel Tower at an altitude of about four thousand feet.

The lights of Le Bourget were plainly visible, but appeared to be very close to Paris. I had understood that the field was farther from the city, so continued out to the northeast into the country for four or five miles to make sure that there was not another field farther out which might be Le Bourget. Then I returned and spiralled down closer to the lights. Presently I could make out long lines of hangars, and the roads appeared to be jammed with cars.

I flew low over the field once, then circled around into the wind and landed.

LANDING IN PARIS

After the plane stopped rolling I turned it around and started to taxi back to the lights. The entire field ahead, however, was covered with thousands of people all running towards my ship. When the first few arrived, I attempted to get them to hold the rest of the crowd back, away from the plane, but apparently no one could understand, or would have been able to conform to my request if he had.

I cut the switch to keep the propeller from killing someone, and attempted to organize an impromptu guard for the plane. The impossibility of any immediate organization became apparent, and when parts of the ship began to crack from the pressure of the multitude I decided to climb out of the cockpit in order to draw the crowd away.

Speaking was impossible; no words could be heard in the up-roar and nobody apparently cared to hear any. I started to climb out of the cockpit, but as soon as one foot appeared through the door I was dragged the rest of the way without assistance on my part.

For nearly half an hour I was unable to touch the ground, during which time I was ardently carried around in what seemed to be a very small area, and in every position it is possible to be in. Everyone had the best of intentions but no one seemed to know just what they were.

The French military flyers very resourcefully took the situation in hand. A number of them mingled with the crowd; then, at a given signal, they placed my helmet on an American correspondent and cried: "Here is Lindbergh." That helmet on an American was sufficient evidence. The correspondent immediately became the center of attraction, and while he was being taken protestingly to the Reception Committee via a rather devious route, I managed to get inside one of the hangars.

Meanwhile a second group of soldiers and police had surrounded the plane and soon placed it out of danger in another hangar.

Gratitude Toward Europe

The French ability to handle an unusual situation with speed and capability was remarkably demonstrated that night at Le Bourget.

Ambassador [Myron T.] Herrick extended me an invitation to remain at his Embassy while I was in Paris, which I gladly accepted. But grateful as I was at the time, it did not take me long to realize that a kind Providence had placed me in Ambassador Herrick's hands. The ensuing days found me in situations that I had certainly never expected to be in and in which I relied on Ambassador Herrick's sympathetic aid.

These situations were brought about by the whole-hearted welcome to me—an American—that touched me beyond any point that any words can express. I left France with a debt of gratitude which, though I cannot repay it, I shall always remember. If the French people had been acclaiming their own gallant airmen, [Charles] Nungesser and [François] Coli, who were lost only after fearlessly departing in the face of conditions insurmountably greater than those that confronted me, their enthusiastic welcome and graciousness could not have been greater.

In Belgium as well, I was received with a warmth which re-flected more than simply a passing curiosity in a trans-Atlantic flight, but which was rather a demonstration by the people of their interest in a new means of transportation which eventually would bring still closer together the new world and the old. Their welcome, too, will be a cherished memory for all time.

In England, I experienced one final unforgettable demonstration of friendship for an American. That spontaneous wonderful reception during my brief visit seemed typical of what I had always heard of the good sportsmanship of the English.

My words to all those friends in Europe are inadequate, but my feelings of appreciation are boundless.

THE 1927 YANKEES: ONE OF BASEBALL'S GREATEST TEAMS

BABE RUTH

The 1927 New York Yankees are considered to be among the greatest baseball teams in history. The legendary Babe Ruth—who hit sixty home runs that season, a record that would stand until 1961—led the team. In the following account, excerpted from his autobiography, *The Babe Ruth Story*, Ruth writes about the Yankees' hitting and pitching prowess, their domination of the American League, and their sweep of the Pittsburgh Pirates in the World Series.

<hr>

A man who has put away his baseball togs after an eventful life in the game must live on his memories, some good, some bad.

DOMINATING THE AMERICAN LEAGUE

Of the good ones the one that stands out most of all is that of the greatest ball club that ever stepped onto a field, one that I played on and starred for—the 1927 Yankees.

We won 110 games that season, the American League record. We could do everything bigger and better than any club in the league and, as far as I'm concerned, any club ever brought together.

We had an individual champ in just about every position.

That was the year I hit 60 home runs, breaking my own

record of 59—set in 1921—and establishing a mark that has not since been touched by the great sluggers who followed me in baseball. [The record lasted thirty-four years.]

We won the 1927 pennant from here to Christmas, and it wasn't a case of knocking over weak competition. There were a couple of clubs in the American League that year which could win pennants in either league today. The Philadelphia Athletics, for one. We beat them easily, though they were loaded with such players as Jimmie Foxx, Mickey Cochrane, Al Simmons, Ty Cobb (who hit .357 in that next-to-last year of his career), Lefty Grove and George Earnshaw.

We murdered the second division teams that year, especially the St. Louis Browns, managed that year by Dan Howley, who once said he'd put a ring through my nose and tame me. We beat the Browns, 21 straight; and then, taking pity on them, we let them win the 22nd game, long after we had clinched the pennant.

A RAISE AND A NEW LINEUP

Before the season started the club gave me another substantial raise. My five-year contract was up, and after my 1926 season I figured I deserved another raise. [Owner Jacob] Ruppert was agreeable. But I made him blink and sputter when I asked for an $18,000 raise to $70,000.

"That's too high, 'Root,'" Jake said. "I agree that you're entitled to more money, but I hadn't thought of anything like that. I was thinking of an $8,000 raise, sending you up to $60,000. Why, any player would be overjoyed with an $8,000 increase, 'Root.'"

At a conference down in St. Petersburg he finally gave it to me. There was a wishing well down there, and he said, "I'm going to throw a coin in that well and wish you success for 1927. Throw one in yourself, Babe, and wish yourself a lot of luck." I did—and I had the luck.

By 1927 [manager Miller James] Huggins moved [Lou] Gehrig ahead of [Bob] Meusel in our batting order and Lou now batted fourth, immediately after me. He remained in that slot in the batting order for the remainder of his active career.

Lou and I broke up a lot of games that season. I drove in 164 runs, my second highest total; but that Dutchman topped me by driving in 175. I scored 158 runs to his 149. Our entire club scored 975 runs, and four men on the club, Lou, Meusel, [Tony]

Lazzeri and I all batted in better than 100 runs.

I don't think I ever would have established my home-run record of 60 if it hadn't been for Lou. He was really getting his beef behind the ball that season and finished with 47 home runs. At one time we were almost neck and neck, and the papers were carrying what they called the home-run barometer showing what Lou and I were doing up to the minute. Pitchers began pitching to me, because if they passed me they still had Lou to contend with.

HITTING AND PITCHING

Well, I liked the big kid and admired him; he had many likeable qualities. But it also was fun to kid the Dutchman by asking him what he ever had learned in Columbia. If he had beaten me out, it would have put a crimp in my kidding. So I really put the wood to the ball in September and eventually left him behind, finishing 13 home runs to the good.

Speaking of my 60 home runs in 1927, they were made before many of the parks had been artificially changed so as to favor the home-run hitter. I hit them into the same parks where only a decade before ten or twelve homers were good enough to win the title. They said they livened the ball up for me, and some of the writers called it the jack-rabbit ball. Well, if they put some of the jack in it around the 1927 period, they put the entire rabbit into it in 1947 and at the same time shortened a lot of fences. But my old record has held up.

We had great pitchers in 1927: [Herb] Pennock, [Waite] Hoyt, [Walter] Ruether, [Bob] Shawkey, [George] Pipgras, and [Urban] Shocker, though poor Urban already was suffering from weak spells. None of us, however, suspected that he'd be dead within a year.

Ed Barrow, always looking for a sleeper in the deck, came up with the pitcher of the year. He was an out-and-out steal. His name was Wilcy Moore, and Barrow pulled him out of a little league in Carolina for $2000. I don't know where Moore was when all the scouts were gumshoeing around those parts, because he was just about the best pitcher in our league in 1927. Hug used him mostly as a relief man, but he was just as good as a starter, winning 19 games and coming up with the best earned-run average in the league.

Wilcy was a farmer who had some cotton acres in Oklahoma. He was a big, easygoing, good-natured guy and the lousiest hitter in baseball history. I took a look at him the first day he worked for us and laid him $300 to $100 he wouldn't get three hits all season. It looked like a cinch, but the double-crosser bore down through the last half of the season and finished with five hits.

Wilcy took the $300 and bought a pair of mules. He named one Babe and the other Ruth, which probably surprised both of them.

FACING THE PIRATES

We won the 1927 World Series the day before it started. The Pirates were the other club, and the first two games were scheduled for Forbes Field. Naturally, we showed up a day early and worked out in the strange park—and we won the Series during that workout.

You see, the Pirates had held their own practice first, and then they had had a little pep meeting and started back to their homes and hotels.

But by the time they came out of their dressing room, to start away from the park, the Yankees were taking batting practice. Most of them had never seen us, so they draped themselves here and there in the empty stands and took a look. Manager Donie Bush should have insisted that they go right home.

The 1927 Pirates had some darn good ballplayers: the Waners [Lloyd and Paul], Pie Traynor, Glenn Wright, old Joe Harris and a good pitching staff. But you could actually hear them gulp while they watched us.

Babe Ruth

We really put on a show. Lou and I banged ball after ball into the right-field stands, and I finally knocked one out of the park in right center. Bob Meusel and Tony Lazzeri kept hammering balls into the left-field seats.

One by one, the Pirates got up and left the park. Some of

them were shaking their heads when we last saw them.

We got off to a good start by winning the first one in Pittsburgh by a score of 5 to 4, though Hoyt almost blew the game in the late innings and Hug had to rush in Wilcy Moore to save it for us.

George Pipgras then was only a kid pitcher on our club, but Hug took a chance on him in the second game and Pip came through fine, winning by a score of 6 to 2. We decided after that game that we'd be the first American League club ever to win four straight in the World Series.

Herb Pennock pitched the third game for us, and it was one of the prettiest pitching performances I saw in my long major league career. Herb almost got away with a perfect game. He retired the Pirates in order in the first seven innings and then got the first man in the eighth—22 consecutive batsmen.

Nobody was letting out a peep on the bench nor making any reference to Pennock's pitching for fear of putting a jinx on him. I rooted for that perfect game as much as if I were pitching it. But I guess it wasn't to be, for Pie Traynor finally slapped a single to left, and, later, Clyde Barnhart doubled to give Pittsburgh its only run.

After the spell was broken it didn't matter much, and Lloyd Waner reached Herb for a third hit in the ninth. I knew the fans were expecting something from me, too, so I hit little Mike Cvengros, who had been in our league with the White Sox, for a homer later in the game. We won it, 8 to 1.

A WORLD SERIES SWEEP

Now we were sure we could make it four straight. Ruppert wasn't a club owner who played for big gate receipts in the World Series, and we knew that nothing would please him better than to have his team score a knockout.

Huggins was so pleased with Moore's relief pitching in the first game that he gave Wilcy a chance to wind it up for us. A pitcher with specs, Carmen Hill, was on the mound for the Pirates. I thought I put the game on ice for us when I rammed a homer into our right-field bleachers in the fifth inning with Combs on base. But our boys booted a couple of plays in the seventh inning, and the score was tied at 3 to 3 when we went into the ninth. And that was one of the craziest innings I ever was in.

By then a big Serb named John Miljus was pitching for the Pirates. He started off by walking Combs, and then Mark Koenig beat out a hit. Mark was our hottest hitter in the Series and batted .500.

While I was up, Miljus let go a wild pitch, putting runners on second and third. Donie Bush then ran out and ordered Miljus to pass me, filling the bases. A run would beat Pittsburgh anyway, and by having the bags filled they had a possible force play at every base.

Miljus had a lot of moxie that day. With the sacks loaded he struck out Gehrig and Meusel, two of the toughest men in baseball. But that still left Lazzeri. Miljus bore down on Tony with everything he had, but when one of his fast balls sailed high and went over catcher Johnny Gooch's head, Combs raced home with the winning run of the World Series.

The play generally was scored as a wild pitch for Miljus, but there were a lot of people who thought Gooch should have stopped the ball. As a former pitcher, I know we often are charged for wild pitches when we think the fault was the catcher's, not ours.

CELEBRATING THE SEASON

What a crazy bunch of guys we were when we reached our clubhouse! Everybody was singing, dancing, yelling his fool head off. Ruppert came into the clubhouse and was so happy he could hardly talk.

"Well, Jake," I yelled at him, "I guess this makes you feel better after the way we blew the 1926 Series on you."

"You're right, 'Root,'" Ruppert beamed. "I never was so happy in my life. The team was wonderful and you were great."

At the dinner of the New York Baseball Writers the following winter they gave me the plaque for being the Player of the Year. They didn't give it to me because I had hit 60 home runs and had helped the club to a four-straight World Series by hitting the only two home runs of the Series. They told me they were giving it to me because of the comeback I had made after my terrible season of 1925, when a lot of them figured, and wrote, that I was all washed up.

I always got a big kick out of these annual dinners of the New York writers. I was at the first one, back in 1924, and I have missed few since then. I recall the first one. They had a character there named Vince Barnett, who played the part of a tough waiter. He insulted everybody, including Ruppert and Judge

Landis, and he finally got on me. He kept poking me in the chest and yelling, "Whoever told you you were a ballplayer?"

Well, he had me crazy. Rosy Ryan of the Giants and I chased him all over the room, and Rosy finally brought him down with a flying tackle. We were starting to beat him up when the writers who had hired Barnett for the gag called us off and told us it was all a rib.

Just when I had him by the neck.

PROSPERITY IN THE 1920S

THOMAS E. HALL AND J. DAVID FERGUSON

In the following selection, Thomas E. Hall and J. David Ferguson describe the prosperity and improvements in living standards in 1920s America. The long-run average growth rate of the American economy is typically 3 percent per year; between July 1921 and August 1929, the average growth rate was 5.9 percent. The automobile helped generate much of this growth, as the mass production techniques implemented by Henry Ford made cars affordable for middle-class families. The sharp increase in automobile ownership led to a boom in related industries, such as tire manufacturing and service stations. The 1920s were also marked by an enormous rise in construction. However, Hall and Ferguson observe that severe income inequality and concerns over the dangers of sudden economic growth accompanied this rise in prosperity. Hall and Ferguson are professors of economics at Miami University in Oxford, Ohio, and the co-authors of *The Great Depression: An International Disaster of Perverse Economic Policies*, the source of the following essay.

T he 1920s were a period of significant prosperity in the United States. From the end of the recession in July 1921 to the economic peak in August 1929 that preceded the Great Depression, economic output growth averaged 5.9 percent per year, and that figure includes output declines during two mild recessions that occurred in 1923–24 and 1926–27. This economic growth is quite remarkable when one considers that

Thomas E. Hall and J. David Ferguson, *The Great Depression: An International Disaster of Perverse Economic Policies*. Lansing: University of Michigan, 1998. Copyright © 1998 by the University of Michigan. Reproduced by permission.

the long-run average growth rate of the U.S. economy is around 3.0 percent per year.

AN IMPROVED STANDARD OF LIVING

This vibrant growth was associated with rapid improvements in living standards for urban Americans. This was the time when many middle-class Americans obtained automobiles, electrical appliances, and their own houses. [Historian Jim] Potter notes that during the 1920s the number of residences rose 25 percent, telephones increased 54 percent, food production went up about 50 percent, the number of automobiles registered went from 9 million in 1920 to 23 million in 1929, kilowatt-hours of electricity generated more than doubled, and there were enormous increases in sales of electrical cooking devices, vacuums, and radios (1974). At the same time, consumption of education and recreational services boomed as well. Potter contends that the decade "amounted to a massive increase in consumption, perhaps greater in total and *per capita* than in any previous decade in American history" (1974).

The output gains of the 1920s were associated with mild deflation as the Gross National Product (GNP) deflator fell at an average annual rate of 0.5 percent from 1921 to 1929. In other words, the aggregate to supply schedule was shifting to the right more rapidly than the aggregate demand schedule was.[1] The major source of the rapid growth of aggregate supply was widespread application of assembly-line techniques in several industries including household appliances, food processing, and tobacco. The resulting productivity gains were such that while total employment in manufacturing was roughly constant from 1920 to 1929, output grew over 60 percent.

The increased ownership and use of autos was an important stimulus to growth. In fact, it is difficult to overstate the role of the automobile in helping to generate the economic gains of the 1920s. Thanks to the cost reductions resulting from the application of modern mass production techniques by Ford Motor Company in 1913, retail prices for the Model T fell from $950 per auto in 1908 to $290 by 1924. At such prices a Model T (and many other competing models) became affordable for middle-

---

1. Aggregate supply is the total production of goods and services available at a range of prices, during a given time period. Aggregate demand is the total real expenditures on goods and services produced that buyers are willing and able to make at different price levels, during a given time period.

During the 1920s, the mass production techniques used by Henry Ford made automobiles affordable for many families.

class families. As a result, auto ownership rose significantly during the 1910s and through the 1920s. At the same time, many roads were being paved, which stimulated the use of the autos. From 1920 through 1929 the number of miles of surface roads nearly doubled from 388,000 to 626,000. The resulting increase in both the number of automobiles and their use generated a massive stimulus to the demand for complementary goods and services. The petroleum industry boomed, as did the production of tires, traffic signals, service stations, and everything else associated with auto use at that time. Experience gained in these growing industries likely resulted in more efficient production techniques and improving productivity. . . .

THE CONSTRUCTION BOOM

Investment spending boomed during the decade as well. Of special note was the enormous rise in spending on both business and residential structures. Investment in business structures peaked at roughly equal values in both 1925 and 1929, and these inflation-adjusted levels were not reached again until 1953. Residential construction peaked in 1928 at inflation-adjusted levels not reattained until 1947.

What factors contributed to the construction boom of the 1920s? The residential construction boom was certainly partly to satisfy pent-up demand generated by low building rates during and shortly after World War I. During the war resources were diverted toward military uses, and then immediately after the war mortgage financing was difficult to obtain. When financing finally became readily available, home building boomed. The automobile, too, was important, because it allowed people to move to outlying areas where the first big subdivisions were being built. Yet another factor was the building cycle of 18 to 22 years, which was based on cycles in population growth. A peak in this cycle was apparently hit during the mid-1920s. Finally, several investigators have claimed that the housing market had a speculative element to it that resulted in an overbuilt market by the late 1920s. For example, [historians and economists] Ben Bolch, Fels Rendigs, and Marshall McMahon contend that speculative overbuilding is demonstrated by the fact that from 1918 to 1926 net household formation exceeded housing starts, while from 1926 to 1929 housing starts exceeded net household formation (1971). Robert J. Gordon and John M. Veitch argue that a speculative element is demonstrated by the fact that from 1924 to 1927 the ratio of residential construction to GNP was "by far its highest level of the twentieth century" (1986). Alexander James Field points out that optimistic entrepreneurs were so busy subdividing acreage into building lots during the 1920s that after the crash in home building America was awash in vacant building lots: "In New Jersey alone . . . [there was] enough prematurely subdivided acreage in 1936 to supply over a million 6,000-square-foot lots, one for every family then resident in the state" (1992). It was also estimated that nationally there were roughly as many vacant building lots as there were occupied homes.

A similar boom occurred in business structures. Much of this construction was of office buildings as the growth of large firms required larger buildings to house their employees. At the same time, the development of safe and reliable elevators allowed far taller buildings to be built than had been built before. So in cities, especially New York, many very large office buildings were built, the Empire State Building being the outstanding example. Another factor in the nonresidential construction boom was the building of electrical generating plants to help meet the increasing demand for electricity in urban areas.

Government purchases were stimulative at the state and local level, but at the federal level spending in 1929 was below the
level of 1921. A good part of state and local spending went for
road construction to meet the increased demand caused by the
proliferation of automobiles, as well as for sewer construction
in the expanding residential areas.

DARK CLOUDS ON THE HORIZON

In the midst of this 1920s prosperity were two features that many
argue were dark clouds on the horizon: the worsening distribution of income and the stock market boom. The distribution-of-
income problem refers to the fact that while most people were
becoming better off, those at the top of the income scale were becoming relatively much more affluent than those in lower income brackets. For example, Johnathan Hughes cites figures
showing that the share of total income accruing to the top 1.0
percent of income earners rose from 12 percent in 1922 to 13.7
percent in 1929 (1987). Over that same period, the share of
wealth held by the top 1 percent of adults rose from 32 percent
to 38 percent. In 1922 the top 1 percent of income recipients accounted for 49 percent of total U.S. saving; by 1929 they accounted for 80 percent of saving. Jeffrey Williamson and Peter
H. Lindert report that using any of a number of measures of income inequality the period of 1928 and the first three quarters of
1929 may include one of "the highest income inequalities in
American history" (1980).

Williamson and Lindert contend that the cause of this increased income inequality was the high rate of unbalanced technological progress during the period, that is, laborsaving technological innovations that favored one group of workers over
another (1980). During the 1920s, laborsaving technological innovations were concentrated in manufacturing. This change
caused a relative demand shift for labor, toward more skilled labor and away from unskilled labor. The laborsaving capital being put into use was replacing jobs at the unskilled level
(assembly-line workers) while creating jobs at more skilled levels (for example, machine repairmen). Thus, wages of skilled
workers rose relative to those of unskilled workers. Williamson
and Lindert conclude that the technological progress during the
1920s raised the skilled labor wage premium by 0.98 percent per
year (1980).

Another important factor helping cause the changing distributions of income and wealth were the changes occurring in the functional distribution of income. Wages grew more slowly than output per worker, which suggests that corporate profits were rising. This change shows up as rising dividends, which constituted 4.3 percent of national income in 1920 and rose to 7.2 percent of national income by 1929. Since 82 percent of all dividends were paid to the top 5 percent of income earners, this clearly helped contribute to the change in income inequality. . . .

The second major problem in the minds of many was the stock market boom during the late 1920s. During much of the 1920s stock prices rose significantly, but especially during the last three years of the decade. Using Nathan S. Balke and Robert J. Gordon's (1986) index of common stock prices, equity values rose 27 percent in 1922, fell 7 percent in 1923, and then rose 16 percent in 1924, 27 percent in 1925, 5 percent in 1926, 25 percent in 1927, 29 percent in 1928, and finally another 30 percent during 1929 up to the peak in September. Certainly holding stocks during the 1920s was a good investment: if an individual had bought a representative basket of stocks at the economic trough in 1921 and had the sagacity to sell at the peak in September 1929 they would have earned a return of 412 percent *excluding dividend payments!* Furthermore, since the price level was falling slightly during that period, the real return would have been even higher.

According to several accounts, the stock market boom on Wall Street generated a great deal of excitement among Americans. While a relatively small number of people were directly involved in the market, only around 1.0 percent of the U.S. population according to John Kenneth Galbraith (1954), Americans got caught up in the mood of the times. Consider the comments of a major commentator of that era, the great social historian Frederick Lewis Allen:

> The speculative fever was infecting the whole country. Stories of fortunes made overnight were on everybody's lips. One financial commentator reported that his doctor found patients talking about the market to the exclusion of everything else and that his barber was punctuating with the hot towel more than one account of the prospects of Montgomery Ward. Wives were asking their husbands why they were so slow, why they weren't getting in on all this, only to hear that

their husbands had bought a hundred shares of American Linseed that very morning (1931).

Or what the noted historian William Leuchtenburg says about the market's effect on the general public:

Even by the summer of 1929 the market had drawn people who never dreamed they would be caught in the speculative frenzy. How much longer could you hold out when your neighbor who bought General Motors at 99 in 1925 sold it at 212 in 1928? There were stories of a plunger who entered the market with a million dollars and ran it up to thirty millions in eight months, of a peddler who parlayed $4,000 into $250,000. The Bull Market was not simply a phenomenon of New York and Chicago; there were brokerage offices in towns like Steubenville, Ohio and Storm Lake, Iowa. Even non-investors followed the market news; like batting averages, it touched the statistical heart of the country (1958).

1929–1933: Depression and Unrest

CHAPTER 3

THE CAUSES AND CONSEQUENCES OF THE STOCK MARKET CRASH

SEAN DENNIS CASHMAN

The economic boom of the 1920s ended in the fall of 1929. Beginning in September 1929, the stock market began to drop significantly in value. On Tuesday, October 29, stock prices fell so drastically that the gains from the previous year vanished completely. The crash led to the Great Depression, an era of poverty and unemployment that lasted until World War II.

In the following essay, Sean Dennis Cashman examines the causes of the crash and the ensuing depression. According to Cashman, the crash was the result of a bad distribution of income, weak corporate and banking structures, a trade imbalance, and the government's lack of useful economic knowledge. Cashman is the author of nine books on American history, including *America in the Age of Titans; America, Roosevelt, and World War II;* and *America in the Twenties and Thirties*, the source of the following selection.

We might characterize the 1920s as an American dream that became a nightmare. Despite the publicity about progress and prosperity, it seemed that, in economic terms, society was digging its own grave, its citizens the victims of an inadequate economic mechanism. American prosperity in

Sean Dennis Cashman, *America in the Twenties and Thirties: The Olympian Age of Franklin Delano Roosevelt.* New York: New York University Press, 1989. Copyright © 1989 by New York University Press. All rights reserved. Reproduced by permission.

the 1920s stood on brittle glass. However, in 1929 the mirror cracked when the economy was shattered by the Wall Street Crash. The crisis for the old order had been brewing for many years and the climax lasted three months—September, October, and November of 1929. The consequences continued for a decade afterward as the Great Depression spread its shadow over the land.

AN OVERSTIMULATED STOCK MARKET

Heedless of the basic flaws in the American economic system, those with money to invest did so eagerly and greedily in the 1920s. For, as historian William E. Leuchtenburg explains, "The prosperity of the 1920s produced the contagious feeling that everyone was meant to get rich." Thus well before the Wall Street Crash of 1929 there was the Florida Land Boom of the mid-twenties, an episode that had all the hallmarks of a classic speculation bubble.

No single individual was responsible for the Wall Street Crash. No single individual was the architect of the babel of speculation that preceded it. Thousands of people contributed freely to the debacle. In the early twenties stock prices were low; in the mid-twenties they began to rise. The main index for these years is provided by the *New York Times* industrial averages, an aggregate of twenty-five leading industrial stocks. Between May 1924 and December 1925 the *Times* averages rose from 106 to 181. By December 1927 the *Times* averages were 245, a gain of sixty-nine points in the year.

The rise was partly a response to a British decision about the exchange rate that had widespread repercussions. In 1925 Winston Churchill, chancellor of the exchequer, returned Britain formally to the gold standard,[1] making the pound sterling the equivalent of £1=$4.86. He did so for mistaken reasons of prestige and failed to recognize the subtle but disastrous effects of overvaluation. The American response was decisive. In August 1927 the Federal Reserve System lowered the rediscount rate from 4 percent to 3.5 percent. It did this partly to discourage the flow of gold from Europe to the United States, partly to encourage the flow of European imports and thus help certain European countries stabilize their currencies, and partly to stimu-

---

1. The gold standard is a system in which monetary units are defined in terms of their value in gold.

late American business. Unfortunately, the Federal Reserve overstimulated the stock market.

The great bull market began in earnest on Saturday, March 3, 1928. For instance, General Motors rose from 140 to 144 that day and in the next week crossed the psychologically significant figure of 150. There was a specific explanation. Since Henry Ford had discontinued the Model T in 1927 and reequipped his plants for the Model A, production of Ford cars would obviously be somewhat impeded. Thus General Motors would gain customers at Ford's expense. One indication that trading was at astonishing, unprecedented levels was the fact that day after day the stock ticker, unable to cope with the demand, was late: on June 12 it was almost two hours late in recording prices on the floor.

The ecstasy of speculation sent American investors in the 1920s into a wonderland where all had won and all must have prizes. The great Wall Street stockbroking firms opened an increasing number of branch offices across the country. Where there had been about 500 branch offices in 1919, in October 1928 there were 1,192. Business was not confined to the New York Stock Exchange, that accounted for only about 61 percent of transactions; the stock markets of Boston, Chicago, and San Francisco were also most active.

Few bankers urged caution. One who did so was Paul M. Warburg of the International Acceptance Bank who was reported by the *Commercial and Financial Chronicle* of March 9, 1929, as calling for a stronger Federal Reserve policy and predicted that, if the exuberant bonanza of unrestricted speculation was not stopped, then there would eventually be a disastrous collapse. A minority of journalists never lost touch with reality. Poor's *Weekly Business and Investment Letter* referred to the "great common-stock delusion." Both the *Commercial and Financial Chronicle* and the *New York Times* warned that a day of reckoning would come.

Of course, very few people were actually buying and selling stocks and shares. In 1929, when the total population of the United States was 121,767,000, the member firms of twenty-nine exchanges had no more than 1,548,707 clients altogether. And of these, 1,371,920 were clients of member firms of the New York Stock Exchange. Those involved in the precarious and potentially damaging marginal trading were only slightly more than 50,000. Thus, as J.K. Galbraith emphasizes, "The striking thing about the stock market speculation of 1929 was not the massiveness of the participation. Rather it was the way it became central to the culture." It was as if by foolhardy, spendthrift actions, a whole society was digging its own economic grave, a victim of its own inadequate economic mechanism. Such foolhardiness was to bring snow in harvest.

THE BEGINNINGS OF THE PANIC

The economy had already entered a depression ahead of the stock market. Industrial production peaked in June 1929, when the Federal Reserve index stood at 126. Thereafter, it began to decline. By October, the Federal Reserve index of industrial production was 117. Thus economist Thomas Wilson later maintained that the ensuing fall in the stock market was reflecting a change that had already occurred in industry, rather than the other way round.

A few shareowners, suspicious of market fluctuations, quietly sold stock at advantageous prices. In time everyone began selling as much as possible. Real panic set in on the morning of "Black Thursday," October 24, 1929, when 12,894,650 shares changed hands in a vicious spiral of deflation. In the mad scramble to sell people were ready to part with shares for next to nothing. Among visitors to the New York Stock Exchange that day was Winston Churchill who might have rued his decision to return Britain to the gold standard four years earlier. To the *New York Herald Tribune* of October 25, 1929, Wall Street on Black Thursday was like a carnival with huge crowds in a holiday mood surging around the narrow streets of the financial centers and with hotels nearby overflowing with brokers' men. The atmosphere was most tense with enraged brokers vandalizing stock tickers and (largely unsubstantiated) rumors of others having jumped from windows. But it was prices that were falling through the floor.

At noon organized support rallied at 23 Wall Street, the offices of J.P. Morgan and Company. Led by Thomas W. Lamont, the senior partner of the House of Morgan, a pool of six bankers was formed to save the situation. Nevertheless, "Black Tuesday," October 29, 1929, was the bitter climax of everything that had gone wrong before. The amount of trading and the fall in prices was greater than ever. Altogether, 16,410,030 sales took place and the *Times* averages fell 43 points, wiping out all the gains of the previous twelve months. The worst losses were sustained by overvalued investment trusts. Goldman, Sachs Trading Corporation fell from 60 to 35; Blue Ridge fell from 10 to 3. The collapse of the stock market was greeted with blunt vulgarity by the weekly stage paper, *Variety*. Its headline of October 30, 1929, was "WALL STREET LAYS AN EGG."

The period of great bankruptcies began. The first major casualty of the crash outside New York was the Foshay enterprises of Minneapolis, a floundering utilities company, supposedly worth $20 million but already deeply in debt. The Wall Street Crash had eliminated potential investors who might have rallied to it. Now their savings had been wiped out. The market continued to fall inevitably until Wednesday, November 13, 1929. The *Times* averages then stood at 224, compared with 542 in early September. Altogether stocks and shares had lost $40 billion in the autumn of 1929.

The crisis continued along its remorseless and inevitable path of economic disintegration. Despite temporary gains in early 1930, the stock market continued to fall until July 8, 1932, when the *Times* averages were 58, as compared with 224 at their low ebb on November 13, 1929.

THE CAUSES OF THE CRASH

The Wall Street Crash exposed the underlying instability of the American economic system—the overexpansion of industry and the farm surpluses, the unequal distribution of wealth, and the weak banking structure. In *The Great Crash: 1929*, J.K. [John Kenneth] Galbraith emphasizes five principal weaknesses of an unsound economy. The first was the bad distribution of income. The top 5 percent of the population took a third of all personal income. This inequality meant that the survival of the economy depended on a very high level of investment by the wealthy few, or a high level of luxury spending, or both. Since there was a limit to the amount of food, housing, and clothing the rich could consume they must either spend their money on luxuries or investment. However, both luxury and investment spending were subject to a variety of changing circumstances. They could not remain steady.

A second unsound feature was the bad corporate structure. The most damaging weakness was the great, and comparatively recent, infrastructure of holding companies and investment trusts. Holding companies controlled a majority of shares in production companies, especially in the fields of railroads, public utilities, and entertainment. Even in economic crises holding companies insisted on their dividends, whatever the essential economic needs of the operating (that is the productive) companies from which they derived their great wealth. Thus the operating companies had to give priority to paying dividends rather than being able to invest in new plants or improved machinery that might have led to higher production. The system kept the operating companies weak and fueled deflation.

A third feature was the inherently weak banking structure of the United States with an excessive number of independent banks. In the first six months of 1929 as many as 346 banks with average deposits of $115 million failed. This was a tyranny of the weak. When one bank failed, others froze their assets, thus inviting investors to ask for their money back. In turn, such public pressure led to the collapse of ever more banks. Thus isolated instances of bank mismanagement led to a chain reaction in which neighboring banks collapsed like a row of dominoes. When a depression hit employment and people withdrew their savings, bank failures proliferated.

A fourth feature was the imbalance of trade. The United States became a creditor nation in the course of World War I. However, afterward the surplus of exports over imports, which had once paid for European loans, continued. High tariffs restricted imports and this factor impeded the ability of other countries to repay their loans. During the twenties they tried to meet their payments in gold while at the same time the United States was increasing its loans to foreign countries. Congress impeded further repayment of foreign loans by trade when it passed the Hawley-Smoot tariff, signed by Hoover on June 17, 1930, that raised tariff levels quite decisively. The upshot was a sharp reduction in trade and general default on repayment.

The fifth feature was the poor state of economic intelligence. The people running the economic machinery simply did not fully understand the system they were operating. Official dependence on outdated clichés—such as maintaining the gold standard, balancing the budget, and opposing inflation—all posed insuperable barriers to an early solution to the crisis. Moreover, it was harmful to the economy as a whole for the people in charge to equate the national interest with the special interests of the businesses they served.

Nevertheless, the greater fell with the lesser. Charles E. Mitchell of the House of Morgan, Ivan Kreuger, the Swedish Match King, and officials of the Union Industrial Bank of Flint,

Michigan, were among financiers found out for various forms of sharp practice.

Another crook who was made a scapegoat was Samuel Insull of Chicago. Insull was an English immigrant whom Thomas Edison had employed successively as secretary, assistant, and then general manager. At the turn of the century he was head of Edison's offices in Chicago and in 1908 formed the Commonwealth Edison Company, a $30 million corporation consolidating the Edison companies around Chicago, of which he became president. Insull's specialty was combining small power companies into ever larger units with improved facilities for generating electric power and then distributing it. He was a director of eighty-five companies, chairman of sixty-five boards, and president of another eleven. He owed his fabulous wealth to a conglomerate of 150 utility companies, serving 3.25 million people, and employing 50,000. It was valued at $3 billion. Unfortunately, he had a sinister side, his mania for creating pyramids of holding companies that were no better than a chaotic financial jumble. He refused to take account of the fact that a fall in profits of the operating companies, fundamental to the whole system, would reduce the unstable tiers to rubble. In early 1932 his empire collapsed, partly because it was overextended and overcapitalized and partly on account of fraud. The value of its stock fell to 4 percent of its 1931 level and two of Insull's investment trusts were declared bankrupt. In July 1932, having been indicted by a Cook County grand jury for outrageous debts of $60 million, Insull fled to Europe. He moved from Paris to Rome and, finally, to Athens because Greece had no extradition treaty with the United States. When an extradition treaty was signed in November 1932, he escaped to Turkey disguised as a woman. He was eventually returned to the United States and stood trial. However, he was found not guilty as a result of a major loophole in the law: holding companies were not subject to regulation.

The causes of the Wall Street Crash were complex. The results were plain for all to see. The tawdry affluence of the twenties went out like a light.

HOOVER'S RESPONSE TO THE GREAT DEPRESSION

STEPHEN GOODE

Herbert Hoover was elected to the presidency in 1928. Within six months of his inauguration, the American economy had begun to collapse. By the end of his first and only term, Hoover was widely disliked for what was perceived as his ineffective response to the Great Depression. However, Stephen Goode argues in the following article that these criticisms are unfair. According to Goode, Hoover took many steps to strengthen the economy. While Hoover did not wish to enact welfare programs, he did initiate government programs that helped provide people with the credit needed to pay mortgages. Hoover also initiated numerous public works projects and drafted legislation such as the Emergency Relief Act and Agricultural Marketing Act. Goode concludes that Hoover's popularity fell because he refused to change his political principles in order to meet the demands of the majority. Goode is a senior writer for *Insight* magazine.

H e must have been on top of the world. In 1928, Republican Herbert Hoover took on Democrat Al Smith, the popular New York governor, and defeated him by the widest spread in electoral votes ever in a presidential election up to that time. Hoover carried forty out of forty-eight states, for an electoral vote tally of 444 to 87.

Stephen Goode, "Herbert Hoover: An Uncommon Man Brought Down by the Great Depression," *World & I*, vol. 16, March 2001, pp. 283–85, 291–95. Copyright © 2001 by News World Communications, Inc. Reproduced by permission.

It was a much-celebrated victory. Times were good. The economy appeared robust, with many Americans sharing in new wealth. Republicans were elated. Only four years later, however, Hoover lost to another New York governor, Franklin Delano Roosevelt, by an even greater margin, setting yet another record in presidential elections. In the 1932 debacle, FDR won forty-two states to Hoover's six, with 479 electoral votes going to Roosevelt and a measly 59 to Hoover.

A SOLID REPUTATION

At the beginning of his presidency, Herbert Hoover was a highly regarded statesman, with a solid reputation as an able mining engineer and self-made millionaire. He was a capable administrator who had organized and supervised the successful feeding and clothing of millions in a Europe ravaged by World War I.

Right after World War I, Harvard law professor Felix Frankfurter, who was later to sit on the Supreme Court, called Hoover "a truly great man." And in 1920, no less a figure than Franklin Roosevelt, who was to defeat him so overwhelmingly in 1932, wrote a friend that "I had some nice talks with Herbert Hoover before he went West for Christmas. He is certainly a wonder, and I wish we could make him President of the United States. There could not be a better one."

Many agreed. Hoover was mentioned as a possible presidential candidate as early as the 1920 election. For quite a number of Americans, he represented the best elements of Republican progressivism, the wing of the party that continued the activist role in politics personified by Teddy Roosevelt and stood opposed to the laissez-faire policies advocated by such Republican presidents as William Howard Taft and Calvin Coolidge.

By 1932, at the end of his one term as president, however, Hoover had become the most despised and ridiculed man in America, the very symbol of cold, uncaring, and inefficient government at its worst. The man who had been known for getting things done and done well was now the man who could do no right at all.

THE DECLINE OF HOOVER'S POPULARITY

What had happened? The Great Depression. On October 29, 1929, hardly eight months into Hoover's administration, the New York Stock Exchange collapsed on what has come to be known as Black Tuesday. Hoover had expected a financial crisis and had warned on several occasions against what he regarded as the soft financial policies (too much easy credit) of President Coolidge and Andrew Mellon, Coolidge's secretary of the treasury, even before he became a candidate for the presidency.

Hoover had thought that the boom of the 1920s was shaky and that the roaring market would falter. But no one anticipated the depth or seriousness of the long economic slump that followed the stock market's crash. Unemployment stood at 3.2 percent in 1929, prior to the collapse. By 1933, it had risen to 24.9 percent and by 1934, two years after Hoover left office, it reached 26.7 percent.

That meant that many Americans went hungry. Many lost their homes, unable to keep up their mortgages, and millions looked for work when there were no jobs to be had. Long lines formed at big-city soup kitchens. In rural America, men and sometimes whole families wandered the country, looking for work.

For all this Hoover was blamed—which wasn't fair, even to contemporary observers. The great political commentator and observer Will Rogers, a Democrat and no great fan of Republicans, saw that it wasn't and pointed this out. "Nobody ever asked Coolidge to fix a thing" when things were going well and people were getting rich, Rogers said. "We just let everything go and everybody grabbed off what he could get and all, and never fixed anything. But now everyone wanted Hoover to fix everything."

And when he didn't fix everything, Hoover found himself despised and his onetime reputation as a wonder worker scoffed at. The common charge leveled against Hoover while he was still president and the Great Depression raged was that he did nothing. This accusation has been held against him ever since—by historians (who should know better) and in the common memory held by many Americans of those difficult times when so many were out of work and a once-vital economy seemed to take forever to right itself.

HOOVER'S EFFORTS TO IMPROVE THE ECONOMY

It was in this vein that William Allen White, editor of the *Emporia Gazette* and one of America's best-known journalists in the first half of the twentieth century, wrote that Hoover "will be known as the greatest innocent bystander in history. But history will also write him down as an earnest, honest, intelligent man, full of courage and patriotism, undaunted to the last."

Hoover was indeed patriotic, honest, intelligent, and full of courage. What he wasn't was inactive and do-nothing, as we shall see. Far from a president who sat on the sidelines, hoping that the economic slump would right itself on its own, he was an activist president, in keeping with the role he'd played as secretary of commerce, willing to bring the powers of government to bear on the problems that faced the country.

Hoover initiated big-government programs that offered vast sums of money to provide credit to those hurt by the Depression so that they could pay mortgages, buy farm machinery, and the like. What he couldn't bring himself to do was offer welfare directly to people who believed they needed it. That, he believed, would make Americans dependent on government largesse and turn them into parasites.

"No man ever sat in the White House with a finer heart or a broader general knowledge," wrote Frazier Hunt, a prominent journalist who knew Hoover well. What went wrong? Hoover "could not shake himself free from the ancient theory that private property and capital, the rewards of the sweat of one's brow, were sacred beyond all else. So it was that he could not get himself to placing hungry mouths and human rights above property rights."

What Hunt chose not to emphasize was that Hoover genuinely believed that he was doing all that he morally could do to relieve the Depression. He could have opened government coffers and handed out cash to the needy. But that would have been turning his back on American traditions of self-reliance and individualism, he believed, and he thought that it was not wise or moral to create a class that looked permanently toward government handouts in order to survive, which he saw himself and government as doing, if he went too far to satisfy the demands that much of the public were making upon him.

Could he have brought an end to the Depression, had he chosen to be more activist? Rancorous debates rage on that question. Leftist scholars tend to believe that Roosevelt's New Deal helped bring the Great Depression to an end; conservatives say that the Depression wasn't over until industry and the economy got a major push when the United States entered World War II.

What is clear is that Hoover stood by principle to a degree amazing in a politician. For many, this proved his callousness, even his cruelty. For others, he set an example. "Choosing personal conviction over political convenience," writes political scientist Charles Dunn in *The Scarlet Thread of Scandal: Morality and the American Presidency*, Hoover "suffered overwhelming political defeat. He became a profile in moral courage.". . .

HOOVER'S INITIAL RESPONSE

Hoover responded [to the beginning of the Great Depression] with the same can-do attitude (at least at first) that he'd brought to all his previous jobs, whether private or public. In his *Memoirs*, Hoover made it clear that he knew at the time that he was broaching new territory, where previous presidents had never trod: "No president before has ever believed there was a government responsibility in such cases as a depression . . . we had to pioneer a new field."

He turned to a familiar tactic, conferences between government officials and business leaders, extracting from the latter early on promises not to lower wages. He cut taxes significantly. A man making $4,000 with a wife and children, for example, paid taxes about two-thirds lower than before.

Hoover also expanded credit, passing the Agricultural Marketing Act[1] and creating the Reconstruction Finance Corporation and other agencies that made money available to banks and loan institutions, which in turn could make it available to those in need who were willing to borrow on credit. In 1932, with the Depression deepening, Hoover added the Emergency Relief Act[2] to the measures created by his administration to deal with the financial crisis.

Federally built public works were another approach. "More major public works were started in Hoover's four years than in the previous thirty," writes historian Paul Johnson. Many of them are still in use and have become household names: Boulder Dam (now Hoover Dam), the Los Angeles Aqueduct, and the San Francisco Bay Bridge, for example. (Hoover wanted another public work: the construction of the St. Lawrence Seaway, but Congress vetoed it.)

Hoover hoped too that state and local governments could help. He urged Americans to perform "voluntary deeds" out of

1. Under the Agricultural Marketing Act, the government purchased surplus commodities and promoted marketing cooperatives among farmers.   2. The Emergency Relief Act provided states with 300 million dollars in loans.

a "sense of responsibility and the brotherhood of man" to alleviate the plight of others. What he wouldn't do was turn Americans into parasites by providing payments directly to them from the federal government, teaching them, he feared, to rely forever on Washington.

At times, he suggested that the crisis was in part brought on by Americans' lack of confidence in business, at one point suggesting that what the country needed was a great poem to inspire optimism and return confidence where there was none. But nothing brought an end to the economic slump, and Hoover didn't help by repeatedly claiming in the midst of the crisis that "conditions are fundamentally sound" and the Great Depression would soon be over.

THE END OF THE HOOVER ADMINISTRATION

In the public's mind, Hoover became identified completely with what had happened. It was Hoover's depression, as though he alone was responsible—an attitude the Democrats were quick to take advantage of and exacerbate. If his name had once meant to make efficient, to Hooverize, it now came to be pejorative. Hoovervilles were jerrybuilt towns of homeless and jobless men and women. A Hoover blanket was a newspaper used to keep warm at night by those forced to sleep in the open.

The first bucket of concrete is poured at Hoover Dam on June 6, 1933. The construction of the dam created over five thousand jobs.

Hoover flags were pockets turned inside out to indicate penury. When he set out on the campaign trail in 1932, Hoover was booed everywhere he went. In the November election, Franklin Delano Roosevelt readily defeated him.

FDR had no definite plan to confront the Depression with when he came to office, and the one that came to be identified with his name, the New Deal, was in large part Hoover's creation. In 1974 Tugwell said: "We didn't admit it at the time, but practically the whole New Deal was extrapolated from programs that Hoover started."

No less a figure than Walter Lippmann came to the same conclusion as early as 1935 in an article in the *Yale Review*, "The Permanence of the New Deal." "The policy initiated by President Hoover in the autumn of 1929 was something utterly unprecedented in American history." How so? Because, Lippmann argued, "The national government undertook to make the whole economic order operate prosperously," which it had never before tried to do. "The Roosevelt measures are a continuous evolution of the Hoover measures," he concluded.

In his first inaugural, FDR proclaimed, "We have nothing to fear but fear itself." This wasn't all that different from what Hoover had been saying all along—that the Depression was in large part a failure in confidence, that the nation needed greater optimism. What Roosevelt did have going for him, of course, was a buoyant, exuberant persona, vastly at odds with Hoover's dour demeanor. FDR's optimism was catching. He seemed to be looking forward, at a time when Hoover appeared to be standing still or even moving backward, paralyzed by inaction, even fear.

The low point of Hoover's four years in office came in 1932, when the Bonus Army marched on Washington. Mostly World War I veterans who wanted a pension that had been promised to them paid twelve years early, they camped in the capital waiting for a government response. Hoover refused to meet with their representatives and ordered the "army"—about fifteen thousand or so—to leave Washington. A confrontation between the protesters and the Army (George Patton, Douglas MacArthur, and MacArthur's aide, Dwight D. Eisenhower, were involved in leadership capacities) became a melee, with the protesters forced to abandon their camps.

Most Americans approved of the Army's effort to bring an end to the protest, but Democrats and the Left made great use of the incident (and still do) to denounce Hoover as a tyrant and his administration as an enemy of the people. It was Hoover's worst day, made even worse by an investigation that followed which cast his administration in even darker hues. Little known is the fact that he quietly arranged to have Congress provide funds for the Bonus Army protesters who wanted to return home. Over five thousand of them accepted the aid.

HOOVER'S VALUES

In retirement, Hoover wrote books and traveled. After World War II, he once again helped organize the feeding of the hungry in Europe. In the 1950s, Hoover sat at the head of a committee set up by President Eisenhower to suggest ways to reorganize government and make it more efficient. His commitment to government service helped mitigate the contempt in which many Americans held him.

But not entirely. He was still regarded by many as the symbol of government at its uncaring worst. In his own defense, he pointed out that throughout his administration he had maintained a "rigid" allegiance to the Constitution and his own principles. With the triumph of FDR's New Deal and Roosevelt's political style, Hoover's self-help and individualistic principles seemed dated indeed, consigned to history's morgue. But were they? In the 1990s, the Democrats, heirs to FDR's paternalism and welfare-state policies, joined Republicans in dismantling many welfare measures long in place, actions of which Hoover could only approve.

What is ironic is that the Democrats pursued welfare reform under a president as different from Herbert Hoover as anyone could be. Bill Clinton tested every move he made according to what polls had to say about U.S. opinion at that moment, governing by carefully testing the direction of the prevailing wind, rather than by principle.

Hoover was temperamentally and morally incapable of approaching policy in that manner. By his adherence to liberty and American ideals as he saw them, Hoover indeed set an example of moral courage, but it was one too severe for most people— and certainly most politicians—to emulate. Hoover cared about what Americans thought about him but didn't find it necessary to reshape his ideas to fit the demands of the majority, a character trait very unusual in a politician. . . . Hoover was finally concerned not so much with immediate situations but with principles that would stand for the next hundred years.

THE SCOTTSBORO TRIAL

ROBERT J. ALLISON

More than six decades after the end of the Civil War, racism was still a serious problem in the South. African American men were lynched merely for being accused of raping white women. One of the most famous rape cases was the 1931 Scottsboro case, in which two white women lied about being raped by nine African American youths. In the following selection, Robert J. Allison provides an overview of the Scottsboro case. He details the racism that marred the trials and the conflict between the liberal, Communist, and African American organizations that worked to defend and support the Scottsboro nine. Allison is an associate professor of history and the director of the American studies program at Suffolk University in Boston.

The freight train rolling from Chattanooga to Memphis, passing through northern Alabama, in March 1931 carried on it dozens of stowaways, teenagers, and young adults from various parts of the South, as they traveled from one place to another in search of work. From Tennessee, Alabama, and Georgia came white and black youths who were leaving desperate circumstances at home to find what they hoped would be opportunity somewhere else. As the train rolled through Jackson County, Alabama, some of the white and black youths got into a fight. The blacks won, forcing the whites from the train.

The whites did not take their defeat easily. They reported on the blacks at the nearest station, and when the train pulled into

Robert J. Allison, *History in Dispute, Volume 3: American Social and Political Movements, 1900–1945*. Detroit: St. James Press, 2000. Copyright © 2000 by St. James Press. Reproduced by permission.

Paint Rock, Alabama, a posse was waiting. They had orders to arrest all blacks on the train. From the rear to the front of the train the posse rounded up nine black youths. Some had been involved in the fight, others had not. Four of the nine—Haywood Patterson and Andy Wright, both nineteen, and Andy's brother Leroy and Gene Williams, both thirteen—were from Chattanooga and were traveling together. The other five, all from Georgia, were strangers to one another. Charlie Weems was the oldest at twenty, and Ozie Powell and Clarence Norris were both in their late teens. Olen Montgomery, who had been traveling by himself, was blind in his left eye and was barely able to see out of his right. Willie Roberson had slept by himself at the back of the train when the posse woke and arrested him. His syphilis was so painful that he could only walk with the support of a cane.

From the front of the train fled two white women, Victoria Price and Ruby Bates, dressed in men's overalls. Price and Bates were traveling with two men and feared being arrested for crossing state lines for immoral purposes. The posse found them, and along with the nine black youths, brought the detainees to the jail in Scottsboro, Alabama. Price was a fast thinker, and seeing the nine blacks in custody, she told the deputies that the nine blacks had viciously raped her and Bates. Bates corroborated the story, and before long word spread through the county about a brutal assault on the freight train.

ON TRIAL FOR RAPE

The mere rumor of the rape of a white woman by a black man was sufficient in most Southern communities to enrage white opinion to the point of a mob gathering to brutally execute the accused black man. Authorities in Alabama, though, wanted to make a point. They would not satisfy the mob that began calling for the blood of the accused. Instead, Alabama would grant the accused a trial, after which, if found guilty, they would be executed. The judge in Scottsboro appointed all seven local lawyers to defend the accused, but each white lawyer found reasons not to defend nine black teenagers from other places who were charged with one of the most brutal and bestial crimes ever recorded in Alabama, if not in the United States. Price embellished her story, giving graphic and outrageous details of the assault; local doctors who examined her and Bates found evidence that the two had experienced sexual relations within the previous two days, but no evidence that they had been brutalized.

In early April the trials began. Patterson would remember the trials as "one big smiling white face." Stephen Roddy, a Chattanooga lawyer hired by black congregations in that city, defended the nine, all of whom were convicted. All but Wright were sentenced to die in Alabama's electric chair. Alabama whites were satisfied with the speedy verdict and awaited equally speedy executions to prevent future assaults like this one. As Alabama prepared to execute the boys and vindicate the virtue of Price, Bates, and white women everywhere, however, the Communist Party, National Association for the Advancement of Colored People (NAACP), and American Civil Liberties Union (ACLU) took an interest in the case.

The NAACP had confined itself in recent years to defending the legal and civil rights of African Americans. In 1925 it had engaged Clarence Darrow to defend Ossian and Gladys Sweet, a black couple who had bought a home in an all-white Detroit neighborhood. When a white mob tried to storm the house, someone inside fired a gun and killed a man sitting on his porch across the street. Every person in the Sweet house was charged with murder, but Darrow's brilliant defense saved them from conviction. In 1930 the NAACP had defeated President Herbert Hoover's nomination of North Carolina judge John J. Parker to the U.S. Supreme Court. When Parker ran for governor of North Carolina in 1920, he had said, "The participation of the Negro in politics is a source of evil and danger to both races and is not desired by the wise men in either race or by the Republican Party of North Carolina." The NAACP moved into action, rousing grassroots opposition, mobilizing black voters, particularly in the Northern and border states, to pressure senators to vote against Parker. It was one of the first and one of the most successful mobilizations of black opinion in American history, and Parker's defeat by a vote of thirty-nine in favor and forty-one against was a triumph for the NAACP.

SUPPORT FOR THE SCOTTSBORO DEFENDANTS

The NAACP and the Communist Party became interested in the case for reasons of their own. The ACLU sent Hollace Ransdell to Huntsville, Alabama, to check on the backgrounds of Price and Bates. She discovered that both women came from the worst neighborhood in Huntsville, where Price was known as a colorful local prostitute. She had recently spent time in jail for adultery. Bates's character was less tainted than Price's, though she came from a desperately poor household. Both Bates and Price lived on the margin of white society. Their status now as victims of a bestial crime made them celebrities among whites; they were now respected by whites, who until this time had regarded them as trash.

As the boys awaited execution, their lawyers appealed the convictions to the Alabama Supreme Court and U.S. Supreme Court, as well as engaged in a battle over who the official representing lawyers should be. The Communist Party wanted complete control over the case and won the loyalty of the boys and their parents. In 1929 the Communist International had called for the beginning of social revolution, had targeted African Americans as a likely group to help organize a revolution, and also had called on American communists to lead the revolution by first smashing all rivals to their radical leadership. Other organizations that professed to speak for American blacks, such as the NAACP, the Urban League, or Marcus Garvey's United Negro Improvement Association (UNIA), were to be castigated as traitors and dupes of the ruling class.

Communists denounced these groups and their leaders much more savagely than they attacked anyone in the ruling class.

The communists saw great propaganda value in the Scottsboro case, as they painted the nine defendants as workers being summarily sent to their execution by the brutal hand of capitalism. The International Labor Defense's (ILD) success in winning the loyalty of the defendants and their parents was a public-relations victory, and rallies throughout the North, featuring the mothers of the convicted men, stirred interest in the communist program, if not membership in the Party.

While the communists saw an opportunity in Scottsboro, the NAACP saw problems. Its legal successes had come in defending the rights of black men and women. It had avoided cases of blacks accused of rape, knowing that little good would come to the organization if it was associated with "bad Negroes." While the NAACP had crusaded against lynching, it could not entirely fault Alabama for preventing lynching in this case by legally trying the nine youths. Communist agitation against the verdict, however, spurred the NAACP into action. NAACP members demanded to know what their organization was doing about the Scottsboro boys. Their organization could do little, since both it and the communist ILD each insisted it have total control over the case. The ILD had already won the loyalty of the defendants and their families, while the NAACP was slow to see the defendants as anything other than troublesome black youths. When NAACP head Walter White visited Alabama to try to win over the defendants, he was told by Wright that his mother had committed him to the ILD. White asked the young defendant if he could be sure his mother's judgment was trustworthy. "Mr. White," the incredulous Wright asked, "If you can't trust your mother, who can you trust?"

The guilt or innocence of the defendants seemed to get lost in the ideological struggle between the ILD and the NAACP as they competed for control of the case. The ILD won the right to represent the defendants and argued that the capitalist system would execute these victims of oppression. W.E.B. Du Bois, editor of the NAACP newspaper *The Crisis,* pointed out that while the ILD said the Scottsboro trial was an attempt to suppress the working class, in Alabama it was the working class that clamored for the execution of the nine boys. Some in the NAACP suspected that the communists would welcome the executions, in order to make the nine defendants martyrs. To their credit, ILD lawyers successfully appealed Powell's conviction to the U.S. Supreme Court. In November 1932 the Court ruled that Powell and the other defendants had been denied fair trials and that they had a right to adequate representation by counsel. After the Court overturned Powell's conviction, the ILD engaged Samuel Liebowitz, a noncommunist but a successful New York criminal lawyer, to represent the defendants. The second round of trials were held in Decatur, Alabama, in April 1933. By this time Bates had recanted her story of rape and testified for the defense. Bates had also been touring the North with the mothers of the accused, joining the ILD in its public campaign supporting the Scottsboro boys. Nevertheless, the Decatur jury found the defendants guilty.

A NEW TRIAL AND APPEALS

The judge in Decatur was so shaken by the fact that the jury convicted the accused on flimsy evidence that he granted a new trial; once again, in December 1933, Patterson and Powell were tried and found guilty of rape. The ILD realized that while Alabama juries would continue to convict the boys, public opinion was turning in their favor. Bates had recanted, the doctors' testimony was strong, and it was clear that racial prejudice was all that kept the Scottsboro boys in jail. In October 1934 the ILD recognized that it could gain an even greater advantage in the court of public opinion if Price also recanted. She, on the other hand, needed money, so the ILD and Price approached one another—it is not clear who made the first move—to see if she could change her story and be rewarded for it. When Liebowitz learned that the ILD had tried to bribe Price, he was furious and began moving to have the communists removed from the case. In December he and other groups interested in the defense formed the American Scottsboro Committee, which would rival the ILD in leading the defense.

In the spring of 1935, leaders in Moscow changed their mind about the relative dangers of fascists as opposed to noncommunist leftists. To prevent fascism from taking power in France, the communists had found it necessary to ally themselves with socialists and others. Now, in May 1935, a convocation of communists in Moscow decided that United Fronts to oppose fascism were a good idea. Communists in America now were free to work with noncommunists. In December the ILD, NAACP, American Scottsboro Committee, and ACLU formed the Scottsboro Defense Committee.

In April 1935, Liebowitz argued Norris's appeal to the U.S. Supreme Court, contending that Norris, Patterson, and the other defendants could not have had a fair trial because no black person had ever been called to serve on an Alabama jury. The Court agreed, and once again Alabama had to retry the defendants, this time without excluding blacks from the jury pool. One hundred jurors were called, twelve of them black. All of the blacks were either challenged or opted not to serve on the jury, but Alabama at least could now say that it had not discriminated in calling potential jurors. In January 1936, Patterson's fourth trial opened. He was once again found guilty, but this time the jury sentenced him to seventy-five years in prison. This was the first time in the history of Alabama that a black man accused of raping a white woman was not sentenced to death. The jury foreman was convinced that Patterson was innocent, but he and the other jurors were afraid to go home if they failed to convict.

As Norris, Wright, and Powell were being taken from the courthouse in Decatur back to the Birmingham jail, Powell produced a knife and cut a deputy sheriff's neck. The deputy shot

Powell in the head, seriously wounding both Powell and the case. Powell and the others had already spent five years in prison for a crime that had never happened, but now Powell was charged with assault on a deputy.

THE CONCLUSION OF THE SCOTTSBORO CASE

Alabama had come under increasing pressure from outside to admit its error in holding these nine defendants. At the same time, some white Alabamians sought an honorable way out of the impasse. Some maintained that Liebowitz, whether he was allied with the communists or not, was tainted by their involvement in the case; he was further handicapped by the fact that he was a New Yorker and Jewish. In May 1936 moderate Alabamians formed the Alabama Scottsboro Fair Trial Committee and sought to find a prominent Southern lawyer to take on the case. They failed to do so and could not find an alternative counsel to Liebowitz, who continued to defend the accused. In July 1937, Norris was once again found guilty of rape and sentenced to death.

At this point the state of Alabama showed that it was tired of trying these cases and coming under attack. After Norris's trial the state declared that Powell was not fit to stand trial and ultimately dropped the rape charge in exchange for Powell's guilty plea to assaulting the deputy. He was sentenced to twenty years in prison. Liebowitz unsuccessfully asked the court to take the six years Powell had already served into account. As Wright's trial opened, the state announced it would not seek the death penalty, and Wright was found guilty and sentenced to ninety-nine years in prison. Weems was also convicted and was sentenced to seventy-five years. The state, having convicted four of the defendants and jailed the fifth on other charges, decided not to prosecute the remaining four: Roberson, Montgomery, Wright, and Williams. Liebowitz sent the four to New York, where they appeared in a revue at the Apollo Theatre.

Alabama's governor, under pressure now from President Franklin D. Roosevelt and other liberal leaders, commuted Norris's sentence to life in prison. Between 1939 and 1943 Alabama refused to parole the remaining prisoners. In November 1943, with little public notice, the state released Weems, now thirty-two years old, and the following year released Norris and Wright, sending them to work in a Montgomery lumber yard. The two escaped to Ohio and were returned to an Alabama prison. Norris was paroled again in 1946, and Powell was released the same year. The state parole board had found Patterson to be "sullen, vicious, and incorrigible," but in 1948 he escaped. When the F.B.I. discovered him in Michigan, that state's governor, G. Mennen Williams, refused to extradite him to Alabama. On 9 June 1950, Wright, the last of the Scottsboro defendants in jail, was freed. He had served nineteen years in prison for a crime that had never taken place.

REMEMBERING THE BONUS MARCH

JIM SHERIDAN, AS TOLD TO STUDS TERKEL

In 1932 more than twenty thousand American veterans marched on Washington, D.C., and demanded that a bill be passed that would provide them with immediate payment of a bonus that the U.S. government had promised them for fighting in World War I. When the Senate did not pass the bill, the marchers refused to return home. In response, President Hoover ordered the army, led by Douglas MacArthur, to forcibly evict the veterans. The marchers' camps were set on fire and they were driven from the capital.

In the following account, Jim Sheridan describes his participation in the Bonus March. Sheridan explains how he and other marchers stole rides on trains in order to get to D.C. and how they were eventually smoked out of the capital. Studs Terkel is a broadcaster and Pulitzer Prize–winning author whose books include *The Good War*, *Division Street*, and *Hard Times*, from which the following account has been excerpted.

The soldiers were walking the streets, the fellas who had fought for democracy in Germany [during World War I]. They thought they should get the bonus [that was promised to them] right then and there because they needed the money. A fella by the name of Waters, I think, got up the idea of these ex-soldiers would go to Washington, make the kind of trip

Jim Sheridan, as told to Studs Terkel, *Hard Times: An Oral History of the Great Depression.* New York: Pantheon Books, 1986. Copyright © 1986 by Studs Terkel. Reproduced by permission.

the hoboes made with Coxey in 1894,[1] they would be able to get the government to come through.

ORGANIZING A MARCH

D.C. Webb organized a group from Bughouse Square to go on this bonus march. Not having been in the army—I was too young for World War I and too old for World War II (laughs)—l was wondering if I would be a legitimate marcher. But the ten or fifteen other fellas were all soldiers, and they thought it would be O.K. for me to go. Webb said, "Come along, you're a pretty good bum." (Laughs.)

We went down to the railyards and grabbed a freight train. Our first stop was in Peru, Indiana. We jungled up there for a little while, and then we bummed the town, so to speak. Go to different grocers and give them a tale of woe. They would give us sausage or bread or meat or canned goods. Then we'd go back to the railroad yards, the jungle, where we'd build a little fire and we'd cook it up in these cans. We'd sit around the fire and eat. . . .

Peru was the first division point outside of Chicago on the [Chesapeake and Ohio Railway]. We'd stop off and rest and scrounge up something to eat. We'd generally be told by the conductors the train was made up and ready to go out. Some of these fellas had come with their families. Can you imagine women and children riding boxcars?

The conductor'd want to find out how many guys were in the yard, so he would know how many empty boxcars to put onto the train. Of course, the railroad companies didn't know this, but these conductors, out of their sympathy, would put two or three empty boxcars in the train, so these bonus marchers could crawl into them and ride comfortable into Washington. Even the railroad detectives were very generous.

Sometimes there'd be fifty, sixty people in a boxcar. We'd just be sprawled out on the floor. The toilet . . . you had to hold it till you got a division point. (Laughs.) That's generally a hundred miles. You didn't carry food with you. You had to bum the town. It was beggary on a grand scale.

In one town, D.C. Webb got up on the bandstand and made a speech. We passed the hat, even, among the local citizenry.

1. In 1894, Jacob S. Coxey led a march of unemployed into Washington. It failed in its purpose. The small size of the group led to the coinage of the derogatory phrase, "Coxey's Army."

The money was used to buy cigarettes for the boys. Townspeople, they were very sympathetic.

There was none of this hatred you see now when strange people come to town, or strangers come to a neighborhood. They resent it, I don't know why. That's one of the things about the Depression. There was more camaraderie than there is now. Even more comradeship than the Commies could even dream about. That was one of the feelings that America lost. People had different ideas, they disagreed with one another. But there was a fine feeling among them. You were in trouble . . . damn it, if they could help ya, they would help ya.

One incident stuck in my memory. We had reached a place in Virginia. It was a very hot day. In this jungle, there was a man, a very tall man. He had his wife with him and several small children. We invited them over to have something to eat with us, and they refused. Then I brought something over to them in an old pie plate. They still refused. It was the husband who told me that he didn't care for anything to eat. But see, the baby was crying from hunger.

Finally, me and some others went down to bum the center of the town. I remember going into a drugstore and bumming a baby bottle with a nipple. Now, can you imagine a guy bumming a baby bottle with a nipple? It took me a few guts to work it up. I explained the circumstances. Then I went and bummed the milk.

When I got back to the jungle camp, it was kinda dark. I first reported in to Captain Webb and then he kidded me about the baby bottle. "Christ," I said, "that baby there's gotta eat." And he said, "This afternoon you got pretty much of a rebuff." "Well," I said, "I'm gonna try again." So I went over and addressed myself to his wife. And I told her: here is the baby bottle. We had even warmed up the milk. But she looked at her husband, and her husband said he didn't want it.

What could I do about it, but just feel blue? I didn't look upon it as charity. It seemed to me that here was a fella's pride getting the best of him.

The tragedy came when the train was going through Virginia.

We had to go through these mountain countries. The smoke from the stacks of the engines, and the soot, would be flying back through the tunnels and would be coming into the boxcars. So in order to avoid getting choked, we'd close the boxcars and hold handkerchiefs over our noses. There was quite a discussion about this. What would happen to the little infant? We was afraid it would smother. The mother was holding the baby, but the baby seemed very still. The mother screamed. We didn't know what the scream was about. After we reached Washington, we found out that the baby had died going through the tunnels.

When the baby died, a feeling of sadness came over those in the boxcar. It seemed that they had lost one of their own.

ARRIVING IN WASHINGTON

When we got to Washington, there was quite a few ex-servicemen there before us. There was no arrangements for housing. Most of the men that had wives and children were living in Hooverville. This was across the Potomac River—what was known as Anacostia Flats. They had set up housing there, made of cardboard and of all kinds. I don't know how they managed to get their food. Most other contingents was along Pennsylvania Avenue.

They were tearing down a lot of buildings along that street, where they were going to do some renewal, build some federal buildings. A lot of ex-servicemen just sort of turned them into barracks. They just sorta bunked there. Garages that were vacant, they took over. Had no respect for private property. They didn't even ask permission of the owners. They didn't even know who the hell the owners was.

They had come to petition Hoover, to give them the bonus before it was due. And Hoover refused this. He told them they couldn't get it because it would make the country go broke. They would hold midnight vigils around the White House and march around the White House in shifts.

The question was now: How were they going to get them out of Washington? They were ordered out four or five times, and they refused. The police chief was called to send them out, but he [General Pelham D. Glassford] refused. I also heard that the marine commander, who was called to bring out the marines, also refused. Finally, the one they did get to shove these bedraggled ex-servicemen out of Washington was none other than the great [Douglas] MacArthur.

The picture I'll always remember . . . here is MacArthur coming down Pennsylvania Avenue. And, believe me, ladies and gentlemen, he came on a white horse. He was riding a white horse. Behind him were tanks, troops of the regular army.

This was really a riot that wasn't a riot, in a way. When these

A World War I veteran and his family join thousands of others in Washington, D.C., to demand bonuses promised by Congress.

ex-soldiers wouldn't move, they'd poke them with their bayonets, and hit them on the head with the butt of a rifle. First, they had a hell of a time getting them out of the buildings they were in. Like a sit-in.

They managed to get them out. A big colored soldier, about six feet tall, had a big American flag he was carrying. He was one of the bonus marchers. He turned to one of the soldiers who was pushing him along, saying: "Get along there, you big black bastard." That was it. He turned and said, "Don't try to push me. I fought for this flag. I fought for this flag in France and I'm gonna fight for it here on Pennsylvania Avenue." The soldier hit him on the side of the legs with the bayonet. I think he was injured. But I don't know if he was sent to the hospital.

This was the beginning of a riot, in a way. These soldiers were pushing these people. They didn't want to move, but they were pushing them anyway.

As night fell, they crossed the Potomac. They were given orders to get out of Anacostia Flats, and they refused. The soldiers set those shanties on fire. They were practically smoked out. I saw it from a distance. I could see the pandemonium. The fires were something like the fires you see nowadays that are started in these ghettoes. But they weren't started by the people that live there.

The soldiers threw tear gas at them and vomiting gas. It was one assignment they reluctantly took on. They were younger than the marchers. It was like sons attacking their fathers. The next day the newspapers deplored the fact and so forth, but they realized the necessity of getting these men off. Because they were causing a health hazard to the city. MacArthur was looked upon as a hero.

And so the bonus marchers straggled back to the various places they came from. And without their bonus.

THE FIRST TWO MONTHS OF THE NEW DEAL

FRANKLIN DELANO ROOSEVELT

Herbert Hoover's perceived inability to end the Great Depression resulted in his loss in the 1932 presidential election to Democratic candidate Franklin Delano Roosevelt. Upon his inauguration in March 1933, Roosevelt began to push for laws—known collectively as the "New Deal"—that would help strengthen the economy. These new measures included the Emergency Banking Relief Act and the Federal Emergency Relief Act.

Roosevelt used radio addresses, known as "fireside chats," to keep Americans informed of the latest legislation and economic news. On May 7, 1933, he delivered his second fireside chat. In this address, the president provides details about the newly established Civilian Conservation Corps, the Farm Credit Act, and the Farm Relief Bill. Roosevelt concludes that the United States is making slow but steady progress in its efforts to regain prosperity.

O n a Sunday night a week after my inauguration [on March 12, 1933] I used the radio to tell you about the banking crisis and about the measures we were taking to meet it. In that way I tried to make clear to the country various facts that might otherwise have been misunderstood and in general to provide a means of understanding which I believe did much to restore confidence.

Franklin Delano Roosevelt, *FDR's Fireside Chats*. Norman: University of Oklahoma Press, 1992.

Tonight, eight weeks later, I come for the second time to give you my report, in the same spirit and by the same means, to tell you about what we have been doing and what we are planning to do.

Two months ago as you know we were facing serious problems. The country was dying by inches. It was dying because trade and commerce had declined to dangerously low levels; prices for basic commodities were such as to destroy the value of the assets of national institutions such as banks, and savings banks, and insurance companies, and others. These institutions, because of their great needs, were foreclosing mortgages, they were calling loans, and they were refusing credit. Thus there was actually in process of destruction the property of millions of people who had borrowed money on that property in terms of dollars which had had an entirely different value from the level of March 1933. That situation in that crisis did not call for any complicated consideration of economic panaceas or fancy plans. We were faced by a condition and not a theory.

Responding to Foreclosures

There were just two alternatives at that time: The first was to allow the foreclosures to continue, credit to be withheld, money to go into hiding, thus forcing liquidation and bankruptcy of banks and railroads and insurance companies and a recapitalizing of all business and all property on a lower level. That alternative meant a continuation of what is loosely called "deflation," the net result of which would have been extraordinary hardships on all property owners and all bank depositors,[1] and incidentally, extraordinary hardships on all persons working for wages through an increase in unemployment and a further reduction of the wage scale.

It is easy to see that the result of that course would have not only economic effects of a very serious nature, but social results also that might bring incalculable harm. Even before I was inaugurated I came to the conclusion that such a policy was too much to ask the American people to bear. It involved not only a further loss of homes and farms and savings and wages, but also a loss of spiritual values—the loss of that sense of security for the present and the future that is so necessary to the peace and contentment of the individual and of his family. When you

---

1. The words "and all bank depositors" were added by the president to his prepared text.

destroy those things you find it difficult to establish confidence of any sort in the future. And it is clear that mere appeals coming out of Washington for more confidence and the mere lending of more money to shaky institutions could not stop that downward course. A prompt program applied as quickly as possible seemed to me not only justified but imperative to our national security. The Congress, and when I say the Congress I mean the members of both political parties, fully understood this and gave me generous and intelligent support. The members of the Congress realized that the methods of normal times had to be replaced in the emergency by measures that were suited to the serious and pressing requirements of the moment. There was no actual surrender of power. Congress still retains its constitutional authority to legislate and to appropriate,[2] and no one has the slightest desire to change the balance of these powers. The function of Congress is to decide what has to be done and to select the appropriate agency to carry out its will. That policy it has strictly adhered to. The only thing that has been happening has been to designate the president of the United States as the agency to carry out certain of the purposes of the Congress. This was constitutional and is constitutional, and it is in keeping with the past American tradition.

The legislation that has been passed or is in the process of enactment can properly be considered as part of a well-grounded, well-rounded plan.

THE LATEST LEGISLATION

First, we are giving opportunity of employment to a quarter of a million of the unemployed, especially the young men who have dependents, to let them go into forestry and flood-prevention work. That is a big task because it means feeding and clothing and caring for nearly twice as many men as we have in the regular Army itself. And in creating this Civilian Conservation Corps we are killing two birds with one stone. We are clearly enhancing the value of our natural resources, and at the same time we are relieving an appreciable amount of actual distress. This great group of men, young men, have entered upon their work on a purely voluntary basis; no military training is involved and we are conserving not only our natural resources, but also our human resources. One of the great values

2. The words "to legislate and to appropriate" were added by Roosevelt.

to this work is the fact that it is direct and requires the intervention of very little machinery.

Secondly, I have requested the Congress and have secured action upon a proposal to put the great properties owned by our government at Muscle Shoals [Alabama] to work after long years of wasteful inaction, and with this goes hand-in-hand a broad plan for the permanent improvement of the vast area included in the whole of the Tennessee Valley. It will add to the comfort and to the happiness of hundreds of thousands of people and the incident benefits will reach the entire nation.

Next, the Congress is about to pass legislation [the Farm Credit Act] that will greatly ease the mortgage distress among the farmers and among the homeowners of the nation, by providing for the easing of the burden of debt that now bears so heavily upon millions of our people.

Our next step in seeking immediate relief is a grant of half a billion dollars to help the states and the counties and the municipalities in their duty to care for those who at this time need direct and immediate relief.

In addition to all this, the Congress also passed legislation as you know authorizing the sale of beer in such states as desired it. That has already resulted in considerable reemployment, and incidentally it has provided for the federal government and for the states a much-needed tax revenue.

PLANS FOR THE FUTURE

Now as to the future.

We are planning within a few days to ask the Congress for legislation to enable the government to undertake public works, thus stimulating directly and indirectly the employment of many others in well-considered projects.

Further legislation has been taken up which goes much more fundamentally into our economic problems. The Farm Relief Bill seeks by the use of several methods, alone or together, to bring about an increased return to farmers for their major farm products, seeking at the same time to prevent in the days to come disastrous overproduction, the kind of overproduction that so often in the past has kept farm commodity prices far below a reasonable return. This measure provides wide powers for emergencies and the extent of its use will depend entirely upon what the future has in store.

Well-considered and conservative measures will likewise be

proposed, within a few days, that will attempt to give to the industrial workers of the country a more fair wage return, to prevent cutthroat competition, to prevent unduly long hours for labor, and at the same time to encourage each industry to prevent overproduction.

One of our bills falls into the same class, the Railroad Bill. It seeks to provide and make certain a definite planning by the railroads themselves, with the assistance of the government, in order to eliminate the duplication and the waste that now results in railroad receiverships and in continuing operating deficits.

I feel very certain that the people of this country understand and approve the broad purposes behind these new governmental policies relating to agriculture and industry and transportation. We found ourselves faced with more agricultural products than we could possibly consume ourselves and with surpluses which other nations did not have the cash to buy from us except at prices ruinously low. We found our factories able to turn out more goods than we could possibly consume, and at the same time we have been faced with a failing export demand. We have found ourselves with more facilities to transport goods and crops than there were goods and crops to be

A Civilian Conservation Corps team works on a reforesting project. The CCC provided over 3 million jobs during the depression.

transported. All of this has been caused in large part by a complete lack of planning and a complete failure to understand the danger signals that have been flying ever since the close of the World War. The people of this country have been erroneously encouraged to believe that they could keep on increasing the output of farm and of factory indefinitely and that some magician would find ways and means for that increased output to be consumed with reasonable profit to the producer.

AN IMPROVING ECONOMY

But today we have reason to believe that things are a little better than they were two months ago. Industry has picked up, railroads are carrying more freight, farm prices are better. But I am not going to indulge in issuing proclamations of overenthusiastic assurance. We cannot ballyhoo ourselves back to prosperity and I am going to be honest at all times with the people of the country. I do not want the people of this country to take the foolish course of letting this improvement come back on another speculative wave. I do not want the people to believe that because of unjustified optimism we can resume the ruinous practice of increasing our crop output and our factory output in the hope that a kind Providence will find buyers at high prices. Such a course may bring us immediate and false prosperity but it will be the kind of prosperity that will lead us into another tailspin.

It is wholly wrong to call the measures that we have taken government control of farming or government control of industry, or a government control of transportation. It is rather a partnership—a partnership between government and farming, a partnership between government and industry, and a partnership between government and transportation. Not a partnership in profits, because the profits will still go to the private citizen, but rather a partnership in planning, and a partnership to see that the plans are carried out.

Let me illustrate with an example. Take for instance the cotton-goods industry. It is probably true that 90 percent of the cotton manufacturers of this country would agree tomorrow to eliminate starvation wages, would agree to stop long hours of employment, would agree to stop child labor, would agree to prevent an overproduction that would result in unsalable surpluses. But, my friends, what good is such an agreement of the 90 percent if the other 10 percent of the cotton manufacturers pay starvation wages and require long hours and employ children in their mills and turn out burdensome surpluses? The unfair 10 percent could produce goods so cheaply that the fair 90 percent would be compelled to meet the unfair conditions. And that is where government comes in. Government ought to have the right and will have the right, after surveying and planning for an industry, to prevent, with the assistance of the overwhelming majority of that industry, all unfair practices and to enforce that agreement by the authority of government. The so-called antitrust laws were intended to prevent the creation of monopolies and to forbid unreasonable profits to those monopolies. That purpose of the antitrust laws must be continued, but those laws were never intended to encourage the kind of unfair competition that results in long hours and starvation wages and overproduction.

And, my friends, the same principle that is illustrated by that example applies to farm products and to transportation and to every other field of organized private industry.

We are working towards a definite goal, a goal that seeks to prevent the return of conditions which came very close to destroying what we alive call modern civilization. The actual accomplishment of our purposes cannot be attained in a day. Our policies are wholly within the purposes for which our American constitutional government was established 150 years ago.

I know that the people of this country will understand this and that they will also understand the spirit in which we are undertaking that policy. I do not deny that we may make some mistakes of procedure as we carry out this policy. I have no expectation of making a hit every time I come to bat. What I seek is the highest possible batting average, not only for myself but for the team. Theodore Roosevelt once said to me, "If I can be right 75 percent of the time, I shall come up to the fullest measure of my hopes."

THE BIRTH OF THE HOLLYWOOD MUSICAL IN THE 1930S

JACK C. ELLIS

The first Hollywood movies to feature sound premiered in 1927. Within a few years, a new genre of movie, the musical, had developed. Jack C. Ellis examines the early years of the Hollywood musical in the following selection. The earliest of these films were revues, which lacked a cohesive narrative, and filmed operettas. This new genre culminated in the narrative musical, best typified in the 1933 film *42nd Street*, which featured elaborate choreography and camera work and a plot that explored the effects of unemployment and job insecurity during the Great Depression. Ellis also examines the films of Fred Astaire and Ginger Rogers, which helped popularize the musical. Ellis is the founder of the film program at Northwestern University and a former president of the Society for Cinema Studies. He is also the author of several books on film, including *A History of Film*, the source of this essay.

O f the narrative forms emerging with the new sound medium, [one of the] most vigorous and characteristic of the thirties [was] the musical. . . .
The musical was dependent on sound for its existence. In such harbingers as *The Merry Widow* of 1925, [director Erich] von Stroheim's most popular film, audiences had to be content with a live pit orchestra or organist providing a potpourri of

Jack C. Ellis, *A History of Film*. Boston: Allyn and Bacon, 1995. Copyright © 1995 by Allyn and Bacon. Reproduced by permission.

[Hungarian composer Franz] Lehar melodies to accompany the pantomimed action and printed titles. Fittingly, the film that caused the revolution, *The Jazz Singer* (1927), foreshadowed the backstage musical, an important early subgenre. What it lacked most essentially was dancing, for the appeal of the musical came to depend as much on choreography as on music. From *The Hollywood Revue of 1929* through *Saturday Night Fever* (1977), *All That Jazz* (1979), *Flashdance* (1982), and *Dirty Dancing* (1987), the creators of musicals have been men and women of dance as well as of song.

EARLY FILM MUSICAL FORMS

The Hollywood Revue of 1929 was a prototype for one line of musical, the revue, which flourished in the thirties and first half of the forties. It disappeared after World War II, with only a few exceptions (*Ziegfeld Follies*, 1946; *New Faces*, 1952). Consisting of separate "acts" unconnected by narrative linkage, like its stage counterpart, the screen revue let audiences throughout the world see the great entertainers whose performances had formerly been confined to Broadway and infrequent tours. Generally presented very much as they might have been on a superstage (by impresario Florenz Ziegfeld, let's say), the film revues substituted the possibility of perfection—ideal performers in their best performances—for the special excitements of live theater.

Another early film musical form deriving from theater was the filmed operetta. It began with the romantic comedies-cummusic of Ernst Lubitsch (starting with *The Love Parade*, 1929) and Rouben Mamoulian (*Love Me Tonight*, 1932). These operetta-like screen originals were made at Paramount and starred Maurice Chevalier and/or Jeanette MacDonald. Moving to M-G-M, in 1934 Lubitsch directed the same stars in his version of *The Merry Widow*. It was at M-G-M that the operetta continued, in a series of standard stage favorites beginning with *Naughty Marietta* in 1935. In them Chevalier was replaced by Nelson Eddy; he and MacDonald helped make a great deal of money for everyone concerned.

If the filmed operetta came out of Paramount and M-G-M, the backstage musical began at Warner Brothers. In 1930 [Jack] Warner imported Broadway veteran Busby Berkeley, who became master of the production number. His ranks and clusters of chorines moving with military precision through elaborate patterns are understandably the subject of "camp" appreciation

today. Those extravagant creations nonetheless contain an authentic if frequently exotic charm. Early in the period Berkeley's
spectacular staging and bravura use of camera, cutting, and special effects were brought together in the narrative musical.

A LOOK AT *42ND STREET*

First of the stories with music and dance (which the term *musical* now generally means) was *42nd Street* (1933). Directed by
Lloyd Bacon (with "Dances and ensembles created and staged
by Busby Berkeley"), the story revolves around production of a
Broadway musical, "Pretty Lady." The tough director of the
show (Warner Baxter) is dependent on an "angel" (Guy Kibbee)
who has put up $70,000 because of his infatuation with its star
(Bebe Daniels). The night before opening she breaks her ankle,
permitting the young unknown (Ruby Keeler) to take her place.
As a result of the crisis, the established star realizes her love for
her former vaudeville partner (George Brent), and the newcomer
hers for the junior lead (Dick Powell). Una Merkel and Ginger
Rogers play seasoned chorines—Rogers as Anytime Annie ("She
only said 'No' once—and then she didn't hear the question.").

The prototypical content elements work largely because of
the pace and dazzle of the film. The lines are witty and delivered in rapid-fire staccato. Characterizations are deftly etched,
stereotypical as they should be. The performers take themselves
only seriously enough to blend in with what would become the
conventional hard-boiled-exterior, soft-on-the-inside view of
show biz. Climaxing the film, and what it's all building toward,
are the three production numbers: "Shuffle Off to Buffalo," "I'm
Young and Healthy," and the title song, "42nd Street." After the
numbing exhaustion of rehearsals and the nervous tension of
the young heroine, we are given an enormous release in the pol-
ished extravaganza, which goes considerably beyond what
could be created on any stage. Each of the numbers exceeds the
preceding one in terms of spectacle, and each pulls farther away
from the possibilities of live theater into strictly cinematic ma-
nipulations of space and time, of image and movement.

In *42nd Street*, Berkeley started full scale on that special kind
of creation we associate with his name. The massed lovelies of
the chorus are viewed by the camera from almost any position
except a stationary one in front of a theater stage. They are seen
from overhead as they form floral patterns or strange concen-
tric rings suggesting interconnecting gears. Or the camera gets

down on the floor and moves through their spread legs in as slyly elegant a bit of erotica—funny in a way, but lovely too—as one could imagine. Costumes and settings are designed to support and underscore the extravagant fantasy of the total choreographic conception; or, to put it the other way around, the dances grow out of and take full advantage of every suggestion provided by the visual decor. The chorus line performs a jerky, syncopated march up stairs, they turn toward the camera and raise cardboard profiles of skyscrapers, covering themselves and becoming a miniature Manhattan. Berkeley would later sustain and elaborate on delights of this sort at their most breathtaking (and bizarre) in the *Gold Diggers* series (of 1933, 1935, 1937).

If on one level *42nd Street* can be seen as the most purely escapist kind of entertainment, on another it seems to be dealing with the insecurity and paralysis of the Depression. It's not just the apple vendor, that symbol of the unemployed, in the "42nd Street" number; in a way the whole film is about lack of money and joblessness. The director insists that the only reason he's doing the show is for the money. Portrayed as a driving entrepreneurial type, he says he's been called a machine, producing a steady succession of hits. Sure he's made a lot of money in the past, but he's spent and lost it all on friends and high living and the stock market. As he delivers these lines he is standing against a window high above the street, suggesting the many suicidal leaps of those who had lost their money in the crash. This time, he says, he's going to sock away his earnings so hard they can never be taken from him. The control exerted by the unattractive and stupid, but wealthy, angel over all members of the production—and on the quality of the show itself, when he insists that Anytime Annie replace the injured star—is made pointedly clear. That two hundred jobs depend on the success of the show is insistently reiterated. Keeping cast and crew from falling back into the ranks of the unemployed is the strongest point made in the pep talk the director gives the young replacement for the star just before she goes on. Surely there was a special poignancy to that plea in 1933.

FRED ASTAIRE AND GINGER ROGERS

In this same narrative line, a series of films starring Fred Astaire and Ginger Rogers were the first to drop the theatrical setting as excuse for music and dancing. Though they play professional dancers, thus making their terpsichorean skill plausible, they move from the theater out into the world, breaking into song and dance whenever the emotional charge is sufficient. This observation covers all ten of their costarring films to one degree or another. In *Shall We Dance* (1937), for example, Astaire (as the great Petrov, a Russian Ballet dancer) is first seen tap dancing in his room to a jazz record. (Really he's Peter Peters from Philadelphia, PA.) Returning from Paris on board the *Queen Anne,* he wanders down into the (extraordinarily stylized) engine room, and sings and dances with the black crew and the rhythmically pumping, eccentrically designed machinery. That number suggests a benign and jazzy *Metropolis,* with the ebullient individual replacing the deadened mass, and the machines beating it out in swing-time. Another number on board ship has Rogers and Astaire walking their dogs to the Gershwin music. In New York they are seen roller skating with a group of extras in a soundstage Central Park. Soon they wander off to sing a song, and traject themselves into an energetic and skillful dance on skates. Astaire and Rogers, whose films together extend from 1933 to 1949, served to link the backstage musical inaugurated by *42nd Street* (same year as *Flying Down to Rio,* the first Rogers and Astaire) and the vintage cluster of M-G-M musicals beginning with *On the Town* (same year as the last Rogers and Astaire, *The Barkleys of Broadway*), which offered song and dance as the normal response to life. But of course the grace and charm, the subtle and sophisticated virtuosity of Fred and Ginger gives its own lasting pleasure, which transcends their place in the history of Hollywood musicals. Their appeal remains as inimitable as it is irresistible.

Of the popular American genres, the musical remains one of the most indigenous and enduring. Surely it is the loveliest, offering aesthetic pleasures that by comparison cause many of the more "serious" films valued contemporaneously to fall behind in lumbering earnestness. As long as a simple and sensible Aristotelian notion is accepted—that art offers beauty and beauty is a good in itself—the musical is assured its deservedly important place in the history of the American film. Long may it talk, and sing, and dance.

1934–1939: The Turbulence Continues

CHAPTER 4

THE DUST BOWL

T.H. WATKINS

Drought and dust storms devastated the American Midwest in the 1930s. T.H. Watkins details the steps taken by President Franklin D. Roosevelt's administration to alleviate crop devastation and farmers' economic distress. The government established soil conservation districts to help repair damaged lands, while the Federal Emergency Relief Administration spent $85 million on purchasing and rehabilitating farmland. However, other steps taken by the Roosevelt administration, particularly scarcity programs for cotton—which required farmers to plow over up to one-half of their cotton crops in order to prevent prices from falling—led to the displacement of numerous tenants and sharecroppers while increasing the income of landlords. Watkins explains that for these displaced farmers, their best opportunity for starting anew was to migrate to the West Coast, especially California. These migrants, derisively given nicknames such as "Okies" and "Arkies," traveled throughout California under harsh and unhealthy conditions in search of seasonal agricultural work. Watkins is the author of more than two dozen books, including *The Hungry Years: A Narrative History of the Great Depression in America* and *The Great Depression: America in the 1930s*, from which the following selection was excerpted.

D rought was nothing new, in this country or any other, but that of the 1930s, which continued through most of the decade—combining in some years with unprecedented heat waves—was "the worst in the climatological history of the country," according to a Weather Bureau scientist. It struck first in the eastern third of the country in 1930, where it crippled agriculture from Maine to Arkansas and where only

T.H. Watkins, *The Great Depression: America in the 1930s*. Boston: Little, Brown and Company, 1993. Copyright © 1993 by Little, Brown and Company. Reproduced by permission.

Florida enjoyed anything that approached normal rainfall. It had been drought that had aggravated the terrible desperation of those farmers who had invaded the little town of England, Arkansas, in January of 1931, demanding food for their children, and drought that in 1930 had given the great Delta bluesman, Son House, the theme for "Dry Spell Blues": "Them dry spell blues are fallin', drivin' people/from door to door,/Dry spell blues are fallin', drivin' people/from door to door./Them dry spell blues has put everybody on/the kindlin' floor."

In 1932, the center of the drought started heading west, and by 1934 it had desiccated the Great Plains from North Dakota to Texas, from the Mississippi River Valley to the Rockies. In the northern Rockies in the winter of 1933–34, the snowpack was less than a third of normal, in the central Rockies less than half, and in areas of the southern Rockies barely a dusting of snow had been seen.

THE DEVASTATING EFFECTS OF THE DROUGHT

Providence, fate, or some other cosmic force might be blamed for the drought itself, but not for the phenomenon that accompanied it over hundreds of millions of acres: most of that was inescapably man-made. The speculative dance of the war years and the twenties had abused millions of acres of farmland in the South and Midwest, as farmers plowed, planted, and harvested as much as they could as often as they could. Much of the topsoil was left so exhausted it could barely support the most undemanding ground cover, much less productive crops. Careless plowing had rutted the fields, leaving the land open to gullying from erosion. "Since the cover was first disturbed [in the nineteenth century]," a state commission of the National Resources Planning Board reported, "Iowa has lost approximately 550,000 tons of good surface soil per square mile, or a total of thirty billion tons." Iowa was not alone. "Approximately 35 million acres of formerly cultivated land have essentially been destroyed for crop production," the 1934 *Yearbook of Agriculture* reported, adding that "100 million acres now in crops have lost all or most of the topsoil; 125 million acres of land now in crops are rapidly losing topsoil. . . ." At the same time, decades of overgrazing by cattle and sheep ranchers in the western plains and valleys had left one former rich grassland after another stripped clean of ground cover, vulnerable to rampant wind and water erosion. Grass, a Texas sheepherder of the time commented, "is what counts. It's what saves us all—far as we get saved. Men and towns and such as that, don't amount to a particular damn anyhow. Grass does. Grass is what holds the earth together." Not everyone had understood that simple fact. Since the first great cattle and sheep herds had been turned out in the last third of the nineteenth century to feed on the rich grasslands of the plains and mountain pastures of the interior West, the grass had been steadily, ruthlessly overgrazed, until the earth over enormous stretches of land was no longer held together by anything but inertia. After the wartime and postwar booms of the teen years and the 1920s, more than half the grazing land in the western states was in a condition of soil depletion described by the Department of Agriculture as "extreme" or "severe."

The soil, loose and dry, lay unprotected from the winds, which repeatedly swept down on the ruined grasslands of the west, scooped them clean and carried the dust into the air, moving east to the exposed and waiting farmlands of the plains. Here, the winds deposited much of it, moved it around, added to it, filled the air now with the western grasslands dust and the plains farmland dust in a great choking geographic mix. Beadle County, South Dakota, November 11, 1933:

> By mid-morning, a gale was blowing, cold and black. By noon it was blacker than night, because one can see through night and this was an opaque black. It was a wall of dirt one's eyes could not penetrate, but it could penetrate the eyes and ears and nose. It could penetrate to the lungs until one coughed up black. If a person was outside, he tied his handkerchief around his face, but he still coughed up black. When the wind died and the sun shone forth again, it was on a different world. There were no fields, only sand drifting into mounds and eddies that swirled in what was now but an autumn breeze.

The dust did not always stay west of the Mississippi. When conditions were right, the wind would carry it east on the jet stream in enormous clouds and drop it in the form of filthy unseasonal snow on Chicago, Indianapolis, Washington, New York, and even on the gently rolling decks of Atlantic liners. During just one storm between May 9 and May 11, 1934, an estimated 350 million tons of soil disappeared from the West and reappeared in the East. Chicago got four pounds of it for every person in the city, and Washington, New York, Boston, and other cities burned their streetlamps in the middle of the day.

RESPONDING TO THE DROUGHT

The government did what it could. Interior Secretary Harold Ickes established the Soil Erosion Service under Hugh Hammond Bennett in August of 1933; the agency later moved over to the Agriculture Department as the Soil Conservation Service and Bennett and his people diligently organized farmers into soil conservation districts, but not all the reeducation, preventive measures, or reclamation work in the world could repair the damage of generations. In June of 1934, Roosevelt signed the Taylor Grazing Act, which authorized the president to withdraw up to 140 million acres of federally owned public land from application under any one of the three thousand or so public land laws on the books and to establish grazing districts whose use by the cattle and sheep industry was to be carefully monitored by a new Interior Department agency, the Grazing Service. The Service would be marginally successful in stabilizing the situation, but could do little to repair historical damage. Between 1933 and 1934, the Federal Emergency Relief Administration would spend $85 million to purchase and attempt to rehabilitate ruined farmland, but this program, too, was nearly helpless to reclaim land that nearly a century of abuse had left ruined.

Little helped. Human strength failed. Hope died. "[The] longing for rain has become almost an obsession," Caroline Henderson wrote in 1935. "We dream of the faint gurgling sound of dry soil sucking in the grateful moisture . . . of the fresh green of sprouting wheat or barley, the reddish bronze of spring rye. But we wake to another day of wind and dust and hopes deferred. . . ." The Hendersons toughed it out and continued to work their land for more than two decades, but for thousands of other farm families the drought alone was more than they could endure.

Many people simply pulled up stakes and abandoned their land, and even for many of those who might have stuck it out in spite of all that nature could do, financial circumstances would make it all but impossible. Resident and absentee owners alike lost their lands to foreclosure proceedings; according to Department of Agriculture reports, nearly two hundred out of every thousand farms in the states of the Midwest, the Central South, and the Plains succumbed to forced sales between

1930 and 1935. And when landlords failed, so did croppers and tenant farmers, and to the ranks of dispossessed owners were added thousands of men and women who were forced off land they had worked as if it were their own. Often, they were forced off the land even when their landlords were doing reasonably well, thanks to the Agricultural Adjustment Administration's [AAA] scarcity program, particularly in the cotton-growing regions of the South.

COTTON CROPS AND THE SCARCITY PROGRAM

After the center of drought had moved west, plantations in Alabama, Arkansas, Mississippi, East Texas, and other areas had a bumper crop of cotton on their hands. But there already was a surplus of 12.5 million bales left over from the 1932 season, and prices had fallen to 6.5 cents a pound. More production would, it was felt, lower prices even further and destroy the industry. So it was that the AAA instituted its scarcity program: the cotton planters would plow under anywhere from a quarter to a half of their cotton plants in order to increase the value of existing and future supplies. "To have to destroy a growing crop," Agriculture Secretary Henry Wallace admitted as he launched the program, "is a shocking commentary on our civilization." But destroy the landlords did, and for the most part did so with hearts full of gladness. The program not only raised the price of cotton by about four cents a pound, as promised, it also compensated the landlord for his plowed-up cotton with an amount equal to anywhere from six to eight cents a pound. "The tighter the government control the better," one landlord rejoiced. "[We] never want to see a relaxation of governmental control. The more inspectors Washington puts on the job, the happier we'll be!" One impediment to their complete happiness was the fact that the law required them to share the government payments with their plantation help—half of what they received was supposed to go to sharecroppers, a quarter to tenant farmers. That was rectified in 1934 with another adjustment: under a complex system of "rental" and "parity" payments, the compensation was deliberately skewed in the landlord's favor—so much so that landlords were making more money for *not* growing cotton than they had for growing it, while tenants and sharecroppers lost money.

From the landlord's point of view, the system worked even better because the local administration of the program remained

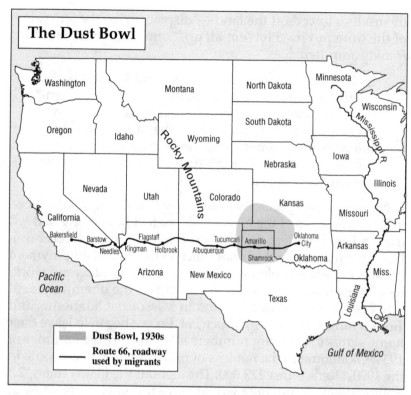

The Dust Bowl

Washington
Oregon
Idaho
Montana
North Dakota
Minnesota
Wisconsin
South Dakota
Wyoming
Rocky Mountains
Nevada
Utah
Colorado
Nebraska
Iowa
Illinois
California
Bakersfield
Barstow
Needles
Kingman
Flagstaff
Holbrook
Tucumcari
Albuquerque
Amarillo
Shamrock
Oklahoma City
Oklahoma
Kansas
Missouri
Arkansas
Miss.
Pacific
Ocean
Arizona
New Mexico
Texas
Louisiana
Gulf of Mexico

Dust Bowl, 1930s
Route 66, roadway
used by migrants

in the hands of locally elected production control committees who were, unsurprisingly, dominated by owners and their friends and relatives, with only occasional oversight by county agents—almost all of them chosen from the same gene pool as the landlords. The opportunities for various forms of theft were irresistible to many owners, who persuaded their croppers and tenant farmers to sign away their shares by threats or subterfuge, or underpaid them, or simply kept the government's payments for themselves without bothering to resort to any special tactics. On one typical plantation, a later government report would say, the owner's gross income had increased from $51,554 in 1932 to $102,202 in 1934, while that of his sharecroppers and tenant farmers had fallen from $379 to $355.

Further, with cotton acreage reduced from 35 million acres in 1932 to 26.5 in 1934–35, the labor force required to plow, plant, and pick the crop was sharply reduced, particularly in those instances when acreage reduction was combined with a rise in the use of tractors and other mechanized equipment. As a consequence, thousands of sharecropper and tenant families found themselves forced off the land—"displaced," as the federalese of the time put it. "I let 'em all go," one Oklahoma landlord frankly admitted.

> In '34 I had I reckon four renters and I didn't make anything. I bought tractors on the money the government give me and got shet o' my renters. You'll find it everywhere all over the country that way. I did everything the government said—except keep my renters. The renters have been having it this way ever since the government come in.

No one knows precisely how many families were displaced in the early years of the New Deal—or just how many had left the land as the direct result of crop reductions or tractor use. However many, there was not much in the way of employment the affected states could offer these suddenly landless and workless thousands; in Arkansas, for example, the unemployment rate was 39 percent in 1933, and in Missouri, Oklahoma, and Texas it ranged from 29 to 32 percent. People began to leave their home states in growing numbers after the terrible summer of 1934. Oklahoma had a net loss of more than 440,000 people in the 1930s. Kansas lost 227,000. Throughout the Plains states, 2.5 million people ultimately would leave for other parts. Most of those parts were nearby; the greater portion of the internal population movement in the American middle in those years was from one state to a neighboring state. But some 460,000 people moved to the Pacific Northwest, where they found work on the building of Bonneville and Grand Coulee dams, found abandoned homesteads they could work in southern Idaho and the eastern valleys of Oregon and Washington, went into the ancient forests of the region as lumberjacks or joined the migrant workers in the hop fields and beet fields—or simply settled in the cities and collected relief checks where and when they could.

STARTING OVER IN CALIFORNIA

Other thousands, particularly from the southwestern Plains states, headed for California. All logic dictated the move, so it seemed. After all, between 1910 and 1930 an estimated 310,000 southwesterners had already moved to the Golden State, lured by the promise of opportunity that had bathed California in the glow of hope ever since the Gold Rush of 1848–52. Residents of Oklahoma, Arkansas, Texas, and other states who had fallen upon hard times now thought of all the cheerful letters they had been receiving from friends and relatives in California, took a look at the tormented land and overburdened cities of their own regions, and put together the wherewithal to get themselves and their families across the plains and deserts to the golden valleys of the West Coast. In one fifteen-month period alone, some 86,000 did precisely that, individually and as families, by car and by bus, most of them taking no more than three or four days to rattle down Route 66 to the border crossing at Yuma, Arizona. By the end of the decade another 220,000 or so would do the same. . . .

Before long, this latest resource of cheap labor would account for nearly half the total of all the state's migrant workers. Like their predecessors, most Anglo migrants confined themselves to journeys up and down the state, following the cycles of planting and harvest from the Imperial Valley to the Sacramento Valley and all the valleys in between, though some backtracked to the cotton fields and other irrigated crops of Arizona or continued straight up California to Oregon and Washington to work the hop fields and beet fields of the north. The average distance traveled from crop to crop every year, the State Relief Administration calculated, was 516 miles. The migrants frequently traveled and worked as families, living in the squalor of work camps either erected by themselves wherever they could with whatever they could or provided by the farmers. Whether self-built or furnished, these feculent little communities, often called "ditch camps" because they were located on the side of roads along which ran filthy water ditches, were disease-ridden and indisputably unfit for human beings. At one point, [journalist and activist] Carey McWilliams reported, fifty babies died of diarrhea and enteritis in one county during just one picking season; children in Tulare County were reported dying at the rate of two a day; and during an inspection tour of eighteen camps in the vicinity of Kingsburg in Kings County, one social worker found "dozens of children with horribly sore eyes; many cases of cramps, diarrhea, and dysentery; fever, colds, and sore throats." Hookworm, pellegra, and rickets were common.

Pay was better than it was in the depressed regions of the South and the Midwest, but whether by the day or by the amount of fruit picked or vegetables dug, wages were still far below what a family needed for decent upkeep. What was more, the seasonal character of the job made it impossible to accumulate a significant stake even when one or more members of the family made up to $3 a day, as many did. The recorded need for seasonal labor in the California fields over one two-year period, for example, ranged from a low of 48,173 workers in March to a high of 144,720 in September. Average annual farm labor income, as a consequence, never got much above $1,300 for each family—nearly $500 less than other Anglo California families (though $315 more than the average for *non-Anglo* Californians).

Huddling to wait out off-season unemployment in makeshift "shacktowns" and "Little Oklahomas" perched on the outskirts of agricultural service centers like Bakersfield, Fresno, and Modesto, collecting state relief, sending their children to local schools, the migrants soon earned the pious contempt of their neighbors in the traditional manner of humans rejecting outsiders who are unfamiliar and therefore vaguely threatening. Whatever their origin, they became known collectively as "Okies" and "Arkies," with a few "Texies" thrown in for good measure, and were subject to the kind of abuse and discrimination that the state's Mexican-American, Filipino, and African-American field workers had endured as a matter of course for decades. "These 'share croppers,'" one woman complained, "are not a noble people looking for a home and seeking an education for their children. They are unprincipled degenerates looking for something for nothing." Interviewing customers at several Sacramento Valley bars, a reporter collected a good run of comments: "Damned Okies." "No damned good. Don't do a damned thing for the town." "Damned shiftless nogoods." "Damned Okies. Damned bums clutter up the roadside."

They possessed a terrible patience, however, these despised migrants, as well as a burning determination and an anger to which someone would be forced to answer sooner or later. But it would be another season or two before the New Dealers [supporters of Roosevelt's economic plan] would comprehend the full dimensions of what had fallen on these wanderers and begin, slowly and indecisively, to give them sanctuary.

LABOR UNIONS IN THE 1930S

CABELL PHILLIPS

In the following selection, Cabell Phillips examines the resurgence of labor unions in the 1930s and the often violent conflicts between the unions and major industries. This resurgence was due in large part to the National Industrial Recovery Act and National Labor Relations Act, which guaranteed collective bargaining rights and established minimum wages and maximum limits to hours worked. As a result of this federal support for labor, unions began to recruit throughout the nation; between 1933 and 1939, the number of people who belonged to unions had increased from 2.6 million to 8.7 million. However, Phillips notes, such increased power led to a number of violent conflicts with employers. Troubled labor relations reached a peak in 1937. During that year, 4,740 strikes—including strikes against General Motors and Chrysler, coal mines, and cotton mills—led to hundreds of casualties and dozens of deaths. However, most of these strikes ended favorably for the employees, further indicating the increased power of labor unions. Phillips was a writer for the *New York Times* and the author of several books, including *From the Crash to the Blitz: 1929–1939*, the source of the following essay.

O rganized labor came of age in the United States in the mid-thirties. After half a century of frustration, and degradation, it burst the bonds of repression and asserted its right to a share in the national council. Its breakout, marked by rioting and bloodshed, was the closest approximation of class warfare the nation had experienced.

AMERICAN LABOR IN THE DEPRESSION

"For the past four and one-half years," the editors of *Fortune* wrote late in 1937, "the United States has been in the throes of a major labor upheaval which can fairly be described as one of the greatest mass movements in our history." And indeed it was. News of strikes, lockouts, and battles on the picket lines, of threats and counterthreats by union bosses and company bosses, dominated the headlines month after month. Debates on the most volatile issue of the day—the rights of labor versus the rights of management—struck sparks in every quarter of society. A new vocabulary was born. Everybody knew what was meant by terms like the stretch-out, the checkoff, horizontal unions, vertical unions. And everybody had opinions about the relative virtues of the open shop, the closed shop, and the union shop.[1] A lot of people who had never linked their destiny to that of the working classes suddenly found it economically feasible and socially acceptable to get into unions themselves: newspaper reporters, schoolteachers, office workers, architects, among others. The picket line became virtually sacrosanct, and the First Lady of the Land set the fashion for regarding it as a moral barricade. In the upsurging cult of liberalism one's credentials were easily established. If you were *for* labor you were a liberal; if *against* labor (or a yes-but equivocator), a conservative.

Out of the turmoil of the years between 1934 and 1939 organized labor reached a pinnacle of numerical strength and of economic and political influence such as had not been dreamed of a decade before.

Like American agriculture, American labor was in a badly demoralized state when the Depression struck. That blow reduced it to a shambles. Labor's "house" consisted principally of the affiliates of the American Federation of Labor, the Railway Brotherhoods, and half a dozen other major independents. The concept of craft unionism—organization according to skills and trades—was almost universal among them. But the protective reach of the unions was spotty—limited largely to the fields of mining, transportation, building construction, metals fabrication, printing, textiles, and the garment trades. There were vast reaches of the industrial landscape where no union man had ever set foot.

1. Employment at open shops is not contingent on whether a potential hire belongs to a union. Only members of a labor union may be hired at a closed shop. Employees do not have to belong to a union to work at a union shop, but they must eventually join a union in order to retain their jobs.

The prosperity of the twenties not only had passed the labor movement by but, perversely, had bled it of some of the vigor it had acquired during the World War. Industry's wartime experience with unions had alerted American businessmen, many for the first time, to labor's potential power, and in the postwar years they bent sedulously to the task of de-fanging the serpent before it could strike. They were fortuitously aided in this by the "Red scare"[2] of the early twenties, which made it easy to suggest to the gullible that labor unions were the tool of the Bolsheviks. The closed shop, which had long been tolerated, was gradually eliminated from many contracts. Injunctions were freely issued by the courts to combat strikes. Union "agitators" were fired from their jobs and blacklisted, and company unions in deceptive guises were foisted on unorganized workers when they showed signs of unrest.

As wages and employment rates rose modestly in the wake of the "Coolidge prosperity," workers had few incentives to join together for mutual protection. Even in the traditional strongholds, such as the mine fields of Appalachia and the mill towns of New England, the prestige of the labor movement waned and its strength eroded. Between 1920 and 1929 the membership of the A.F.L. skidded downward from 4.1 million to 2.7 million. By 1933 it had lost at least half a million more, and the labor movement as a whole was closer to extinction in this country than it had been in half a century.

THE EFFECT OF THE NATIONAL INDUSTRIAL RECOVERY ACT

The National Industrial Recovery Act [NIRA] did for labor what it was supposed, but failed, to do for business—put it on its feet and gave it an infusion of hope and vitality. This achievement was more an inadvertence than a calculated aim. Section 7(a) of the NIRA, which was designed to assure collective bargaining rights for labor under the industrial codes, was written into the law almost as an afterthought and over the objection of [army officer and government administrator] Hugh Johnson, the principal architect of NIRA. Johnson regarded inclusion of a bargaining provision as merely a trouble-making caprice. He was certain that the magical benevolence of the Blue Eagle would shine upon

2. The years of 1919 and 1920 were known as the "Red Scare." Americans at that time distrusted immigrants and anyone else who held anarchic or socialist political views. Several thousand aliens were rounded up for deportation.

the workingman simply in the natural order of things. Frances Perkins, the gentle but doughty Secretary of Labor, was less certain. If businessmen were to be encouraged into collusive action through suspension of the antitrust laws, she argued, workingmen should be granted a compensating opportunity to band together to protect their share of the partnership. What's sauce for the goose is sauce for the gander, she told the President.

Her concern over this was reinforced by a parallel development from another quarter. As the National Recovery Act [NRA] package was being readied for Congressional consideration, Congress was about to pass a mandatory thirty-hour-week bill which had been pushed independently of the Administration by Senator Hugo Black. In the Secretary's view the Black bill promised to do more harm than good. While it might increase the number of jobs, it made no provision for minimum wages to compensate for the reduced working time. The net result, as she saw it, would be a cut in the already dismally low level of the workers' take-home pay, which would, in effect, accentuate the depression spiral. She argued this viewpoint with the President and won his agreement to withhold his support from the Black bill while incorporating a substitute for it in the National Recovery Act.

Thus provisions covering minimum wages and maximum hours for labor were built into the NRA formula. They became basic to each of the industrial codes. To give workers some leverage in enforcing these standards, they were guaranteed under Section 7(a) ". . . the right to organize and bargain collectively through representatives of their own choosing, and they shall be free from interference, restraint or coercion of employers in the designation of such representatives . . . or in other concerted activities for the purpose of collective bargaining or other mutual aid or protection."

Never in the history of capitalist America had the cause of unionism won such a resounding sanction. Liberals hailed it as "labor's Magna Carta"[3] (later they transferred this accolade to the Wagner Act).

The long-dormant labor movement came suddenly to life. From national headquarters of the big unions and on down

3. The Magna Carta, an important step in the development of constitutional governments, was a document signed by England's King John in 1215 that increased the rights and freedoms of English barons. The freedoms listed in the document were gradually expanded to include more of the English citizenry.

through the musty, cobwebby warrens of state and city centrals and the hundreds of grimy local union halls, many of which had been boarded up and in disuse for years—an intense activity burst forth. Recruiters and organizers fanned out in every direction, posted themselves at mine tipples and factory gates, called shop meetings and public rallies, and passed out bales of leaflets and membership blanks. Coal miners coming off their shifts in West Virginia and Kentucky had fliers thrust into their hands proclaiming, "The President says you must join the union." Dropouts, holdouts, and those with no present job responded eagerly. Defunct locals came back to life. Shop stewards and walking bosses asserted their authority, and union buttons were openly worn on the job without fear of reprisal.

The results were spectacular. The United Mine Workers claimed to have gained 135,000 new members within three weeks after the signing of the NRA bill. Within a year the International Ladies Garment Workers Union trebled its membership to approximately 200,000. A score of other unions swelled impressively. Between 1933 and 1935 total union membership rose from 2.6 to 3.6 million, and by 1939 it had reached 8.7 million, almost a fourfold increase in six years. The 1939 figure represented 28.6 percent of the entire nonfarm labor force, a level of strength that has not been greatly exceeded since. (It was 35.5 in 1945 and 28.0 in 1966.) Thus, in terms of numerical growth alone, labor made a long leap forward.

This great upsurge created not only an internal turbulence among dissident elements in the unions but also a counterwave of resistance from management. What little most businessmen knew about labor unions in 1933 added up to fear and distrust. For more than twenty years they had devoted a large part of their personal and corporate effort to preventing unions from getting a foothold in their plants. Or, if a union had already made an entry they used every wile to minimize its effectiveness. Now that the New Deal[4] had virtually forced open the door of their nonunion and open shop citadels, they pooled their talents and energies to find ways of neutralizing the hated strictures of Section 7 (a). A few followed the lead of Henry Ford, who flatly proclaimed he would not do business with any union that had links outside his own plants, NRA or no NRA.

4. The New Deal was President Franklin D. Roosevelt's domestic program. It was a series of policies intended to end the Great Depression and strengthen America's economy.

Others dismantled their plants and moved them to the South and to other regions free of union contamination. A greater number sought to head off invasion by the big national unions by quickly devising company unions embellished with group insurance, pensions, and recreational programs but devoid of meaningful collective bargaining rights.

In all substantive ways these company unions were the captives of management. Starting practically from scratch in 1933 (a few had been carried over from the twenties), they proliferated almost as rapidly as the independents and by 1935 had an estimated membership of 2.5 million. They could be made to look legitimate within the meaning of Section 7(a) as long as management could stave off a secret election by employees under the supervision of the National Labor Board, which had been set up for that purpose. And even where the company lost in such a showdown (which they did more often than not), litigation through the courts offered a long and rewarding respite before capitulation became inevitable.

Thus the battle lines were drawn for an historic era of industrial strife. Initially the unions fought chiefly for the right to organize and for recognition as promised them under the NRA. As their flying squadrons of recruiters and organizers collided with sheriff's deputies and vigilantes in the cotton-mill towns of Alabama and Georgia, with armed guards and militiamen at the auto assembly plants of Flint and Toledo, with the stony intractability of a [chairman of the board] Tom M. Girdler at the gates of the Republic Steel Company, the map of the nation came to resemble a mine field erupting with spasmodic violence. . . .

A VIOLENT YEAR

Nineteen thirty-seven was the most critical and tumultuous year in the history of labor relations in this country. It was the year in which American industry mounted its last great, concerted assault against union encroachment. That year, too, union labor felt the first full surge of its offensive strength. The destruction of NRA, along with Section 7(a) by the Supreme Court in 1935 gave management the hope that it could undo the iniquities of compulsory union recognition that had been forced on it. But labor had developed too much momentum to be turned aside. The legal vacuum left by the demise of the NRA had been filled in 1935 by new legislation, the National Labor Relations Act (the so-called Wagner Act), which recreated the provisions of Section 7(a) in statutory form. The new law came under immediate attack in the courts as being just as vulnerable to the charge of unconstitutionality as the law it replaced, and employers were widely urged by their lawyers and trade associations to ignore it.

"I won't have a contract, verbal or written, with an irresponsible, racketeering, violent, communistic body like the C.I.O.," hard-nosed old Tom Girdler fumed. "And until they pass a law making me do it, I won't do it." Labor was just as determined to use every weapon it possessed or could lay its hands on to widen the beachhead it had carved out on the enemy's shore. It locked Girdler's Republic Steel and the other "little steel" mills in a bruising, costly, and protracted strike.

In this climate of open hostility and last-ditch defiance, the labor wars of the thirties mounted to a climax. Communists and their sympathizers, who had streamed into the new unions, added to the turmoil. So did labor spies, whom industry hired by the thousands to infiltrate and sabotage the organizational effort. Strikes for recognition multiplied in frequency and violence—some 10,000 of them between mid-1933 and the end of 1937, involving over five million workers. There were more

Union members stage a sit-down strike at an auto body plant in Cleveland, Ohio. During the 1930s, many strikes resulted in violence.

strikes in 1937 than in any previous year—a total of 4,740, cost-ing a record 28.4 million man-days of work. The great General Motors strike, which came in January, spread to six states and pulled 45,000 men off the production lines. The Chrysler strike in March idled 63,000. The "little steel" strike, beginning in May, shut down dozens of plants in seven states and affected 90,000 workers. Tens of thousands of workers in the rubber plants of Akron, the coal mines of Pennsylvania and Illinois, the cotton and rayon mills of South Carolina and Georgia, and the docks of the East Coast and the Gulf ports abandoned their jobs and went on the picket lines. Retail clerks in New York and Philadel-phia joined the pickets.

Violence erupted on both sides. Strikers broke windows, smashed machinery, dynamited mine tipples, beat up (or were beaten up by) scabs and strikebreakers. Police, the National Guard, and armed mercenaries hired from the Pinkertons and other professional "security" organizations clashed in bloody hand-to-hand combat with battalions of angry strikers. Dozens of combatants were killed—ten in the bloody "Memorial Day massacre" at South Chicago alone—and hundreds were hospi-talized with bullet wounds, cracked heads, and broken bones.

No state and no city, it seemed, was wholly free of violence, or at least the threat thereof, but its epicenter appeared to be De-troit and the surrounding domain of the auto-makers. Here the labor militants perfected their newest and most invulnerable weapon, the sit-down strike. The workers simply shut down their machines and refused to leave the plant. This nonviolent tactic baffled management, which could clear the plants forcibly only at the price of itself committing violence. General Motors, facing this dilemma for the first time in January, appealed to Michigan Governor Frank Murphy to send the National Guard to liberate its factories in Flint from occupation by a boisterous, song-singing army of the U.A.W. Murphy refused the troops but intervened as a mediator. Six weeks later General Motors threw in the towel and signed with the U.A.W., granting most of the union's demands. Chrysler followed suit a few weeks later. (Ford held out successfully until 1941.) Of the more than 4,000 strikes called in 1937 the Department of Labor estimated that 82 percent were settled on terms favorable to the unions.

Two other events of 1937 were landmarks in labor's progress toward maturity and power. The Supreme Court upheld the National Labor Relations Act as constitutional in all its parts, and in the summer of that year Congress passed the Fair Labor Standards Act, which gave statutory sanction to the establishment of minimum wages and maximum work-week hours in interstate commerce. The Social Security Act, which had been passed by Congress in 1935 with provisions for workers' pensions and unemployment insurance, was another benefit obtained largely through labor's pressure on the government. American labor had at last pulled abreast of its counterpart in other advanced countries of the world in terms of fundamental guarantees and prerogatives. Indeed, it had something of a bonus in the Wagner Act, for it won certain privileges of collusive action in the prosecution of its demands—privileges that were denied to employers under the antitrust laws. The New Deal had balanced the scales for labor; it in fact, had slightly overbalanced them.

A HOBO RECOUNTS HIS EXPERIENCES

STEAMTRAIN MAURY, AS TOLD TO JACQUELINE K. SCHMIDT

For countless people during the depression, the best way to stay employed was to travel by train throughout the United States in search of work. These people, who were typically men, were known as hobos. One of these men was Steamtrain Maury, a five-time National King of the Hobos. In the following selection, told to Jacqueline K. Schmidt, Maury describes his life during the depression and explains the history and ethics of hobos. According to Maury, hobos are not bums, but rather people who choose to live a nomadic lifestyle. Another trait that sets them apart from bums is that hobos have trades and skills that allow them to be self-supporting. Schmidt, also known by the hobo nickname Gypsy Moon, is the former executive director of the Indiana Transportation Museum and a National Queen of the Hobos.

A t first, I just went in the summertime. I was just a teenage boy then. I got acquainted with a lot of the old men in those days. A lot of people think hoboing originated during that time, but of course it didn't. Hoboing started after the Civil War. The original hobos were all veterans of the Civil War. And after World War I, big numbers hit the road.

They were veterans coming home from the war. A lot of them were still on the road when the Great Depression hit in the 1930s. During the Depression years, thousands of men hit the road and went out looking for work when there wasn't any work. They were just restless men, unemployed. They'd pick up a little work in the harvest fields. That was about all they

Steamtrain Maury, as told to Jacqueline K. Schmidt, *Done and Been: Steel Rail Chronicles of American Hobos*. Bloomington: Indiana University Press, 1996. Copyright © 1996 by Indiana University Press. Reproduced by permission.

found during the Depression. There was about a thousand men for every job. They just roamed the country on freight trains and slept out along the rivers. They did chores for something to eat, either for housewives or restaurants. A lot of them lived off the land. Some hunted and fished and ate greens.

BECOMING A HOBO

I was born in '17. I was thirteen the first year I hit the road, in 1930. 1 went again in the summer when I was fourteen, went in the summer when I was fifteen. Then I went on the road for three or four years, just staying on the road, finding work here and there.

My dad lived in Toledo. My mother died when I was about twelve. My dad didn't like what I was doing very well, but he didn't do anything about it either. I had a brother and two sisters, but they all were much older than I was. I was the youngest of the family. They were all married and had families by then.

Part of my boyhood, I'd been raised in Idaho. I'd come to Toledo to live with my dad, and I wanted to go back to Idaho where I had been raised the early part of my boyhood. I was set to go back there, and the only way to get there was ride the freight trains.

At first I spent summers in the western states working. I listened to a lot of the oldtime hobos. I listened very carefully to them. They handed me down their histories. At that time those men were in their sixties, seventies, some of them in their eighties. That's how I learned about the oldtime history. There I was a young lad, and I was getting acquainted and listening to all the oldtime hobos that had come from way back before the turn of the century. And I felt like a historian from the very beginning.

In the '30s I stopped hoboing because I got to working steadily and got married. Then later on in life I got crippled up and couldn't work anymore. I was too young to retire. I was only about fifty, and I got hoboing again. Just a little bit at first, and then more and more and more. Finally ended up spending another ten years hoboing—1971 to '80, something like that. I had a wife at home. She was working. She got mad about that. It took a lot of sweet-talking to get back home.

THE HOBO WAY OF LIFE

A hobo is a man that worked along the way. People argue about this, but this is the way it was handed down to me. I knew them from back in the old times. The hobos were men that followed the railroads, and they worked here and there. They all had a trade or craft to work at. The tramps were a group of men that also came out of the services of the army, but they were men that walked wherever they went. The word *tramp* means "walker." "Tramp, Tramp, Tramp, the Boys Are Marching." Remember that old song? Tramp, tramp, meant marching in the service. A professional walking man, he was called a tramp. And he worked. A lot of people argue about that too, but a tramp does do work. He was just a different kind of vagabond than a hobo.

Another difference is hobos were clannish, they were a brotherhood, and they rode the freight trains. They were organized, they had conventions, they had leaders, district leaders, and they had national leaders. It was like that then, and it still is today. The hobos still have a convention every year in Britt, Iowa. It's been held there for eighty-five years. I was elected the hobo king five different times.

They was in Chicago before they moved to Iowa at the turn of the century. In the year 1900 they wanted to change because Chicago was getting to be such a large city. People would throw rocks at them, and there were big crowds gathering around too much. Sometimes the police would bother them. They wanted to get away from that big crowd, that big city. They wanted to get in a small community, someplace centrally located. Britt, Iowa, was a little town out on the prairie. They said, "Let's invite them out here." And they did. Some of the kings and some of the leaders of the hobos went out there, and they had a meeting. They decided to start having the convention there that year. They met just periodically from then on for twenty years. They didn't have a yearly convention, but it was their headquarters. They would have meetings there and small gatherings. Then in 1933 they started having regular national conventions every year. They also held regional meetings.

Now, there's an early conception about how the word *hobo* began. It has to do with these fellows around the turn of the century that used to carry a hoe with them. They would make a living with a hoe. Every woman in town had a garden, and all the farmers had gardens, and the field also had to be worked with a hoe. And a lot of the oldtime hobos carried their own hoes with them. People would say, "There goes a hobo, a traveling man with a hoe, a 'hoe boy.'"

They might be called a boy. But men, they'd say, "Hey, I'm a man, you speak to me as a man." So they called him "bo." A "bo" is a man, an adult. They called them "ho bo." And that's where the name started.

There was even a few women during the Depression years. Women that hoboed. Boxcar Bertha was one. She retired and lived in Burlington, Iowa, for quite a while. Died about five years ago. She wrote a book [*Boxcar Bertha, An Autobiography, as told to Ben L. Reitman*, with an introduction by Kathy Racker].

COMPARING HOBOS AND BUMS

Very few of them that I ever heard of did it out of necessity. They did it because they wanted a free life. You know, street people that are on the streets today, thousands of homeless street people, they're out there because of necessity. They're out there because they can't make it. But hobos were not like that in any way. They were men that left home and chose that kind of life.

There never was any bums among us. A bum is a person that can't make it, won't make it. A bum is a local person around town that won't work or can't work, maybe even handicapped. Doesn't travel unless it's just down to the next town. Now, there's been some bums that got out and traveled around, a little of them up and down the coast or someplace. But bums are usually alcoholics or men that can't work, or won't work. But the hobos all had good trades and good arts and crafts that they worked at. And they made their way. They didn't bum their way.

I have seen whole families on the road—riding the freight trains, working and picking fruit, working in the harvest fields. And women were safe in those days. I can remember one woman who got in a boxcar with twenty-five men, and nobody even thought about bothering her—not one. Now, that wouldn't happen today. But it was that way back in the '30s. And they were just as safe out there as they would have been at home. Most of the men worried about them, thought they shouldn't be out there. They didn't see that as a life for a woman. And there wasn't a lot of them, just very, very few of them.

When you weren't on freights, the jungles were your home. You stayed in the jungle camps. Men would go out in all different directions and come in with vegetables, meat, and things to throw in the stew. They would make a big old stew, and they'd always hunt wild animals, and they'd fish. They'd wash their clothes; the hobos kept themselves clean. A lot of times the jungles were located near rivers or creeks. Near rivers or a place where there was plenty of water so that they could wash clothes and cook—and they could fish a lot, too. A lot of the hobos were good at living off the land. They knew all the wild food to eat.

A lot of men got out on the road during the Depression because they didn't have no place to live. They'd leave home because they had to. A lot of men went out on the road because they were dropouts, they couldn't make it. But hobos weren't dropouts. Hobos chose their lives because they wanted adventures, outdoor life.

Jesse Owens's Record-Setting Olympics

Timothy Kelley

Despite the protests of many Americans and Europeans over Germany's racist and anti-Semitic policies, Berlin hosted the 1936 Summer Olympics. In the following article, Timothy Kelley explains how Nazi Germany and its chancellor, Adolf Hitler, had hoped that the games would garner positive publicity for the country and prove the superiority of Aryan (white, non-Jewish German) athletes. However, Germany's hopes were thwarted by African American Jesse Owens, who won four gold medals and set two world records. Unfortunately, when Owens returned to the United States, he was met with racist attitudes similar to those that Americans had protested before the games. Kelley is a writer for the *New York Times*.

Put yourself in the shoes of history's most notorious racist dictator, Adolf Hitler. You've spent a ton of your country's money to host the biggest, gaudiest Olympic Games ever [in Berlin in 1936], and you want them to prove that your white countrymen are the world's master race. If one athlete is to win a record number of medals, what color would you like that athlete to be? . . .

Hitler's Bigotry

The Olympics had long been a peaceful outlet for competitive national feelings, and Hitler spared no expense in trying to

Timothy Kelley, "Stealing Hitler's Show," *New York Times Upfront*, vol. 133, no. 1, September 4, 2000, pp. 32–34. Copyright © 2000 by Scholastic, Inc. Reproduced by permission.

make the Games a propaganda coup for his three-year-old National Socialist (Nazi) regime. For the Nazis, nationalism was tied up with bigotry. They blamed Jews for many of Germany's problems, and believed "Aryans"—non-Jewish white Europeans—were superior to all other racial groups and should therefore win international athletic competitions. But the superstar of that year's Olympics turned out to be a black American, Jesse Owens.

In 1936, people did not yet know that Hitler's aggression would plunge the world into its most destructive war (World War II, 1939–1945). But they knew he had come to power advocating racism and an all-powerful Germany. In his 1925 book *Mein Kampf* (*My Struggle*), Hitler had set forth with remarkable candor his plans for ruling his nation and conquering the world in its name. He had also made clear that, while reserving his bitterest hatred for Jews, he had extreme contempt for blacks too:

> From time to time illustrated papers report . . . that some place or other a Negro has for the first time become a lawyer . . . or something of the sort. . . . the Jew shrewdly draws from this a new proof for the soundness of his theory about the equality of men that he is trying to funnel into the minds of nations. . . . It is criminal lunacy to keep on drilling a born half-ape until people think they have made a lawyer out of him, while millions of members of the highest culture-race must remain in entirely unworthy positions.

When Hitler came to power in January 1933, his policies quickly proved that the book was no bluff. In the Nazis' first year, Jews in Germany were excluded from many leading professions. Soon they were deprived of citizenship, and eventually some 6 million would be killed.

GERMANY PREPARES FOR THE OLYMPICS

At first the Nazis had mixed feelings about the Olympics, which Berlin had already been chosen to host. A Nazi Party newspaper demanded that the Games be limited to whites only—a policy clearly at odds with International Olympic Committee rules. But Hitler's propaganda minister, Joseph Goebbels, apparently persuaded him that hosting the Olympics could win prestige for the Fatherland. So Germany promised to welcome Olympic athletes of every color, and even vowed—with the equivalent of fingers crossed behind its back—to let its own Jewish athletes have a fair chance to compete. Unconvinced, U.S. and European critics of the Nazis called for moving the Games to another city—or boycotting them. But Olympic officials overruled them.

The Germans spruced up Berlin and built a colossal, 110,000-seat Olympic Stadium. Writes William L. Shirer, then a reporter in Berlin:

> The signs "Juden unerwuenscht" (Jews Not Welcome) were quietly hauled down from the shops, hotels, beer gardens, and places of public entertainment, the persecution of the Jews and of the two Christian churches temporarily halted, and the country put on its best behavior. No previous games had seen such a spectacular organization nor such a lavish display of entertainment.

To put on a false face of tolerance, the Germans put two athletes of partly Jewish background on their team for show—while barring other Jews. And when a Nazi paper sneered about the "black auxiliaries"—that is, African-American athletes—the U.S. team was bringing to the Olympics, the paper was officially rebuked. But everyone knew that Hitler wanted Germany's white, non-Jewish athletes to prove their racial superiority on the field.

On August 1, more than 100,000 people cheered Hitler at the opening ceremonies (although U.S. athletes declined to give him the straight-armed "Heil Hitler!" salute). For the dictator it was "a day of triumph, exceeding perhaps any that have gone before," the *New York Times* reported. But the triumph soon went sour. Though Germany did win the most medals, the 1936 Olympics had one big hero, and he was 22-year-old Jesse Owens of Cleveland, Ohio—a black.

JESSE OWENS'S ACCOMPLISHMENTS

On August 3, Owens won a gold medal by finishing the 100-meter run in a world-record 10.3 seconds. The next day he took a second gold with an 8.06-meter long jump, another world mark, and the day after that he won a third gold medal by running 200 meters in 20.7 seconds. No one had ever won four gold medals in an Olympics before, but Owens did so when he led the U.S. team to victory August 8 in the 400-meter relay. Even the Germans cheered, and the *Times* called him "the world's fastest human."

Press reports created an enduring myth by claiming that Hitler snubbed Owens, refusing to congratulate him after his first victory because he was black. Actually, Hitler had left the stadium before the event. But the myth symbolized a larger truth: a black man had left Hitler's claims of Aryan superiority in the dust.

Owens returned home to reminders that the Nazis had no monopoly on racism. Years later he recalled:

> After all those stories about Hitler and his snub, I came back to my native country, and I couldn't ride in the front of the bus. I had to go to the back door. I couldn't live where I wanted. Now what's the difference?

Indeed, racial discrimination was still the law in much of the U.S. in 1936. It wouldn't end till nearly 30 years later—after a war for freedom against Hitler's Germany had helped to shine a moral spotlight on racism at home.

DEMOCRACY AND EDUCATION

JOHN DEWEY

John Dewey was one of the most important philosophers and educators of the twentieth century. In the early 1900s, he helped lead the evolution of American education from a system that emphasized authority to one that focused on students and was based on experimentation and practice; education in the 1930s continued to be influenced by his ideas. Dewey believed that this new approach to education would teach students how to live in a democratic society.

In the following essay, written in 1938, Dewey addresses the situation in Europe and the relationship between political doctrines and education. Germany and Italy were antidemocratic states, led respectively by Adolf Hitler and Benito Mussolini. Both nations used propaganda to shape the thoughts and opinions of their citizens. According to Dewey, the United States needs to use education to teach the value of the individual while at the same time stressing each citizen's duty to society. Dewey concludes that the United States has the resources to develop a genuine democracy.

I t is obvious that the relation between democracy and education is a reciprocal one, a mutual one, and vitally so. Democracy is itself an educational principle, an educational measure and policy. There is nothing novel in saying that even an election campaign has a greater value in educating the citizens of the country who take any part in it than it has in its immediate external results. Our campaigns are certainly not always as educational as they might be, but by and large they certainly do serve the purpose of making the citizens of the country aware of what is going on in society, what the problems are and the various measures and policies that are proposed to deal with the issues of the day.

[Prime minister and dictator of Italy, Benito] Mussolini remarked that democracy was passé, done with, because people are tired of liberty. There is a certain truth in that remark, not about the democracy being done with, at least we hope not, but in the fact that human beings do get tired of liberty, of political liberty and of the responsibilities, the duties, the burden that the acceptance of political liberty involves. There is an educational principle and policy in a deeper sense than that which I have just mentioned in that it proposes in effect, if not in words, to every member of society just that question: do you want to be a free human being standing on your own feet, accepting the responsibilities, the duties that go with that position as an effective member of society?

DEFINITIONS OF DEMOCRACY

The meaning of democracy, especially of political democracy which, of course, is far from covering the whole scope of democracy, as over against every aristocratic form of social control and political authority, was expressed by Abraham Lincoln when he said that no man was good enough or wise enough to govern others without their consent; that is, without some expression on their part of their own needs, their own desires and their own conception of how social affairs should go on and social problems be handled.

A woman told me once that she asked a very well-known American statesman what he would do for the people of this country if he were God. He said, "Well, that is quite a question. I should look people over and decide what it was that they needed and then try and give it to them."

She said, "Well, you know, I expected that to be the answer that you would give. There are people that would *ask* other people what they wanted before they tried to give it to them."

That asking other people what they would like, what they need, what their ideas are, is an essential part of the democratic idea. We are so familiar with it as a matter of democratic political practice that perhaps we don't always think about it even when we exercise the privilege of giving an answer. That practice is an educational matter because it puts upon us as individual members of a democracy the responsibility of considering what it is that we as individuals want, what our needs and troubles are.

THE VALUE OF INDIVIDUALS

[American educator] Dr. Felix Adler expressed very much the same idea. I am not quoting his words, but this was what he said, that "no matter how ignorant any person is there is one thing that he knows better than anybody else and that is where the shoes pinch on his own feet"; and because it is the individual that knows his own troubles, even if he is not literate or sophisticated in other respects, the idea of democracy as opposed to any conception of aristocracy is that every individual must be consulted in such a way, actively not passively, that he himself becomes a part of the process of authority, of the process of social control; that his needs and wants have a chance to be registered in a way where they count in determining social policy. Along with that goes, of course, the other feature which is necessary for the realization of democracy—mutual conference and mutual consultation and arriving ultimately at social control by pooling, by putting together all of these individual expressions of ideas and wants.

The ballot box and majority rule are external and very largely mechanical symbols and expressions of this. They are expedients, the best devices that at a certain time have been found, but beneath them there are the two ideas: first, the opportunity, the right and the duty of every individual to form some conviction and to express some conviction regarding his own place in the social order, and the relations of that social order to his own welfare; second, the fact that each individual counts as one and one only on an equality with others, so that the final social will comes about as the cooperative expression of the ideas of many people. And I think it is perhaps only recently that we are realizing that that idea is the essence of all sound education.

Even in the classroom we are beginning to learn that learning which develops intelligence and character does not come about when only the textbook and the teacher have a say; that every individual becomes educated only as he has an opportunity to contribute something from his own experience, no matter how meager or slender that background of experience may be at a given time; and finally that enlightenment comes from the give and take, from the exchange of experiences and ideas. The realization of that principle in the schoolroom, it seems to me, is an expression of the significance of democracy as the educational process without which individuals cannot come into the full possession of themselves nor make a contribution, if they have it in them to make, to the social well-being of others.

THE CONNECTION BETWEEN DEMOCRACY AND EDUCATION

I said that democracy and education bear a reciprocal relation, for it is not merely that democracy is itself an educational principle, but that democracy cannot endure, much less develop, without education in that narrower sense in which we ordinarily think of it, the education that is given in the family, and especially as we think of it in the school. The school is the essential distributing agency for whatever values and purposes any social group cherishes. It is not the only means, but it is the first means, the primary means and the most deliberate means by which the values that any social group cherishes, the purposes that it wishes to realize, are distributed and brought home to the thought, the observation, judgment and choice of the individual.

What would a powerful dynamo in a big power-house amount to if there were no line of distribution leading into shops and factories to give power, leading into the home to give light? No matter what fine ideals or fine resources, the products of past experience, past human culture, exist somewhere at the center, they become significant only as they are carried out, or are distributed. That is true of any society, not simply of a democratic society; but what is true of a democratic society is, of course, that its special values and its special purposes and aims must receive such distribution that they become part of the mind and the will of the members of society. So that the school in a democracy is contributing, if it is true to itself as an educational agency, to the democratic idea of making knowledge and understanding, in short the power of action, a part of the intrinsic intelligence and character of the individual.

I think we have one thing to learn from the anti-democratic states of Europe, and that is that we should take as seriously the preparation of the members of our society for the duties and responsibilities of democracy, as they take seriously the formation of the thoughts and minds and characters of their population for their aims and ideals.

This does not mean that we should imitate their universal propaganda, that we should prostitute the schools, the radio and the press to the inculcation of one single point of view and the suppression of everything else; it means that we should take seriously, energetically and vigorously the use of democratic schools and democratic methods in the schools; that we should educate the young and the youth of the country in freedom for participation in a free society. It may be that with the advantage of great distance from these troubled scenes in Europe we may have learned something from the terrible tragedies that have occurred there, so as to take the idea of democracy more seriously, asking ourselves what it means, and taking steps to make our schools more completely the agents for preparation of free individuals for intelligent participation in a free society. . . .

BUILDING A STRONGER DEMOCRACY

With our fortunate position in the world I think that if we used our resources, including our financial resources, to build up among ourselves a genuine, true and effective democratic society, we would find that we have a surer, a more enduring and a more powerful defense of democratic institutions both within ourselves and with relation to the rest of the world than the surrender to the belief in force, violence and war can ever give. I know that our schools are doing a great deal to inculcate ideas of peace, but I sometimes wonder how far this goes beyond a certain sentimental attachment to a realization of what peace would actually mean in the world in the way of cooperation, goodwill and mutual understanding.

I have endeavored to call your attention first to the inherent, the vital and organic relation that there is between democracy and education from both sides, from the side of education, the schools, and from the side of the very meaning of democracy. . . . And I wish to close (as I began) with saying, that after all the cause of democracy is the moral cause of the dignity and the worth of the individual. Through mutual respect, mutual toleration, give and take, the pooling of experiences, it is ultimately the only method by which human beings can succeed in carrying on this experiment in which we are all engaged, whether we want to be or not, the greatest experiment of humanity—that of living together in ways in which the life of each of us is at once profitable in the deepest sense of the word, profitable to himself and helpful in the building up of the individuality of others.

THE NEW DEAL PROLONGED THE GREAT DEPRESSION

JIM POWELL

The New Deal—the name given to Democratic president Franklin D. Roosevelt's domestic reform program during his first two terms in office—was a collection of laws that was intended to end the Great Depression and rebuild the American economy. Major New Deal legislation included the establishment of the Civilian Conservation Corps and the Federal Deposit Insurance Corporation, stricter banking and finance regulations, and the establishment of Social Security.

In the many decades since the Great Depression, liberal politicians and constituents have praised the New Deal for its effectiveness. However, Jim Powell asserts in the following article that Roosevelt's programs failed to end the Great Depression and in fact prolonged U.S. economic woes. According to Powell, the New Deal failed to reduce unemployment because the policies forced employers to pay above-market wage rates; in response, employers eliminated hundreds of thousands of jobs. Banking laws such as the Banking Act of 1935 and the Glass-Steagall Act weakened the banking system and led to a cut in lending. Powell also writes that Roosevelt's tax increases prolonged the depression, while the Robinson-Patman Act, National Industrial Recovery Act, and several other pieces of legislation forced up prices at a time when consumers had little disposable income. Powell concludes that Roosevelt's aim was to restrict business rather than help the United States recover

Jim Powell, "Did the New Deal Actually Prolong the Great Depression?" *American Enterprise*, March 2002, pp. 48–49. Copyright © 2002 by the American Enterprise Institute. Reproduced by permission.

from the Great Depression. Powell is a senior fellow for the lib-
ertarian public policy organization Cato Institute and a writer
whose works have appeared in the *New York Times, Wall Street
Journal,* and *Esquire.*

T he Great Depression was the most important economic
event in twentieth-century American history, yet we
know surprisingly little about it. Though the popular impression is that Franklin D. Roosevelt's New Deal policies
brought about recovery, economic research developed in recent
decades suggests the New Deal prolonged the Depression.

THE NEW DEAL PROLONGED HIGH UNEMPLOYMENT

The most troubling issue is the persistence of high unemployment throughout the New Deal period: At no point during the
1930s did unemployment go below 14 percent. Living standards
remained depressed until after World War II. Stanford University's David Kennedy seems to be the only major political historian to mention any of the research about the effects of New Deal
policies. In the Pulitzer Prize–winning *Freedom from Fear* published in 1999, Kennedy concluded flatly that the New Deal "was
not a recovery program, or at any rate not an effective one."

It's true the Great Depression was an international phenomenon. But compared to the United States, as economic historian Lester V. Chandler observed, "in most countries the depression was less deep and prolonged." While the U.S. made
a modest recovery between 1933 and 1937, the 1937 peak was
still lower than our previous economic peak in 1929, a highly
unusual occurrence.

Scholarly investigators have raised some provocative questions about this. Why did New Dealers make it more expensive
for employers to hire people? Why did New Deal policies discourage private investment, without which private employment was unlikely to revive? Why so many policies to push up
the cost of living? To what extent did New Deal labor laws pe-
nalize blacks? Why was so much New Deal relief spending
channeled *away* from the poorest people? The list of provocative questions goes on and on. And when researchers try to answer them, considerable evidence emerges that New Deal policies actually prolonged high unemployment.

THE TRUE CAUSE OF THE GREAT DEPRESSION

During the 1930s, the Great Depression was widely blamed on stock market speculation, reckless banking practices, and a concentration of wealth in too few hands. The New Deal laws were drafted accordingly. Subsequent investigations, however, have convinced most economists that the Depression had little to do with any of those things. The most influential single work is *A Monetary History of the United States, 1867–1960*, published in 1963 by Milton Friedman and Anna Jacobson Schwartz, which documented the catastrophic one-third contraction of the money supply between 1929 and 1933. Princeton University economist Paul Krugman remarks that, "Nowadays, practically the whole spectrum of economists, from Milton Friedman leftward, agrees that the Great Depression was brought on by a collapse of effective demand, and that the Federal Reserve should have fought the slump with large injections of money."

Yet the Roosevelt administration didn't address Fed mistakes until FDR signed into law the Banking Act of 1935. Here the idea was to expand the power of the Federal Reserve Board in Washington, which meant that Fed mistakes could have an even bigger impact on the economy. The new Federal Reserve Board's first bad call came soon. Concerned about what appeared to be excess bank reserves which might lead to a surge of lending and inflation, the Fed doubled bank reserve requirements between August 15, 1936, and May 1, 1937. The strategy backfired: In an effort to rebuild excess reserves, banks cut their lending, contributing to the severe recession of 1938.

Nor did FDR do anything about unit banking laws that had doomed thousands of rural banks to failure in bad times. These laws limited banks to a single office, preventing them from diversifying their loan portfolios and their source of funds. When local depositors withdrew their funds, and local borrowers defaulted on their loans, the banks collapsed. Because Canada didn't have unit banking laws, even rural banks were able to diversify, and there weren't any bank failures in Canada during the Great Depression.

What FDR did, of course, was support federal deposit insurance. This has involved charging reckless banks the same premiums as prudent banks. Federal deposit insurance subsidizes reckless banks and passes the resulting losses to taxpayers—during the 1980s, the tab exceeded $500 billion.

WEAKENING THE ECONOMY

Another of FDR's major banking reforms, the second Glass-Steagall Act,[1] actually weakened the banking system by breaking up the strongest banks in order to separate commercial banking from investment banking. Universal banks (which served depositors *and* did securities underwriting) were much stronger than banks pursuing only one of these activities. Very few universal banks failed, and securities underwritten by universal banks were less risky. Why did Congress break them up? Two of the biggest lobbyists for Glass-Steagall were the Investment Company Institute and the Securities Industry Association—representing competitors of commercial banks who would benefit from having banks banned from their own business field.

FDR's tax increases also did much to prolong the Great Depression. Federal taxes more than doubled from $1.6 billion in 1933 to $5.3 billion in 1940. FDR raised personal income taxes, corporate income taxes, excise taxes, estate taxes, gift taxes, and liquor duties, and he introduced Social Security payroll taxes (Social Security taxes began in 1937, but Social Security benefits didn't begin until 1940). All these levies meant there was less capital for businesses to create jobs, and consumers had less money in their pockets.

THE EFFECTS OF ABOVE-MARKET WAGES

Black people were among the major victims of the New Deal. Large numbers of blacks were unskilled and held entry-level jobs, and when New Deal policies forced wage rates above market levels, hundreds of thousands of these jobs were destroyed. Above-market wage rates encouraged employers to mechanize and in other ways cut total labor costs.

At a time when millions of people had little money, New Deal policies made practically everything more expensive. In 1933, the worst point of the Depression, FDR pushed through Congress the National Industrial Recovery Act which promoted cartels in over 700 industries, aimed at maintaining consumer prices above market levels. People were jailed for discounting! Then came the Robinson-Patman Act, the Retail Price Maintenance

---

1. The Glass-Steagall Banking Act, which became a law in June 1933, protected investors by creating the Federal Deposit Insurance Corporation (FDIC) and by increasing the powers of the Federal Reserve Board.

Act, and the Civil Aeronautics Act, which maintained prices of thousands of products and services above market levels.[2]

DISPROPORTIONATE RELIEF

Perhaps the worst of the New Deal laws, from a consumer's point of view, were those like the Agricultural Adjustment Act which aimed to raise farm incomes by destroying food and forcing up food prices. These laws mainly enriched big farmers since New Deal farm subsidies were based on the amount of land one had. The laws displaced poor sharecroppers and tenant farmers. High farm foreclosure rates persisted during the New Deal, indicating that the Act did almost nothing for the poorest farmers.

While FDR authorized the spending of billions for relief and public works projects, a disproportionate amount of this money went not to the poorest states such as in the South, but to Western states where people were better off—apparently because these were "swing" states which could yield FDR more votes in the next election. The South was already solidly Democratic, so there wasn't much to be gained by buying support there.

Government spending was touted as a cure for the Depression, but it didn't work. In 1933, federal government outlays were $4.5 billion, and by 1940 had more than doubled to $9.4 billion. Unemployment remained stubbornly high.

REFORM AND RECOVERY

Despite his charismatic personality and comforting "Fireside Chats," FDR failed to make the recovery of private, productive employment his top priority. Along with advisors like Louis Brandeis, Felix Frankfurter, Rexford Tugwell, and Thomas Corcoran, FDR viewed business as the *cause* of the Great Depression, and he did everything he could to restrict business. His goal was "reform," not recovery. Leading newspaper columnist Walter Lippmann observed at the time that New Dealers would "rather not have recovery if the revival of private initiative means a resumption of private control in the management of corporate business. . . . The essence of the New Deal is the re-

---

2. The Robinson-Patman Act barred sellers of commodities in interstate commerce from practicing price discrimination. The Retail Price Maintenance Act allowed manufacturers to set the price and discount structure for their merchandise. The Civil Aeronautics Act freed airlines from the control of the U.S. Post Office Department and established the Civil Aeronautics Board.

duction of private corporate control by collective bargaining and labor legislation, on the one side, and by restrictive, competitive, and deterrent government action on the other side."

Economic research on the effects of New Deal policies strongly suggests that the best way to promote a speedy recovery from depression is to let people keep more of their money, remove obstacles to productive enterprise, let markets rather than regulators make decisions, and provide stable money and a political climate where investors feel that it's safe to invest for the future.

1940–1945:
America
at War

CHAPTER 5

THE POLITICAL VIEWS OF THE AMERICA FIRST COMMITTEE

JUSTUS D. DOENECKE

Although World War II did not begin until September 1939, Europe had been the site of numerous conflicts in the 1930s; by March 1939, Germany had taken over Austria and Czechoslovakia, while Italy had invaded Ethiopia. Instead of becoming involved in these battles, the U.S. Congress passed Neutrality Acts that were intended to prevent American entry into future European wars. As these acts suggest, the 1930s were the height of American isolationism—the belief the United States should avoid military conflict.

In the earliest years of World War II, the America First Committee (AFC) was the standard bearer of the isolationist movement. Justus D. Doenecke examines the committee's views in the following selection. According to Doenecke, the AFC supported peace negotiations and argued that Germany did not pose a dangerous military threat. The AFC also provided an economic argument in favor of isolationism, claiming that regardless of the outcome of the war, America's domination of trade in the Western Hemisphere guaranteed that its industries would remain strong. Doenecke is a history professor at the New College of Florida in Sarasota and the editor of *In Danger Undaunted: The Anti-Interventionist Movement of 1940–1941 as Revealed in the Papers of the America First Committee*, from which the following article has been excerpted.

Justus D. Doenecke, *In Danger Undaunted: The Anti-Interventionist Movement of 1940–1941 as Revealed in the Papers of the America First Committee*. Stanford, CA: Hoover Institution Press, 1990. Copyright © 1990 by the Board of Trustees of the Leland Stanford Junior University. Reproduced with permission.

Once money was raised and leaders recruited, the America First Committee [AFC] wasted no time in publicizing its views. In a series of instructions for speakers drafted during the lend-lease debate,[1] America First offered its own interpretation of the nature and causes of what was to become World War II. It is not the least of ironies that an organization backed by believers in capitalism advanced in part a modified Leninist argument: namely, that the conflict was fundamentally a struggle between competing empires. Expressing a viewpoint popular in the 1930s, the AFC speakers bureau still thought in terms of "imperialist war" and "have-not" powers. Of course, unlike the communists, the AFC saw the Soviet Union as simply another imperialist regime.

VIEWS ON GERMANY

The war, said the speakers bureau, was simply "another chapter in the series of conflicts between European states that have been going on in war and peace for hundreds of years." A new German empire was attempting to compete with well-established ones, and when Britain learned that Germany would be expanding at Britain's expense, not that of the Soviet Union, it declared war on the Third Reich. The bureau denied that Nazism embodied a worldwide revolution. In fact, if the United States preserved its democracy, it would insulate itself from National Socialism. Even if Britain were victorious, it would be unable to restore the governments destroyed by Germany. Moreover, any restored states would be too small to defend themselves, and the unstable political order created by the Versailles peace[2] would simply continue. One thing remained clear: neither the survival of democracy nor the preservation of the global balance of power was at stake.

The speakers bureau drafted questions designed to embarrass the Committee to Defend America by Aiding the Allies [CDAAA] speakers. For example, the AFC denied that war could destroy the ideologies of Nazism, fascism, or communism. "How can philosophies be stamped out?" it asked. In an effort to show that the mere existence of a hostile ideology con-

1. The Lend-Lease Act, signed by Roosevelt on March 11, 1941, allowed America to send arms and other war supplies to Britain and other nations considered vital to America's defense. 2. Under the Versailles Treaty, which brought World War I to a conclusion, Germany was disarmed and required to pay reparations to the Allies for the losses they had suffered.

tained no threat, the bureau noted that the United States had enjoyed "quite amicable" trade relations with the German and Italian dictatorships until war broke out in 1939.

The AFC accused the Roosevelt administration of participating in the war without the consent of Congress or the people. In so doing, it said, the United States was neglecting its two primary concerns: preserving a democratic form of government and building an adequate national defense. Certainly there was no indication that U.S. belligerence would preserve democracy. And it was equally certain that the American people had made no commitment to fight outside the Western Hemisphere.

The AFC staff also promoted specific books, including Charles A. Beard's *A Foreign Policy for America* (1940), Norman Thomas's *We Have a Future* (1940), and Maj. Gen. Johnson Hagood's *We Can Defend America* (1937). It also kept tabs on friendly elements within the press and held Hanson W. Baldwin, military columnist for the *New York Times,* in particularly high esteem. Occasionally it praised specific articles, even if they appeared in such interventionist magazines as *Life* and *Collier's.*

WAR AND PEACE AIMS

If the AFC had a solution to the international crisis, it lay in a negotiated peace. Negotiation was the one real alternative to the continuous fighting—and to what it saw as the perilous interventionism of Franklin D. Roosevelt. Even the popular slogan "V for Victory" was suspect, and [Charles] Lindbergh and [R. Douglas] Stuart suggested an alternative, "A is for America." Although the AFC as an organization did not officially endorse the position, it promoted pleas for negotiation made by others.

Furthermore, its individual leaders were far from silent on the whole matter of war and peace aims. In January 1941 General [Robert E.] Wood claimed a victorious Germany would seek economic control of Europe but would leave most states politically independent. Two weeks later, Clay Judson claimed that a compromise peace would give the world a chance to recover from the wreckage of war. In February, [William R.] Castle noted that John Cudahy, a former ambassador to Belgium, had told him a negotiated peace was Britain's only hope.

[Ruth] Sarles kept careful tabs on any peace talk. In late May 1941 she suspected that John Winant, U.S. ambassador to Great Britain, had come home with "Hitler's latest peace proposal." In July she noted that any peace could be made only on Hitler's terms. Hence, for America First publicly to urge peace in the abstract, or to make specific peace proposals, would be self-defeating. It was better, she wrote Stuart, to have local chapters study peace aims. Another month later, she was even more pessimistic. The president, she said, had decided on a limited war, not involving mass numbers of army troops but drawing upon American marines and sailors.

THE THREAT POSED BY GERMANY

The German invasion of the Soviet Union led to more peace talk. In October 1941, Sarles suspected that a victorious Hitler might propose a peace, while resigning as chancellor because his work was done. [Chester] Bowles thought that Britain, seeing ahead the possibility of the Soviet Union's defeat, might make peace in return for German restoration of the Western democracies. Stuart, also looking at the Russian front, asked Robert Hutchins to launch a mediation movement. In November, [John T.] Flynn predicted that if the Soviet Union fell, Roosevelt would abandon Britain. America First, he continued, should support prominent clergy in an independent peace effort. Wood, however, was uncertain whether the time was ripe, and the matter of negotiation was not raised again.

The Roosevelt administration had continually stressed that Germany posed a devastating military threat. Many historians have concurred, claiming that Hitler's goals far surpassed rectification of the Versailles treaty. His "Greater Germany" was merely a way station to larger aims—hegemony in Europe, including the Soviet Union; the projection of German power overseas; a broader global struggle with the United States. But even though Hitler had continually expressed hostility toward the United States, the AFC denied that Hitler could conquer it. To America First there was a great difference between intention and capability, and it focused on what it saw as great weaknesses in the German war machine.

On this point, materials prepared for speakers raised important questions: Was the United States next on Germany's list of conquests? Would it not be better to fight now, with allies, than later without them? Could the prestige acquired by a victorious Nazism bring fascism to the United States? What damage could a German "fifth column" do?

Another series of questions centered on German designs overseas: Could Germany invade the continental United States from any European base? From the Caribbean or Central America? From any base south of the Caribbean? What would happen if Germany defeated Britain and then sought Canadian and Caribbean outposts? Or sought French and Dutch colonies as bases for an assault on the United States?

A third group of questions centered on naval defense. Excluding the British navy, was not the combined tonnage of the Axis powers greater than that of the United States? If Germany captured the British fleet and used the shipbuilding facilities of the nations it had conquered, could it isolate the United States from the rest of the world? Was the British fleet the first line of a U.S. defense?

America First had to confront other arguments as well. Interventionists warned constantly that an Axis victory would result in a crippling loss of U.S. markets and raw materials. Therefore the AFC had to devise rebuttals on such questions as How dependent is the U.S. economy on foreign trade? Could Germany capture world commerce and thereby strangle American industry? Must the United States fight in order to secure needed tin and rubber? Could Germany cause the world to abandon the gold standard, thereby making U.S. currency valueless?

SUSTAINING U.S. TRADE

The speakers bureau stressed that the United States already held the lion's share of Latin American trade and was doing as much business as Germany, Italy, England, France, and Japan together. It noted that needed raw materials were located in the Western Hemisphere, an area the U.S. Navy could protect.

In addition, the position papers of the AFC's research bureau argued that even if Hitler were victorious over Europe, North Africa, and the Near East, he could not destroy U.S. trade; that Germany might well find victory over the Soviet Union counterproductive; and that within the Western Hemisphere lay all raw materials needed for U.S. industry. While denying the administration's claim that the United States faced an oil shortage, the AFC sought economic integration of the entire hemisphere. The research bureau was especially critical of Roosevelt's economic policies. Accusing the administration of poorly allocating raw materials and misinterpreting the Lend-Lease Act, it found the United States on the verge of another depression.

General Wood maintained that the United States could always dominate the trade of the upper half of Latin America.

The products of the continent's temperate zone, however—Brazil's cotton, Chile's copper and nitrates, and Argentina's meat, cotton, and wool—were bound to compete with U.S. goods. "We cannot sell unless we buy," the general said, "and that is a far greater obstacle than all nazidom."

AFC's ECONOMIC ARGUMENT

The anti-interventionist economic argument at its most sophisticated level can be found in excerpts from an eighty-four-page manuscript, "The Economic Consequences of American Intervention," written by Lawrence Dennis. Dennis was a journalist and economist who advocated what he called "a desirable fascism," by which he meant nationalization of banks and major monopolies, redistribution of wealth and income through progressive taxation, subsidization of small enterprises and farming, one-party rule, and reorganization of the Congress on vocational lines. Two weeks before Pearl Harbor, Wood sought to raise funds for the publication of Dennis's manuscript, possibly under the signature of someone better known and less controversial.

Hitler, said Dennis, could not deprive the United States of its Latin American markets. Neither, for that matter, would Japan be able to withhold rubber from the United States even if it conquered Southeast Asia. Moreover, by skillful use of the economic weapon of barter, the United States would be able to build a powerful economic presence in the Western Hemisphere. If Germany dominated all the Near East and Africa and Europe to the Urals, the United States could not only ward off German economic penetration, it could actually emerge, claimed Dennis, a much stronger power.

If Dennis's manuscript had been published under AFC auspices, it would have constituted the most extensive public challenge yet to the interventionist economic arguments popularized by columnist Walter Lippmann and diplomat Douglas Miller. Lippmann had claimed that Germany would undersell the United States, Miller that the United States would become a Nazi economic colony. Publication of the manuscript would also have shown the AFC was willing to sponsor, at least surreptitiously, the views of a man who espoused a corporate state and who would soon be branded in the popular press as "America's No. 1 fascist author."

THE AFTERMATH OF PEARL HARBOR: AMERICA ENTERS THE WAR

FRANKLIN DELANO ROOSEVELT

The relationship between the United States and Japan had been tenuous throughout 1941. Following Japan's military occupation of Indochina in July, President Franklin Delano Roosevelt froze all Japanese assets in the United States, and the United States ceased trading with Japan. Later that fall, Japan realized that it would have to defeat the American navy in order to increase its power in Asia. In a surprise attack on December 7, 1941, Japan bombed the American naval facilities at Pearl Harbor, Hawaii. The attack destroyed or damaged twenty-one vessels, killed 2,388 people, and wounded another 2,000. The next day, Congress declared war on Japan.

In the following article—excerpted from a radio address delivered on December 9—Roosevelt explains the United States' decision to enter World War II and describes the challenges Americans will face and sacrifices that they will have to make. The president declares that the United States is fighting for the right to live in freedom. Roosevelt also details government policies on war production and urges his country to accept the financial and material sacrifices that must be made in order to ensure victory. Roosevelt was the thirty-second president of the United States.

Franklin Delano Roosevelt, *FDR's Fireside Chats*. Norman: University of Oklahoma Press, 1992.

M y fellow Americans. The sudden criminal attacks perpetrated by the Japanese in the Pacific provide the climax of a decade of international immorality.
Powerful and resourceful gangsters have banded together to make war upon the whole human race. Their challenge has now been flung at the United States of America. The Japanese have treacherously violated the long-standing peace between us. Many American soldiers and sailors have been killed by enemy action. American ships have been sunk; American airplanes have been destroyed.

The Congress and the people of the United States have accepted that challenge.

A RIGHT TO PRESERVE FREEDOM

Together with other free peoples, we are now fighting to maintain our right to live among our world neighbors in freedom, in common decency, without fear of assault.

I have prepared the full record of our past relations with Japan, and it will be submitted to the Congress. It begins with the visit of Commodore Perry to Japan eighty-eight years ago.[1] It ends with the visit of two Japanese emissaries [Admiral Kichisaburo Nomura and Ambassador Saburo Kurusu] to the secretary of state [Cordell Hull] last Sunday, an hour after Japanese forces had loosed their bombs and machine guns against our flag, our forces, and our citizens.

I can say with utmost confidence that no Americans, today or a thousand years hence, need feel anything but pride in our patience and in our efforts through all the years toward achieving a peace in the Pacific which would be fair and honorable to every nation, large or small. And no honest person, today or a thousand years hence, will be able to suppress a sense of indignation and horror at the treachery committed by the military dictators of Japan, under the very shadow of the flag of peace borne by their special envoys in our midst.

A PATTERN OF INVASIONS

The course that Japan has followed for the past ten years in Asia has paralleled the course of [Adolf] Hitler and [Benito] Mus-

---

1. Commodore Matthew C. Perry (1794–1858) led a naval expedition in 1853 to open Japan to American trade. He signed a treaty with the Japanese on March 31, 1854, after undertaking a second mission.

solini in Europe and in Africa. Today, it has become far more than a parallel. It is collaboration, actual collaboration, so well calculated that all the continents of the world, and all the oceans, are now considered by the Axis strategists as one gigantic battlefield.

In 1931, ten years ago, Japan invaded Manchukuo[2]—without warning.

In 1935, Italy invaded Ethiopia—without warning.

In 1938, Hitler occupied Austria—without warning.

In 1939, Hitler invaded Czechoslovakia—without warning.

Later in '39, Hitler invaded Poland—without warning.

In 1940, Hitler invaded Norway, Denmark, the Netherlands, Belgium, and Luxembourg—without warning.

In 1940, Italy attacked France and later Greece—without warning.

And this year, in 1941, the Axis powers attacked Yugoslavia and Greece and they dominated the Balkans—without warning.

In 1941, also, Hitler invaded Russia—without warning.

And now Japan has attacked Malaya and Thailand—and the United States—without warning.

It is all of one pattern.

We are now in this war. We are all in it—all the way. Every single man, woman, and child is a partner in the most tremendous undertaking of our American history. We must share together the bad news and the good news, the defeats and the victories—the changing fortunes of war.

A DIFFICULT BEGINNING

So far, the news has been all bad. We have suffered a serious setback in Hawaii. Our forces in the Philippines, which include the brave people of that commonwealth, are taking punishment, but are defending themselves vigorously. The reports from Guam and Wake and Midway islands are still confused, but we must be prepared for the announcement that all these three outposts have been seized.[3]

The casualty lists of these first few days will undoubtedly be large. I deeply feel the anxiety of all of the families of the men in our armed forces and the relatives of people in cities which

2. Manchukuo was the name given by the Japanese in 1932 to the former Manchuria and the Jehol province of China.   3. Guam fell to the Japanese on December 11, and Wake Island on December 23. The Americans managed to hold Midway, which was the site of a key naval and air battle in early June 1942.

have been bombed. I can only give them my solemn promise that they will get news just as quickly as possible.

This government will put its trust in the stamina of the American people, and will give the facts to the public just as soon as two conditions have been fulfilled: first, that the information has been definitely and officially confirmed; and, second, that the release of the information at the time it is received will not prove valuable to the enemy directly or indirectly. . . .

TWO WAR POLICIES

It will not only be a long war, it will be a hard war. That is the basis on which we now lay all our plans. That is the yardstick by which we measure what we shall need and demand; money, materials, doubled and quadrupled production—ever-increasing. The production must be not only for our own Army and Navy and Air Forces. It must reinforce the other armies and navies and air forces fighting the Nazis and the warlords of Japan throughout the Americas and throughout the world.

I have been working today on the subject of production. Your government has decided on two broad policies.

The first is to speed up all existing production by working on a seven-day-week basis in every war industry, including the production of essential raw materials.

The second policy, now being put into form, is to rush additions to the capacity of production by building more new plants, by adding to old plants, and by using the many smaller plants for war needs.

Over the hard road of the past months, we have at times met obstacles and difficulties, divisions and disputes, indifference and callousness. That is now all past—and, I am sure, forgotten.

The fact is that the country now has an organization in Washington built around men and women who are recognized experts in their own fields. I think the country knows that the people who are actually responsible in each and every one of these many fields are pulling together with a teamwork that has never before been excelled.

A PRIVILEGE, NOT A SACRIFICE

On the road ahead there lies hard work—grueling work—day and night, every hour and every minute.

I was about to add that ahead there lies sacrifice for all of us. But it is not correct to use that word. The United States does not consider it a sacrifice to do all one can, to give one's best to our nation, when the nation is fighting for its existence and its future life.

It is not a sacrifice for any man, old or young, to be in the Army or the Navy of the United States. Rather it is a privilege.

It is not a sacrifice for the industrialist or the wage earner, the farmer or the shopkeeper, the trainman or the doctor, to pay more taxes, to buy more bonds, to forego extra profits, to work longer or harder at the task for which he is best fitted. Rather it is a privilege.

It is not a sacrifice to do without many things to which we are accustomed if the national defense calls for doing without it.

A review this morning leads me to the conclusion that at present we shall not have to curtail the normal use of articles of food. There is enough food today for all of us and enough left over to send to those who are fighting on the same side with us.

But there will be a clear and definite shortage of metals for many kinds of civilian use, for the very good reason that in our increased program we shall need for war purposes more than half of that portion of the principal metals which during the past year have gone into articles for civilian use. Yes, we shall have to give up many things entirely.

VICTORY MUST BE THE ONLY RESULT

And I am sure that the people in every part of the nation are prepared in their individual living to win this war. I am sure that they will cheerfully help to pay a large part of its financial cost while it goes on. I am sure they will cheerfully give up those material things that they are asked to give up.

And I am sure that they will retain all those great spiritual things without which we cannot win through.

I repeat that the United States can accept no result save victory, complete. Not only must the shame of Japanese treachery be wiped out, but the sources of international brutality, wherever they exist, must be absolutely and finally broken.

LIFE IN A JAPANESE INTERNMENT CAMP

MINÉ OKUBO, AS TOLD TO DEBORAH GESENSWAY AND MINDY ROSEMAN

One of the most controversial decisions made by President Franklin D. Roosevelt during World War II was the signing of Executive Order 9066 on February 19, 1942. The order authorized the evacuation of all Japanese Americans living on the West Coast; these evacuees were sent to camps in the Southwest until 1945. Roosevelt had signed the order because of concerns expressed by California politicians and residents of California, Oregon, and Washington that Japanese Americans were working on behalf of the Japanese government and military.

One of these evacuees was Miné Okubo. In the following account, she recalls her life in two internment camps during World War II. Okubo explains how she learned to cope and turned to art and teaching as ways to occupy her time. She concludes that while life in these camps allowed her to study people, she wants to ensure that evacuation never happens again.

Deborah Gesensway is a freelance journalist and Mindy Roseman is a research specialist at the Program on International Health and Human Rights. They are also the co-authors of *Beyond Words: Images from America's Concentration Camps*, the source of the following article.

W e were suddenly uprooted—lost everything and treated like a prisoner with soldier guard, dumped behind barbed wire fence. We were in shock. You'd be in shock. You'd be bewildered. You'd be humiliated. You can't

Miné Okubo, as told to Deborah Gesensway and Mindy Roseman, *Beyond Words: Images from America's Concentration Camps*. Ithaca, NY: Cornell University Press, 1987.

believe this is happening to you. To think this could happen in the United States. We were citizens. We did nothing. It was only because of our race. They did nothing to the Italians and the Germans. It was something that didn't have to happen. Imagine mass evacuating little children, mothers, and old people! . . .

I had always wanted to come out East, but I didn't know anybody and I was shy. So when the evacuation came, I said, "God has answered my prayers!" All my friends asked why don't I go East instead of going to camp. I said, "No, I'm going camping!"

At the time I was working for the Works Progress Administration [WPA] doing artwork—murals in mosaic and fresco for the army in Oakland. I was working in the daytime when Pearl Harbor was bombed on December 7, 1941. We were taken completely by surprise, but we thought the citizens wouldn't be evacuated.

There was a curfew from 8 P.M. to 6 A.M. I had to get a special permit from the government so I could go beyond the five-mile radius to go to Oakland for work. I worked and finished the murals a few days before the evacuation day.

THE FIRST STAGE OF EVACUATION

My mother had died before evacuation, so my youngest brother came to live with me in Berkeley. Another brother was drafted in the army before Pearl Harbor. My father was living alone in Riverside. My sister came from Pomona to visit him one day and the whole house had been ransacked—everything we had, all the old Japanese suitcases filled with parents' old kimonos, my parents' past life. Everything had been stolen. Everything. It looked like he had been taking a bath and cooking when the FBI came to take him away. My sister made inquiries and found him in the Riverside jail. But they wouldn't let her see him. You see, anyone who was connected with any Japanese organization was considered potentially dangerous and when Mother died, Father started helping at the Japanese church. He was shipped to a [U.S. Department of Justice] camp in Missoula, Montana.

My brother and I were evacuated to Tanforan racetrack for six months and then to Topaz, Utah, for one and one-half years. I would get letters from my father. It would read: "Dear Miné, Block, block, block" [blocked out by the censor] and his name signed. So I never found out what happened. Then I received letters from Louisiana. It was the same: block, block, block, block. Finally I had a letter from him saying they were releasing him. That was while I was still in camp. They had cleared him. He decided to go to Heart Mountain to be with my sister and brother. But before evacuation he had met a widow in the Japanese church and she was in the Poston camp. Father was very lonely so I told him he should transfer. He did go there and they were finally married and eventually moved back to Japan. He died there.

In Tanforan, before we went to Utah, all those that had any business problems that they wanted to settle could get out for one day, with a guard. This poor fellow went out of his mind! I took him to the University of California. Met all the professors. And fed him at the faculty club. Bought lots of candy; we weren't allowed candies at that time. We just made it back to camp in time. It was crazy. I mean if you were guilty or something, fine. But it's a strange feeling to have a guard along. But everything was insane when you didn't do anything. All these people—young babies, pregnant mothers—how can they be dangerous? The whole thing is so outlandish that you can't believe it.

LIFE IN THE EVACUATION CAMPS

Tanforan was awful. My brother and I didn't have proper clothing or equipment—just had a whisk broom to sweep out all the manure and dust in our stable. The smell! We cleaned the stall, stole lumber, and turned our stall into a home. Adapt and adjust right away, that's my whole nature.

You could hear all the people crying, the people grinding their teeth; you could hear everything. Even lovemaking. It turned out that the barrack that my brother and I were in was a special stable for young married couples. Later on this neighbor came quietly to me and said we ought to move because we weren't married. I said, "If there's any moving to be done, it's going to be you because we're all settled." But everything ended well. We were never home.

I was always busy. In the daytime I went around sketching. There wasn't any photographing allowed so I decided to record everything. Observing. I went around doing all these minute sketches of people and events. I didn't sleep much.

I worked all night at the newspaper. It was lunacy to work all night, going twenty-four hours a day. I was art editor for the daily newspaper and art editor for *Trek* literary magazine.

I made many friends in camp. Those working on the newspaper and many others. With ten thousand people in a mile-square area, everybody knew everybody. There were many interesting people. I was considered quite a character. There was absolutely no privacy, so I nailed up a quarantine sign to discourage visitors. I would say I had hoof and mouth disease. I still have the sign. You have to live the camp life to know what it was like.

When visitors came, they had to stand in the middle of the highway. And all the cars would go by and they would yell, "You Jap lovers!" So I discouraged my friends from coming.

In Topaz the barracks were better—clean except for the alkali powder dust. We stole right away all the lumber and things. Those that came late didn't have anything. We went out at night, falling into ditches and pipes. It was just chaos. Deep ditches with humps of dirt because they were still building the camp. It was dark as the ace of spades with no lights anywhere. It was quite an experience.

LEARNING TO KEEP BUSY

They had hobby shows in camp, very well received. Everybody in camp displayed their talents. They made use of everything in camp. Rocks, pebbles, fruit wrapping, seeds, cardboard, fence, anything they could find. Clever, beautiful, interesting. I did a huge collage using rolls of toilet paper. They didn't know what to make of it. Gave many a good laugh though!

I taught art in camp to children. I liked the children and students. It is a two-way learning—we learn from each other. Each one is an individual and needs individual attention. It was interesting. I remember the girls drew pictures about camp and camp life. The boys were more imaginative. Their pictures were on war, airplanes, circus, and subjects out of camp.

But for the children, camp wasn't too bad. Children can take anything. Everything was a circus to them. But it was hard on the old people and mothers with children. Children attracted children and they would run off to play.

In camp I kept myself busy. I knew what I wanted to do. All my friends on the outside were sending me extra food and crazy gifts to cheer me up. Once I got a box with a whole bunch of worms even. So I decided I would do something for them. I started a series of drawings telling them the story of my camp life. At the time I wasn't thinking of a book; I was thinking of an exhibition, but these drawings later became my book *Citizen*

13660. So I just kept a record of everything, objective and humorous, without saying much so they could see it all. Humor is the only thing that mellows life, shows life as the circus it is.

After being uprooted, everything seemed ridiculous, insane, and stupid. There we were in an unfinished camp, with snow and cold. The evacuees helped sheetrock the walls for warmth and built the barbed wire fence to fence themselves in. We had to sing "God Bless America" many times with a flag. Guards all around with shot guns, you're not going to walk out. I mean . . . what could you do? So many crazy things happened in the camp. So the joke and humor I saw in the camp was not in a joyful sense, but ridiculous and insane. It was dealing with people and situations. The humor was always, "It is fate. It can't be helped. What's going to happen next?" I tried to make the best of it, just adapt and adjust. . . .

LOOKING BACK

I am not bitter. Evacuation had been a great experience for me because I love people and my interest is people. It gave me the chance to study human beings from cradle to grave, when they were all reduced to one status. And I could study what happens to people. At the beginning they were all together—comradeship and humor—but as camp grew, they started becoming status conscious, bettering their homes, being better than Mr. Jones. Just like what happens in the establishment. People are people; everywhere it's the same. Only the backdrop and stage is different. Just have to change the scenery. People have the same concerns for home, family, comfort, security, and loads of problems. That's all there is when you come to think of it.

So how people reacted to the evacuation depends. There are different personal reactions to everything. Disaster always brings change both good and bad. Certain people get bitter, vengeful. I am a creative, aware person. Like I said before, an observer and reporter. I am recording what happens, so others can see and so this may not happen to others.

WOMEN AND THE WAR EFFORT

LUCILLE GENZ BLANTON TEETERS, AS TOLD TO NANCY BAKER
WISE AND CHRISTY WISE

Sixteen million men served in the American military during
World War II. Their departure to Europe and Asia brought new
economic opportunities to American women. During the war,
the number of working women increased from 12 million to 19
million. Many of these women chose to help with the war effort
by taking jobs in the defense industry, such as in shipyards and
aircraft factories. These jobs, including those outside the defense
industry, enabled women to adopt traditionally male roles and
experience greater levels of freedom and equality. A popular
symbol of these working women was the wartime character
"Rosie the Riveter."

In the following account, Lucille Genz Blanton Teeters—
whose husband went off to war—describes her wartime job at
the Consolidated Aircraft factory in Fort Worth, Texas. According to Teeters, helping to build airplanes was difficult but en-
joyable work. However, the long hours provided little time for
a personal life, and Teeters was quick to leave Consolidated
when her husband returned home.

Nancy Baker Wise, a journalist, worked as a copywriter during the war and also held positions at the Office of War Information and the Phoenix Metal Cap Company. Christy Wise is a
freelance journalist whose articles have appeared in the *New
York Times* and the *Wall Street Journal*. Baker Wise and Wise are
the authors of *A Mouthful of Rivets: Women at Work in World War
II*, from which the following account has been excerpted.

M y husband went into the Seabees,[1] and then I took a three-month course learning how to put airplane wings together. They placed us in Fort Worth at the airplane factory there, the B-24s, the bombers. But I had to pull out. My husband was fixing to go overseas and he wanted me to come to Rhode Island to see him before he left, so I went up there for two or three weeks, and when I got back the class had gone off. I had to go back and finish my course. And when they placed us over there at Ranger, Texas, they helped us find a room. We had room mothers and dorms and got up and went to work and everything, real neat.

STARTING THE JOB

I knew some ladies from Coleman and we lived together. I worked the day shift and started in the wing, the wing tip department. Then I got to shoot on that big B-36 that they were bringing out. I got to shoot explosive rivets. When you shoot it, there's a certain kind of tool and then it explodes. We had partners on these wings, and I'd rivet part of one, she'd rivet, and then I'd have to buck on the other side where you couldn't see each other. If you wanted to stop, you tapped. If you didn't, the rivet would go through. Of course, they had men that went by all the time and kept your time sheets, what you were working on, how many hours you spent on this. I worked on the wing tip for a while and then I worked on the wing, they called them the skin, big sheets of aluminum for the wing.

I enjoyed the work. It was in this big, big building. It was, oh, to walk from one end to the other, I'm going to say it would be a mile. The noise was terrible. And we didn't wear ear protectors. We wore these blue caps so your hair wouldn't get caught in the drill.

They knew about what position to place you in with a certain group. I feel I was in with a real super group. And you just worked hard. I'd rather shoot rivets than buck them. But this lady who was my partner, she'd prefer to shoot rivets, too. So we'd swap. When you buck rivets you have a bucking bar, a big old bar, and you hold it in your hand. It's like a block. If you didn't hold it right it wouldn't buck right, and the inspector would come around all the time and inspect this, and if it wasn't

---

1. Seabees are members of U.S. Navy construction battalions. They build naval shore facilities in combat zones.

Women apply fixtures to the fuselage of a B-17 bomber. Many women took jobs in the defense industry during World War II.

right, he'd mark it and you'd have to take it out. If you drilled that out many times, that hole, you got marks against you. I don't know what happened if you got too many marks. I don't guess I got very many. I guess they moved you, transferred you to somewhere else.

LIFE OUTSIDE THE JOB

They called me to the office one day there at Consolidated, and I thought, what have I done? I got over there and they took my picture and put it in the little old newspaper, our newspaper. I guess the mailman had reported I had written a letter to my husband every day since I'd been in the department, and that I had received about as many from him. So it was a real sweet write-up. But I was afraid I'd done something wrong.

We were off Saturday and Sunday. We did our laundry and our hair and things like that. But it was mostly hard work.

One time I got to the end of my rope, I guess, and I took off and went over to the middle and crawled up in one of those airplanes. I decided I wanted to see what they looked like. I didn't realize that they kept up with each worker so much. I went over there and was climbing up in that, and I was looking this thing over, and then the foreman came up to me and said, "You mean you've never seen? Come here, I'm going to show this to you." And he got me through, and he went over that whole plane with me. But I never did leave my place of work anymore.

There may have been outside activities, but I didn't go. By the time you bathed and wrote your letters, bed, and then we got up so early the next morning. And then our ride comes by and honks and we ride to work, that's the routine. It was just a routine, just work.

Two years of work and they called me at work one day and told me they had a message. I hadn't heard from my husband for a couple of months, and I thought maybe he's been killed. They called me at the office. They had a message from the War Department, and I was scared to death—everybody else was, too—saying that he was on his way home. Boy, I threw my toolbox down and I left there and I didn't go back. They begged me not to go. I just thought the war was over. They begged me not to go, and this girlfriend brought my check to me. When he came home, I came home, and then I went back to San Francisco with him. I enjoyed my work at Consolidated but I never went back after that.

A FIRSTHAND ACCOUNT OF D DAY

RICHARD L. STROUT

One of the turning points of World War II took place on June 6, 1944, when Allied forces, led by General Dwight D. Eisenhower, stormed the coast at Normandy, France, in the largest amphibious invasion in history. By the end of the day, which was known as "D day," the Allies had successfully secured five landing beaches, which would enable 1 million Allied soldiers to land in France by month's end. The attack was successful, but it also resulted in the loss of thousands of American, British, Canadian, and French lives. The Germans suffered major casualties as well.

Richard L. Strout, who was a staff correspondent for the *Christian Science Monitor* during World War II, provides a detailed account of the events of D day. Strout was stationed on the heavy cruiser USS *Quincy,* which departed from England on June 5. He details the crew's preparation for the following morning's invasion as the ship sails to France. He then describes the bombardment of the beach and the Allied arrival on shore. Strout concludes that the battle proved that the Allies could not lose the war. Strout earned a Pulitzer Prize in 1978 for lifetime achievement and died in 1990 after more than six decades as a journalist. His account appears in the anthology *Typewriter Battalion: Dramatic Frontline Dispatches from World War II.*

Richard L. Strout, "Shot-by-Shot Story of D Day," *Typewriter Battalion: Dramatic Frontline Dispatches from World War II,* edited by Jack Stenbuck. New York: William Morrow and Company, Inc., 1995. Copyright © 1944 by Richard L. Strout. Reproduced by permission.

On board the heavy cruiser U.S.S. *Quincy* off France, June 7, 1944—This is a round-by-round story of the invasion of France and the opening of the Second Front.[1] It covers the secret passage of the invasion fleet under fire and the most glorious sight of the arrival by glider of 10,000 airborne troops.

The battle continues as this is written.

The ship jolts with the explosion of shells.

But one thing is certain. Our beachhead is established.

The degree of organization disclosed is so amazing as to augur [Adolf] Hitler's overthrow.

The story begins on the open bridge of a United States heavy cruiser (the U.S.S. *Quincy*), Capt. Elliott M. Senn, United States Navy, commanding.

THE EVENTS OF JUNE 5

It is 2 P.M. Monday, June 5. I am standing under the sky. I am dictating this story as it happens.

We have just left our anchorage. We are headed almost due east in a single line of capital ships flanked by outriders. History hangs on the weather.

On our left are the cliffs of England. We are in an Anglo-American task force. The ships' names mingle like a chant. Those of the British have come down through history. The American names sing of the New World.

Our vessel, with its home port at Boston, is one of the fleet's newest and finest. There is another task force. The combined flotilla with landing craft will be vast. There are French, Dutch and Norwegian ships.

Already, another convoy is visible carrying its own barrage balloons.

The sky is overcast. The sea is lead-colored but quiet. There is hardly any wind. Even a squall no worse than last night's would hamper landing craft, result in thousands of casualties, maybe upset the whole show. Well, we have done what we can—the weather is nature's business.

This high, open bridge covers three sides. Forward and below are three decks and gun turrets. The biggest turrets carry triple sticks of long range, dangerous-looking guns.

The prow comes to a razor edge. Like most of man's weapons,

1. The Second Front was Western Europe (the First Front was the Soviet Union).

this appears beautiful. It is slim as a race horse, rhythmic as a poem.

It is so new that 1,000 of its crew are green. They speak every American accent. This spot is a magnificent grandstand seat for history's greatest show.

DEPARTING ENGLAND

5 P.M. We have overtaken and are passing the landing craft fleet formerly seen on the horizon. They make slow headway; their barrage balloons tied front and stern of larger craft tug ahead as though pulling.

These craft are chock-full of assault troops and supplies. They will catch up to us as we anchor in the night.

6 P.M. We have hoisted a fresh, clean battle flag. It will fly there till the engagement is over. Blue-coated figures in steel helmets are sweeping the sky and sea around me, chanting observations like football quarterbacks.

The air is tense and the men are consciously trying to break the suspense by horseplay. This has gone on for weeks. Our ship has known its mission and has been sealed. Now it is coming. The gun crew is skipping rope.

We are leaving England. The great adventure begins. The coastline fades as we steam slowly. Right under the haze close to the distant shore is another line of vessels, alternating big and little ones, moving our way stealthily under the shore line.

We look and wonder. Something marvelous is going on. All the world's ships seem to be going our way.

Rumors fly about. Yesterday, at the peak of uncertainty, came the radio news that a New York press association had falsely reported the invasion already under way. I have been asked dozens of times if this kills the whole thing.

7 P.M. A voice breaks the silence over the loudspeaker system. A battle message has been received for this task force.

"I will read it," says the voice. It is terse, pungent, without false heroics.

"Let's put the Navy ball over for a touchdown," it concludes. The sailors chuckle.

And now the chaplain offers the final prayer before the battle. All over the ship, out here in the breeze and down in the engine room beneath the surface of the sea, the men pause with bared heads.

The voice goes over the ship and into the evening air: "Our

help is in the Lord."

"Ask and it shall be given, seek and ye shall find," the solemn voice concludes.

FINAL PREPARATIONS

8:30 P.M. Zero hour tomorrow is 6:30. There will be general quarters tonight (which means battle stations) from 10:30.

That is the loudspeaker announcement. A hush falls on the crew, only two hours before night and day watches set in, with compartments sealed watertight.

Hurried last minute preparations are made. I walk through the compact crew compartments. Some men sit by themselves, others write letters home, some are on bunks in the canvas tiers. The voices are cheerful.

I turn in for a final nap.

10:30 P.M. The boatswain just piped, followed by the electrifying cry, "All hands man your battle stations!" Now the bugle blows "general quarters."

The sky is overcast. Somewhere up there the moon is one night from being full. Behind us are a few red streaks of sunset. Will this thick cloud conceal us? Is it possible German planes haven't spotted these great ship lines? All afternoon the number has been swelling. But the enemy has given no sign.

Midnight. It is June 6, D-day.

The breeze has freshened. France is off ahead. There is a spurt of distant tracer bullets and a failing meteor that is really a falling airplane.

There is a gray light and we can see one another. We keep peering out, wondering when the enemy will go into action, but nothing happens.

Here is a wonderful thing: Out here in the open Channel we are following mine-swept safety lanes clearly marked so even a landsman can read them, for there are little pinpricks of buoys. Nothing that has happened has so given me the sense of extraordinary preparation.

We steam slowly. Our ship is flanked by shadowy destroyers. Only occasionally does a muffled signal flash and even on ship in the corridors, there are only his red battle lights. Now and then there is a hint of moon in the cloud blanket.

1 A.M. For an hour, airplanes have gone over us. Occasional star shells fall off there in France. Once, the moon glowed out and cast us in full relief and a silvery patch. As I dictate this,

suddenly a batch of lights twinkles like July 4 sparklers. Anti-aircraft stuff! Now it is gone.

I keep thinking of home. It's 7 P.M. there now. The family is just finishing supper. It's the same in millions of American homes, children doing homework, mothers at dishes, fathers reading papers. And here we are on the dark sea moving at half speed toward history.

REACHING FRANCE

2 A.M. France is just over there twelve miles off. There must be hundreds of ships around us. It is impossible to see. I couldn't have believed we would get so far undetected. The Germans must know we are here. But nothing happens. Just bombers.

A few minutes ago a great flock came back from France flying low and scudding past like bats showing the prearranged signal of friends.

Behind tiny wedges come stragglers, some with limping motors. Again and again the lights blaze on the French coast. The moon dodges in and out.

Something extraordinary in bombing must be going on. When I was a child, I could see the distant glow of fireworks at Coney Island. This is like that. Just as I dictate, a fountain of sparklers sprays upward—dotted lines of tracer bullets shoot out. This must seem pretty bad on shore, but they don't know what's to come.

3 A.M. We have arrived. And the slower landing craft meet us here. Then we go in with them to six miles offshore.

There will be simultaneous attacks by the Americans and British. Our beachhead is the one farthest north, the one nearest Cherbourg.

Here on the open bridge I hear the order, "Be ready to fire."

It just doesn't seem possible they don't see us. If they do, why don't they fire?

This must be the greatest concentration of bombing in the war. Everything is going off. We strain to read its meaning.

The only thing we know is that we are in Act 2.

Our performance is to reverse Dunkerque.[2]

---

2. Also known as Dunkirk, this French seaport was the site of an Allied evacuation in late May and early June 1940. Germany had attacked the city after British, French, and Belgian troops had retreated from Belgium and headed toward Dunkerque, following Germany's conquest of Belgium. Between late May and June 4, more than 800 vessels led an evacuation of approximately 338,000 Allied troops from Dunkerque to England.

4 A.M. Well, this is the most spectacular bombing display of all. This must be the commotion kicked up by our parachute landings.

As I write, the roar of planes is like an express train going over a viaduct. I dictate this to Chief Yeoman Charles Kidder. As I speak now, flares blaze out in fifteen to twenty clusters. I can read my watch. Flames still drop. They coil out long wriggling trails of white smoke. The water seems jet. I am so wrought up I can hardly hold still. The tension on the ship is reaching a peak.

We are going inshore. The bombs on land are so near and so big I feel the concussions. Our big guns are trained ahead.

Everybody is tense for the shore battery which does not come.

The moon is gone and it is darker than it has been. We are getting an acrid smell of torn-up soil. The eerie flares have gone out.

Well, here we go!

THE BOMBARDMENT BEGINS

4:50 A.M. We are a few miles offshore. And no comment from the enemy. More fireworks stuff. I never imagined anything like it. The most horrible thing was two falling planes—ours, I suppose—that crashed down with great bubbling bursts of oily flames when they hit.

All nine big guns are pointed at the beach. It's getting lighter. There are yellow streaks in the cloud blanket.

5:30 A.M. It's come!

This is the bombardment. My ears pound. Our big guns are just under me and every time they go off—as just then—I jump and the ship jolts.

We all have cotton in our ears, but it is noisy just the same and we feel the hot blast on our faces.

We crouched behind the rail for the first one and are bolder now. We will pound the beach for an hour, picking up where the bombers quit.

Enemy shore batteries are ineffectual so far. They produce only geysers of water.

I hear the crunch of our neighbors' big guns. We all are pounding away for miles off the coast.

Here is the picture:

Dawn is breaking. There's more light every second. The sea is calm as a lake. The sky is mostly overcast.

By moving around the semi-circular bridge, I can see two-thirds of the horizon. We are in a sort of bay. We have moved in and the landing craft are coming in.

Dawn found us on Germany's doormat like the milk bottle.

The big ship to our left is firing tracers and they go in like pitched baseballs.

The whole bowl of sky echoes with our din. While we are concerned mostly with our own beach, we see tracers from other ships zipping ashore, see the flame from guns and a few seconds later, get the report.

I can see the flag waving at our mast and the long streaks of sun-touched cloud are like its stripes.

6 A.M. We bang away regularly like a thunderbolt worked by clockwork. The individual drama goes on all around. Somehow I never imagined it would be like this.

I thought it would be all a motion picture close-up. Actually, the immensity of sky and land dwarfs everything and you have to strain at the binoculars to see what is going on. I guess that is true of all battles.

If you are right in them, you can't figure what is happening. But here are details:

An airplane laying a smoke screen for the landing just crashed. It looked as though it was hit in midair.

We are smashing in salvos at specific objectives and every time the guns go off the whole ship jumps and so do I.

A sound like milk cans is the shells being ejected from the five-inch batteries.

Our third salvo seems to have silenced one shore battery and we have moved to the next.

HITTING THE BEACHES

Now at 6:30 the landing craft should be hitting the beaches.

It is H-hour.

7 A.M. An American destroyer has been hit. It is heartbreaking to watch. The enemy fire splashes again and again. We shift our guns to knock off a battery.

A whaleboat leaves the destroyer.

Distress signals blink. A cloud of steam or smoke appears. A sister ship moves in right under the fire to pick up survivors.

Forty-five minutes later, the same din, the same animated scene.

A line of ships goes ashore. And empties are coming back.

A little French village with a spire nestles at the cliffs that look so like England across the Channel.

The drama has shifted from ship to harbor.

Things probably are moving fast, but it seems amazingly slow.

8 A.M. The sun shines gloriously. This probably is the best weather ever picked for an invasion—cloudy at night, bright by day now.

Our destroyers are practically walking on the beach, blazing into the cliffs as they move. We get radio word that one emplacement in concrete and the destroyer can't rack it. Our turrets sweep around.

Bang they go! Now a second time!

It is almost impossible to stand still, so great is the will to urge that long new line of invasion barges forward. Any one of the runny little amphibious beetles makes a story in itself.

It is like picking a particular ant.

Here in my binoculars I see an ugly squarish little craft making for shore with a lace of foam in front. It reaches the beach, the white disappears, it waddles up. I can't see, but its guns are probably going.

On the sands are hulks of other boats—motionless. They have hit mines.

Allied forces land on the beach at Normandy under heavy machine-gun fire on June 6, 1944.

9 A.M. No sleep—and a plate of beans for breakfast. It seems as though it must be afternoon.

Our radio has just picked up a German radiocast denying any troops are ashore. They seem thoroughly befuddled.

They say we made an attempt at Dunkerque and Le Havre.[3] It seems a complete surprise.

Noon. Everything depends on speed. We have a landing, but we had that at Dieppe.[4] Can we stick and can we go in fast enough to pinch off Cherbourg?

The whole drama is that line of ships. What it looks like is an ant line.

One line moves an army with crumbs and another returns to the crust. Here they are moving like that—little black ships, but all sizes.

A big one with a whole rear end that unfolds on the beach or a little one with a truck or two. They are all pretty squat and ugly—and the most beautiful sight I ever saw.

Yet it looks so quiet and peaceful. The splashes of water look like top splashes. Except when the splashes come in our direction.

There is one persistent battery that keeps trying to get us. It quiets after we fire and then comes on again after we shift to something else.

One earlier target we got in the first salvo.

LISTENING TO THE BATTLE

2 P.M. I have just had on the head phones in the communications room. Shore groups with walkie-talkies are telling the parent control what they find.

It is all in a jargon of communications nomenclature. The parent voice calls out loudly and commandingly through the static.

More and more crackling static. Suddenly a quiet voice identifies itself.

"I am pinned down," says the quiet voice. "I am between machine-gun and pill-box cross fire." So that's it.

And now our radio leaves him.

A station reports that "firing from the bluff is continuing." It reports that the water obstacles are being taken care of. The incoming tide is helping.

3. Le Havre is a French seaport that suffered heavy damage during World War II due to Allied bombing.   4. The French port of Dieppe was the site of a British raid in August 1942.

That's what a battle sounds like under the scream of shells. We can't really tell what's happening. We are in it, but we might be losing for all we know.

4 P.M. Well, things are going well. We know because we have just heard a British Broadcasting Corporation (BBC) broadcast! BBC seems delighted. It says reports are splendid. O.K. by us.

That far bluff is still spitting fire, though, and the elusive shore battery has splashed us with water. What does BBC advise?

But we are so weary now we are going to sleep on our feet anyway.

6 P.M. Six of the clumsy mechanized landing crafts (LCM's) go by—the most angular craft ever built. Their front end, that ought to be high, is low, and vice versa. Not even its mother could love it. They are like wallowing watering troughs.

They carry a five-man crew and will lug a tank ashore. They come in abreast closer than anything so far. Those six, somehow, epitomize the whole affair. I can pick out figures—almost faces—with my glasses. To the men on shore they must look like ministering angels.

I can see the burly captain and even at this distance notice his arms akimbo. He is contemptuously looking at our towering warship and staring it out of counterance.

Then he sweeps the battle with uncomplimentary eye—the very image of a Hudson River tugboat captain. If I talked to him, I bet he would have a tough Jersey accent and would take backtalk from nobody, see—not from the Germans, nor from a warship.

We let go an eight-inch gun salvo over his right ear that must at least establish a feeling of joint respect.

A GLORIOUS SIGHT

All the time I have been typing, the ship has been blasting ahead. The typewriter jumps with the jolt.

Midnight. We are, I think, winning the battle. And here is the place to stop because I have just seen the most glorious sight of all. The paratroopers have come in. It was a scene of almost unbelievable romance and it probably revolutionizes warfare.

Right out of the east came suddenly a bigger and bigger roar of sound, as if all the planes in England were droning, and then here appeared line on line of big bombers, each towing a glider.

They curved over us in a mighty crescent and sped over the shore into the sunset.

Then, as the first batch passed and the second appeared, the bombers of the first were coming back again singly, this time having released their gliders filled with crack troops to reinforce the weary invasion companies that have battled all day.

Just at 11 o'clock, a new batch, even bigger than before, skimmed over in the late dusk of double summer time. They were so close you could see the rope that bound plane and glider taut as a fiddle string—all in perfect formation.

In each of the three earlier flights, there were many planes and as many gliders. Just now there are even more.

It was a fantasy out of the future.

Last week, when correspondents on the battle fleet were briefed, we were told something about airborne troops. It seemed fantastic—the number was so large. But I am beginning to believe it.

What a sight that overhead reinforcement must have been to the muddy, blackened men below. It had the dash and elan of a cavalry charge.

After seeing the things I have in the past 24 hours, I know one thing—the road may be tough, but we can't lose.

AMERICAN ATTITUDES TOWARD THE HOLOCAUST

DEBORAH BACHRACH

The Holocaust, which took place between 1939 and 1945, was Germany's attempt to kill all Jews who lived under German rule. The Nazis first relied on troops known as the Einsatzgruppen to shoot Jews. In 1942, Germany started to build concentration camps and evacuated Jews from the ghettos in which they had been forced to live since World War II began. When the Jews reached the camps, the strongest people were put to labor, while the weakest were executed in gas chambers. Six million Jews died during the Holocaust, largely from the gas chamber, disease, and starvation; the Nazis also killed 6 million non-Jews who were from groups Germany considered undesirable, such as Gypsies and homosexuals.

In the following essay, Deborah Bachrach examines American attitudes toward Jews and the Holocaust, as well as the reluctance of the government to assist European Jews. According to Bachrach, although many Jewish and left-wing organizations did speak out on behalf of Jews in Nazi-occupied Europe, Americans were largely indifferent or unsympathetic to the stories of persecution. In fact, anti-Semitism was greater during the war than at any other time in American history. The government in particular ignored the plight of European Jews until the war had nearly reached a conclusion. Bachrach writes that President Franklin D. Roosevelt, along with anti-Semitic forces in the State Department, focused on defeating Germany instead of

Deborah Bachrach, *The Holocaust Library: The Resistance*. San Diego: Lucent Books, 1998. Copyright © 1998 by Lucent Books, Inc. Reproduced by permission.

saving the lives of Jews in concentration camps or allowing more Jewish refugees to enter the United States. Bachrach has written several books, including *The Holocaust Library: The Resistance,* the source of the following selection.

T he United States emerged from World War I as the most important industrial power in the world. In addition, her moral influence was so strong that President Woodrow Wilson, through the establishment of the League of Nations,[1] essentially imposed his own views of international organization on a war-weary world. And, although the United States did not join the League, the country's influence was felt both there and throughout the Americas, where the United States largely dominated the affairs of most of Latin America.

For these reasons the refusal to aid Germany's Jews even before the Holocaust greatly influenced the attitudes adopted by other countries toward the Jews of Europe. Tragically, the perceived national interests of the United States did not appear to coincide with the needs of the Jews of Europe.

Franklin D. Roosevelt became president at a time when many influential people believed that it had been a mistake for the United States to become involved in European affairs, and consequently, in World War I. These people were called isolationists. They had lobbied against further immigration and had succeeded in passing very restrictive immigration legislation in 1924.

AMERICAN ANTI-SEMITISM IN THE 1930S

Americans' dislike of foreigners fanned an increasing amount of anti-Semitism in the United States. This was fueled by the depression, which resulted in the loss of so many jobs. Americans did not want foreigners, particularly Jews from eastern Europe, coming to the country and competing for the few jobs available.

The terrible events of *Kristallnacht* in November 1938, when Jewish shops, synagogues, schools, and homes throughout Germany were set on fire and Jews were attacked and killed in the streets by Nazi thugs, did not alter these attitudes. Nor did the news that Germans were placing Jews in concentration camps in Germany, where they were brutally tortured.

---

1. The League of Nations was an international organization formed after World War I
to help promote peace and cooperation.

The results of a series of polls taken in 1939 and 1940 reflect the generally hostile attitude of the American people toward Jews. Seventeen percent of those polled saw Jews as a menace to the United States. Another 12 to 15 percent of the population indicated that they were ready to support a campaign of anti-Semitism in the United States. An additional 20 percent were sympathetic to such a campaign while 30 percent indicated they would oppose action against Jews in the country. According to these polls, "The remainder did not care much either way."

Americans read stories of Jewish persecution and for the most part ignored them or thought that they were exaggerated. Some people simply did not care. A depression-weary nation did not have the energy to worry about people in other countries, especially if those people were Jews. In addition, suggests historian David S. Wyman, "Comparatively few American non-Jews saw that the plight of the Jews was their plight too." That is, they hardly understood that Hitler's attack on Jewish citizens in Germany was a threat to those moral principles on which Western civilization was based.

In addition, many religious bigots in the United States believed that Jews must have done awful things to be the object of such terrible treatment. Many religious people in the United States still believed that all Jews deserved to suffer because they held Jews responsible for the death of Jesus of Nazareth two thousand years earlier.

For these reasons, the United States in the 1930s did not provide a bright beacon of welcome to the tormented people of Europe, especially to the Jews. The government offered a lukewarm response to an international attempt to deal with refugees in the 1930s when, for a price, Hitler was still willing to let German Jews escape.

LIMITING JEWISH IMMIGRATION

In July 1938 Roosevelt indicated how he intended to respond to the plight of the Jews fleeing Germany and Austria. He sent Myron C. Taylor [his personal representative to the Vatican] as the American representative at the conference at Evian, France, a resort town on the shores of Lake Geneva, to discuss the worsening refugee crisis. Speaking on behalf of Roosevelt, Taylor wistfully expressed the hope that other nations would prove to be generous and take in Jews desperate to leave Germany.

The other countries represented at Evian took their cue from the United States. Since the United States did not display great sympathy for the plight of these people, the other representatives expressed diplomatic platitudes and kept their gates shut to the doomed Jews. Four South American countries—Argentina, Chile, Uruguay, and Mexico—adopted particularly strict limitations on Jewish immigration.

The U.S. Congress did not even permit its limited legal immigration quotas to be filled. People with entry visas found it difficult to negotiate the red tape barriers erected by Congress against their entry. People with family members in the United States, even those with sons serving in the American armed forces, were unable to gain entry. Refugee ships were turned away from the shores of the United States. Their doomed occupants were forced to return to the death camps of Europe.

Some groups and some newspapers denounced these actions. An editorial in the *Churchman* on October 1, 1940, which noted the media attacks on Jews by American hero Charles Lindbergh and Republican senator Gerald P. Nye, concluded:

> Strangely enough, many otherwise decent citizens, even members of Christian churches, have fostered the Nazi-directed efforts by indulging in anti-Semitic talk. When Lindbergh came out in the open with his anti-Semitic brutality large members of such cooperators began to see the ultimate meaning and danger of such talk. It is a pity that many Christians, whose anti-Semitism has denied them their right to the name Christian, have to be awakened.

Journals such as the *Nation* and *New Republic* used their front pages to publish all news they received regarding the extermination camps. Most others published limited stories which appeared on the back pages where they could be overlooked.

THE STRUGGLE TO RESCUE JEWS

Only a tiny number of representatives in the Congress were Jewish. Among them Samuel Dickstein and Emmanuel Celler spoke out in efforts to increase rescue efforts. Their calls were not answered.

Before the United States entered World War II in late 1941 some funds found their way into Europe to assist the victims of the Nazi onslaught. Most of this money came from Jewish organizations such as the World Jewish Congress and the Joint

Distribution Committee (JDC). It was distributed through the efforts of the Joint American Distribution Committee, known as the Joint. The Joint had offices in Geneva, Switzerland, and Istanbul, Turkey.

The Joint worked with the YMCA, the Quakers, the Red Cross, and other assistance organizations. These American funds were used primarily to secure places of safety for Jewish children who were left orphaned as a result of the Holocaust.

Once the United States became a participant in the war, it became illegal to send funds to German-controlled Europe. Jewish relief organizations continued to collect money in the United States and most of it found its way into the hands of rescue workers in Europe. Now, however, such organizations worked under the threat of prosecution by the American government. Their rescue efforts became more difficult. So, increasingly, they directed their efforts from neutral countries such as Switzerland and Spain, rather than France, Holland, Belgium, and elsewhere where Jews were in hiding.

Still, though restricted, those working to rescue Jews fought their limitations. Historian Leni Yahil writes that "While scrupulously observing the legality of its operations, in conformity with American law, the JDC tried to lend support to every kind of rescue action—official, secret, and even some that were illegal according to the laws and ordinances of one country to another." Saving Jews was their most important consideration.

American Jews continued to try to assist their families and their coreligionists in Europe, but at home, they too felt themselves to be endangered. They knew that anti-Semitism in the United States was greater during the war than it had been before.

A Threatening Environment

Many synagogues were defaced. Jewish children were taunted and beaten in American cities. The radio blasted hate-filled tirades by such fascists as Father Charles Coughlin and others who shared his racist views. An American Fascist Party, called the Silver Shirts, received support from such famous Americans as Charles Lindbergh. They held marches in several cities. They took part in large public demonstrations. The Silver Shirts made many American cities dangerous places for Jews.

In such a threatening environment at home, many American Jews found it extremely difficult to speak out on behalf of their fellow Jews in Europe. This was the case particularly before news of the gas chambers and ovens became known in the middle of 1942.

By that point it became impossible to ignore the facts of the extermination campaign Hitler and his armies waged against the Jews of Europe. News from Geneva, London, Warsaw, and elsewhere arrived at the State Department in Washington, D.C. The reports were based on information smuggled out of the death camps by survivors of the extermination campaign. They provided detailed information regarding the gassing, the shootings, the starving people, the barbed wire, the forced labor camps, and the mounds and mounds of dead, emaciated bodies. Names such as Majdanek, Treblinka, Sobibor, and Auschwitz conjured up images of torture and death.

ANTI-SEMITISM IN THE STATE DEPARTMENT

Many newspaper editorials in the United States tried to play down the enormity of the murders. A group of people at the State Department, led by Breckenridge Long, a virulent anti-Semite and nationalist, deliberately tried to hide this information entirely. Long ordered that reports from American consulates could no longer include information regarding the Holocaust. Breckenridge Long and his cohorts simply refused to concern themselves with the slaughter of innocent men, women, and children, especially if they were Jewish.

They kept the official information they received from Geneva from becoming public to help prevent open debates on the subject in Congress. Their major concern was that if news of its suppression came to the attention of influential Jews, there might be a scandal.

Paul T. Culberton of the State Department, Division of European Affairs, expressed just such an opinion: "I don't like the idea of sending this [information from Dr. Gerhart Riegner, the representative of the World Jewish Congress in Geneva about mass Jewish murders] on to [Rabbi Stephen Wise] but if the Rabbi hears later that we had the message and didn't let him in on it he might put up a kick. Why not send it on and add that the Legation [in Geneva] has no information to confirm the story."

At the same time the president and his cabinet could always deny knowledge of these events. Certainly, however, the president and his immediate advisers knew about the extent of the murders through U.S. intelligence agencies. American intelligence officers such as Allen Dulles, head of the Office of Strategic Services (OSS) in Bern, Switzerland, from 1942 to 1945, held secret meetings with members of the Abwehr, the German intelligence agency, during the course of the war.

ROOSEVELT'S OBLIGATIONS

Roosevelt found himself in a difficult situation. He was aware of what was happening in Europe. First lady Eleanor Roosevelt urged him to take action to resist the Holocaust. Roosevelt himself had many Jewish friends and appointees.

Yet above all else Franklin Roosevelt was a politician. He would not act contrary to the views and prejudices of the political forces whose votes in Congress enabled him to wage war against Hitler. Winning World War II was his main concern. Roosevelt knew that he would lose that political support if the isolationists and anti-Semitic forces in the country believed that he was waging a war just to save the lives of Jews. For Roosevelt the most important objective in World War II was to defeat the Axis powers, Germany, Japan, and Italy. They had to be defeated in order to defend the interests of the United States.

Roosevelt had additional obligations. For instance, he had an important agreement with Winston Churchill, prime minister of Great Britain, which spelled out their joint war aims. The two leaders agreed that World War II would be fought until Germany surrendered unconditionally. That meant that no special deals could be made with anti-Hitler factions in Germany, even if that meant saving the lives of Jews in the concentration camps.

The Soviet Union, the wartime ally of the United States and Great Britain, understood the policy of unconditional surrender of Germany to be absolute and final. Any change in that policy might drive the Soviet Union into signing a separate peace treaty with Germany. If that happened, the United States and Great Britain might even lose the war.

So, in response to appeals by American Jews to resist the Holocaust, the American government had a ready answer. The faster Germany was defeated, the government maintained, the faster Jewish lives would be saved.

SECRET CONVERSATIONS

Many people, particularly the Jewish youth fighters in Hungary, sent messages urging the United States to bomb the concentration camps and the railroad lines leading to them. The government, however, left that decision in the hands of the military authorities, who determined that only considerations of military necessity, not humanitarian concerns for Jews, should influence the location of air strikes in Europe.

The United States also refused to engage in discussions toward the end of 1943 that might have resulted in the saving of hundreds of thousands of Jews. At that time some unusual and secret talks took place between representatives of Heinrich Himmler and people close to humanitarian groups in the United States. Himmler saw that the war would be lost and considered himself the natural successor of a defeated Hitler.

Himmler needed tens of thousands of trucks to continue his efforts against the Russians, whom he feared far more than he did the West. Himmler also understood that if such a deal could be made, the alliance between the United States and Britain on the one hand and the Soviet Union on the other would be threatened. Joseph Stalin surely would have regarded such a deal as a threat to his own country.

The highly secret conversations dealt with the possibility of releasing 1 million Hungarian Jews in exchange for the trucks as well as other military equipment urgently needed by the German army. This equipment, the Germans promised to various secret agents, would of course only be used against the Russians, not against the armies of the Western powers.

There was to be no deal. The transfer of money to Europe became even more difficult. Funds then available in Switzerland for humanitarian purposes were frozen to avoid any appearance of dealing with the Germans. In fact the United States even reported the talks to Stalin in Russia to avoid the appearance of taking action behind his back. Besides, it was not clear that any country was interested in taking in a million Jews.

Given all these circumstances, it is possible to understand why no massive acts of resistance to the Holocaust in the United States occurred. However, many organizations and many thousands of men and women did what they could to relieve the suffering of the Jews in Europe. The Quakers and the Red Cross, for example, made great but largely futile efforts to bring children to the United States.

SOME JEWS SPOKE OUT

Many American Jews did speak up. The American Jewish press actively urged the government to resist the Holocaust. So too did the American Jewish Congress, the World Jewish Congress, the Union of Orthodox Rabbis, the Jewish Labor Committee, and the American Jewish Committee. Reform rabbi Stephen S. Wise, a longtime activist in the social justice movement and the most important American spokesman for Zionism, never ceased his efforts.

Rabbi Wise first began to organize an American movement to boycott German goods in 1933 in response to early German outrages against German Jews. The American Jewish Congress continued to press for such a boycott and by 1937 Wise was able to gain the support of American trade unions for a mass rally in Madison Square Garden in New York. Addressing a crowd consisting of both Jews and non-Jews, Wise declared: "The Boycott, moral and economic, is a warless war against the war makers. The Jews in Germany were but one element of the civilization that Nazism had sworn to destroy."

Many left-wing organizations in the United States, including trade unions, socialist groups, and communist organizations, encouraged the government to speak up on behalf of the tormented people in Europe. And many public personalities such as William Randolph Hearst openly and continually spoke out. But they represented a tiny fraction of the population. Their words and actions fell on a government resistant to such pressures.

Finally, a small group of brave men within the Treasury Department decided to challenge the government's decision not to act on behalf of Europe's Jews. These men detested the efforts of Breckenridge Long and his group to subvert the Constitution of the United States by withholding information from the president and by making foreign policy instead of Congress. The group included John W. Pehle, Raymond Paul, and Joshua E. Dubois Jr. They were all non-Jews who endangered their own careers in the interests of a principle. That principle was their refusal to permit the officials of the State Department to thwart the policies of the American government.

All these men had information regarding the restriction of relief funds which could be sent to Europe. They came to believe that the U.S. State Department was "guilty not only of gross procrastination and willful failure to act, but even of willful attempts to prevent action from being taken to rescue Jews from Hitler." During 1943 they spent many months searching government files for documents that would reveal the way in which Long suppressed information. When they had amassed considerable incriminating evidence, they took their report to

Henry Morgenthau, the secretary of the treasury. The title of the report was "Report to the Secretary on the Acquiescence of This Government in the Murder of the Jews."

ROOSEVELT FINALLY TAKES ACTION

Morgenthau was the highest-ranking Jew in the Roosevelt administration. He read the report and immediately made an appointment to speak to the president. On January 17, 1944, he told Roosevelt that unless the president acted on behalf of the remnant of the Jewish population in Europe, he, Morgenthau, would reveal to the press the details of the report indicating corruption was rampant in the State Department.

Roosevelt knew that Morgenthau would carry out his threat. The president also knew that the war was coming to an end. And he sensed that in the United States, the attitude of the American people toward the suffering of the Jews of Europe was beginning to turn. The grim reports and photographs sent to the United States by escapees of the camps and by the Jewish Palestinian organization Yishuv, had been verified to the satisfaction of most Americans and many began to want to help the Jews.

On January 22, 1944, Franklin Roosevelt signed an order establishing the War Relief Board, or WRB. The board was ordered to "take all measures . . . consistent with the successful prosecution of the war . . . to rescue the victims of enemy oppression." The board had the authority to engage in all measures of relief, including negotiations with the enemy if necessary in order to save lives. At long last, and almost too late, the government of the United States took active steps to resist the Holocaust.

Roswell D. McClelland became the main representative of the WRB, centered in Bern, Switzerland. McClelland immediately established contacts with the International Red Cross, the Swedish government, and the Vatican in Rome in an effort to save the last remaining sizable Jewish population in Europe, the Jews of Hungary.

At the same time, Zionists in the United States sensed that politicians of both major political parties were willing to turn their support to the establishment of a Jewish national homeland. Nineteen forty-four was an election year and the Jewish vote in many large cities was important. Both Roosevelt and the Republican candidate for the presidency, Thomas Dewey, pledged their strong support for a Jewish homeland in Palestine.

At the political conventions held that summer both parties included support for unrestricted Jewish immigration into Palestine as a plank in their platforms. Coming very late in the game, too late to save the lives of 6 million slaughtered people, in 1944 the United States finally made effective gestures toward assisting the survivors of the Holocaust.

THE STORY OF G.I. JOE: THE DEPICTION OF AMERICAN SOLDIERS IN MOVIES

CLAYTON R. KOPPES AND GREGORY D. BLACK

During World War II, Hollywood studios produced numerous war films. These movies served as propaganda, typically depicting the virtues of the Allied forces in contrast to the dangers posed by Germany, Italy, and Japan. However, toward the end of the war, Hollywood produced a film that depicted military life in largely realistic terms. In the following selection, Clayton R. Koppes and Gregory D. Black evaluate *The Story of G.I. Joe*. According to the authors, *G.I. Joe* stands apart from most wartime films because it depicted the randomness of death and the homesickness of soldiers without relying on histrionics or sentimentality. Koppes and Black conclude that the movie provides an epitaph to combat films while standing apart from the genre. Koppes is the dean of the College of Arts and Sciences at Oberlin College in Oberlin, Ohio, and a history professor. Black is a professor of communication studies at the University of Missouri at Kansas City. They are the co-authors of *Hollywood Goes to War: How Politics, Profits, and Propaganda Shaped World War II Movies*, from which the following essay has been excerpted.

Clayton R. Koppes and Gregory D. Black, *Hollywood Goes to War: How Politics, Profits, and Propaganda Shaped World War II Movies*. New York: Free Press, 1987. Copyright © 1987 by Free Press. Reproduced by permission.

T he ultimate example of World War II combat films was a
story of the Italian campaign, produced late in the war:
The Story of G.I. Joe. This picture has a maturity and relentless realism that was possible only as the war neared its end.
The mud; the seeming endlessness of war (you took one ridge
only to find another beyond it); the randomness of death—these
things could neither have been shown nor comprehended in
feature films until late in the war. *The Story of G.I. Joe* is so far removed in its seriousness and candor from early battle films like
Wake Island as to seem to be from a different war.

THE MOVIE'S PLOT

Directed by William Wellman, *The Story of G.I. Joe* was based on
the reporting of Ernie Pyle, whose accounts of the common foot
soldier earned him a Pulitzer Prize in journalism and the undy-
ing respect of the G.I. Pyle's stories of courage, tragedy, fear, and
humor were matter-of-fact tributes to the infantrymen who bore
the brunt of the war under the most miserable conditions. He
went along with the troops, asked for little, and died as they
died when a Japanese sniper killed him on Okinawa in 1945. *The
Story of G.I. Joe,* which began as a salute to the common soldier,
became also a tribute to the writer who understood them best.

Building on Pyle's material, Wellman achieved a remarkable
degree of realism in a wartime entertainment film. He inter-
wove scenes from the graphic documentary, *The Battle of San
Pietro;* the fictional scenes are good enough that the fit between
them and those from the documentary is almost seamless. A
Lester Cowan production, the film featured Burgess Meredith
as Pyle and Robert Mitchum in a strong performance as Captain Walker. Most of the cast were unknowns, and included 150
combat veterans who were assigned to the film for a six-week
working leave. Wellman gave several of them speaking parts,
and he forced all the actors to train with the vets. After their
stint before the cameras, the G.I.s were shipped to the Pacific.
Only a few returned.

The Story of G.I. Joe follows a group of American infantrymen
who fight their way toward Rome after the Allied landing on
the Italian peninsula in September 1943. [Benito] Mussolini had
been deposed in favor of Marshall Pietro Badoglio, and the Italians left the war that month. But the Germans decided to turn
Italy into a battleground and put up such a fierce resistance that
Allied forces did not enter Rome until June 1944, and Milan un-

til April 1945. Pyle goes along to record the G.I.'s experiences in this bloody campaign. For the most part the film avoids false heroics, pronouncements about beating the fascists, and sermons about winning the war for democracy. In one scene Pyle and the captain talk about writing and the war. Walker tells Pyle he writes too, but he writes home to parents, girlfriends, and wives about men who have been killed. They were scared kids who did not know what this was all about—just scared stiff. "If only we could create something good out of all this energy," he says. Pyle just looks at him. Nothing said. Nothing needed.

DEPICTIONS OF BATTLES AND MILITARY LIFE

The relatively few battle scenes are stark and spare. As the men advance into a bombed out town, they run from street to street, building to building against an unseen enemy. Walker and the sergeant move into a bombed out church. The captain shouts "lousy kraut swine" in an attempt to flush the hidden enemy. It works, and one German is killed. "Funny place to be killing men in, isn't it," says the sergeant, and kneels to pray. Suddenly a German soldier fires from the bell tower, but Walker picks him off. Nothing is said. No histrionics about wiping savages off the face of the earth.

The film does not lose sight of the ordinary rhythms that pace army life. It rains constantly, and the relentless mud is almost as grim as the fight against the enemy. Light touches relieve the monotony. A soldier's concern for his puppy—a familiar, hokey touch in too many war pictures—comes off as a deft comment on the contrasting roles a soldier has to assume. A G.I. gets a record with the voice of his infant son; he wears it literally next to his heart; and in every town he searches frantically for a phonograph so that he can hear his son's first words. This depiction of a father's separation from his family is more believable than any windy, sentimental dialogue.

The most serious lapse in the picture is the handling of the hotly controversial bombing of the Benedictine monastery, Monte Cassino, the cradle of western monasticism. Allied troops believed the Germans were holed up in the monastery high on a ridge, from which they trained a withering fire that halted the Allied advance. The high command hesitated to bomb the shrine because of a policy to spare religious and cultural monuments. But the G.I.s are unequivocal. "I'm a Catholic and I say bomb it," avers one. "Think I want to die for a piece of stone?"

When headquarters finally decides to bomb the monastery, the troops break into ecstatic cheers. The treatment of the incident beckons the audience to join in the applause. In reality, however, the Germans were not holed up in the monastery, and, ironically, pounding it to rubble simply created an ideal landscape where they could dig in. The foot soldier had to go in and slug it out anyway. In contrast to the film's propaganda, General Mark Clark in his memoirs concluded the bombing of the monastery was a military and propaganda mistake of the first order.

Having finally dislodged the Germans from Monte Cassino, the Allies are again advancing toward Rome. As they rest by the side of the road, a pack train slowly moves by. The bodies of dead soldiers are slung over the backs of the mules. The men watch mutely until they see the corpse of the captain. They are devastated. Some gaze in uncomprehending silence and then plod on to the next battle. One soldier kneels beside his dead captain and murmurs how sorry he is, another holds his hand. Walker's closest buddy, overcome with emotions for which he has no words, bends over the dead man for an eternal moment and tenderly, somewhat furtively, strokes his face. Then he straightens up and digs his boots into the road to Rome.

Pyle says in a voice-over: "This is our war. We will carry it with us from one battleground to another. In the end we will win. I hope we can rejoice in our victory, but humbly. . . . As for those beneath the wooden crosses we can only murmur, thanks, pal, thanks."

Those flat, hopeful, wary words provided a fitting epitaph to a four-year cycle of combat pictures. They could not have been spoken in 1942, and they were still rare in 1945. No Office of War Information (OWI) records have been found for this film, but it seems unlikely that the propagandists would have approved of its non-ideological, often bleak, portrait of war. Throughout the war the uneasy collaboration of Hollywood and OWI had produced a fairly consistent interpretation of American soldiers—who they were, where they came from, and what they became. The capstone of that interpretation, *The Story of G.I. Joe* also stood somewhat outside that corpus.

THE VIRTUES OF MILITARY EXPERIENCE

The movies presented the military experience as an enactment of civic virtue and as an exercise in collective self-improvement. Military service became yet another variation on Hollywood's favorite theme: the success story. The war took average guys from every corner in the land—Flatbush, or Smith Center, Kansas, or El Centro, California—and gave them purpose, commitment, and courage. The war may shake a young man out of a period of personal drift (Rusty Marsh), or represent a higher calling (John in *Tender Comrade*), or offer a break from a pleasant but monotonous routine (Al Schmid in *Pride of the Marines*). The young men are characters of studied innocence who have to be taught the art of war; they are a far cry from the bloodthirsty savages of Japan or the coldly efficient killers of Germany. Some have moral qualms that have to be assuaged. Sergeant York [in the movie of the same name] had to find a way to rationalize killing at all; the new recruit in *Bombardier* had to find a justification for bombing innocent civilians. The men fight with an innate sense of the rules, and deviations from the code of war are justified by the enemy's routine crimes. (One of the few Allied fighters to swerve from the code, [Humphrey] Bogart in *Passage to Marseilles*, is a French civilian.) Foxholes are miniature democracies: all races, creeds, and classes are welcomed on a basis of equality. The movies do not yet have a Sergeant Croft, the sadistic platoon leader in Norman Mailer's *The Naked and the Dead*, who kills Japs out of blood lust, drives his own men beyond endurance for no rational purpose, and is responsible for the needless death of the weak private he found contemptible.

The citizen soldiers and sailors are led by tough, heroic, yet sensitive men, most of them only recently out of civilian clothes. The troops respect, even revere their leaders. With the mourning of Captain Walker, *The Story of G.I. Joe* came as close as the movies dared to speaking of male love. The exalted ranks of generals are almost as divine as Lionel Barrymore's cloud-swathed heavenly staff room in *A Guy Named Joe*. Generals and admirals appear almost exclusively in remote cameos of command and decisiveness. There are no generals like Mailer's Cummings, who can deal with his ambivalent, part homoerotic, part competitive feelings towards his aide only by banishing him to a senseless and inevitably fatal reconnaissance. Nor do movie officers yet worry, like Mailer's general, whether the way they conduct a battle will generate another star. When *A Bell for Adano* tried to deal with [General George S.] Patton's much publicized shooting of a peasant's mule out of pique, the incident had to be converted into an instance of overzealous pursuit of a reasonable objective.

In the end the military experience culminated in upward mobility—a societal expression of personal fulfillment. Some men died, to be sure, but they and their loved ones understood why. They usually died as heroes, taking a clutch of enemy soldiers with them, not with the utter randomness and sheer impersonality of *The Story of G.I. Joe*. Some men like Al Schmid were badly wounded, but a welcoming society, and a woman's love, assured a relatively easy readjustment to civilian life. For the rest the postwar, though not without ominous possibilities, promised greater happiness and personal advancement than these young G.I.s had ever known. The depression was behind, they had new skills and self-confidence, and the G.I. Bill of Rights was society's way of paying them back. As the wounded men of *Pride of the Marines* debate postwar prospects in an immaculate San Diego veterans hospital, they expect their prewar fantasies to be realized. One is going to buy that store on the corner; another intends to use the G.I. Bill to become a lawyer and enter politics; they will all own a home of their own. A pessimist is shouted down. As the Jewish soldier says: If we just pull together, in peace as in war, we can make this thing work.

For many, though not all, it happened that way. For others the propaganda was a cheat. But for everyone, veterans and audiences alike, the war success stories were a deception. Few pictures besides *The Story of G.I. Joe* dared breathe what everyone knew but found hard to voice aloud—that death was random and success only partly related to one's desserts. Faced with some of the most profound of human experiences, Hollywood and OWI could only graft the prepackaged emotions of the success story onto the war.

THE POTSDAM CONFERENCE

ROBERT JAMES MADDOX

The war in Europe reached a swift conclusion in spring 1945. During a two-week span in April and May, the Soviets entered Berlin, deposed Italian dictator Benito Mussolini was hung, Adolf Hitler committed suicide, and Germany surrendered to the Allies. All these events occurred after the death of Franklin D. Roosevelt, who died of a cerebral hemorrhage on April 12, 1945, and was succeeded by Vice President Harry Truman.

On July 17, 1945, Truman, British prime minister Winston Churchill (who was replaced by Clement Atlee midway through the conference after losing a national election), and Soviet leader Joseph Stalin gathered at Potsdam, a town outside Berlin, to discuss numerous issues relating to Germany's surrender. In the following selection, Robert James Maddox examines the bargaining that occurred between the three allies. According to Maddox, the Soviets gained the upper hand throughout the conference, in part because Truman was willing to offer concessions despite British objections. Those concessions would later prove costly because Truman did not recognize how great the differences were between American and Soviet interests. Maddox is professor emeritus of American history at Pennsylvania State University in State College and the author of numerous books, including *The United States and World War II*, the source of the following article.

The last summit conference of the war, code-named TER-MINAL, began July 17, 1945, in Potsdam on the outskirts of Berlin. [President Harry] Truman arrived at the "little White House," former home of a German publisher in nearby Bablesburg, on July 15. The following morning, he was visited by [British prime minister Winston] Churchill, and the day after by [Soviet leader Joseph] Stalin. His reactions to the two men are revealing. Churchill, Truman noted in his diary, "gave me a lot of hooey about how great my country is and how he loved Roosevelt and how he loved me, etc. etc." He thought they would get along, Truman wrote, unless the Briton tried "to give me too much soft soap." He was more favorably impressed by Stalin, who "looked me in the eye when he spoke." "I can deal with Stalin," he concluded, "he is honest—but smart as hell."

On the evening before the first formal session, Secretary of War [Henry L.] Stimson conveyed to the president word from the United States that the first atomic test had succeeded beyond expectations. Truman did not, as he later claimed, regard the atomic bomb as just another weapon. "We have discovered the most terrible bomb in the history of the world," he wrote in his diary; "it may be the first destruction prophesied in the Euphrates Valley era, after Noah and his fabulous ark." Although naturally pleased by the prospect of ending the war against Japan more quickly, Truman's order of priorities was little changed by the news. As Secretary of State [James F.] Byrnes later pointed out, there was no guarantee that a bomb "would of certainty explode when dropped from a plane." Besides, only two such weapons would be available in the near future, and it could not be known whether Japan would surrender even if they did work.

INTERPRETING THE YALTA ACCORDS

Most of the discussions at Potsdam involved differing interpretations of the Yalta accords.[1] The issue of reparations from Germany is a case in point. At Yalta, FDR and Stalin had agreed to use the Soviet request for $20 billion as a "basis for discussion" in subsequent negotiations. Just as Churchill had predicted, the Soviets had since begun claiming that the figure rep-

1. Franklin D. Roosevelt, Winston Churchill, and Joseph Stalin met at Yalta in Crimea from February 4–11, 1945. At the meeting, Stalin agreed that the Soviet Union would enter the war against Japan within three months of Germany's surrender. In exchange, the Soviets would receive territorial concessions in the Far East.

resented a commitment rather than a target to be sought. All along, American officials had assumed that on-site inspections of the German economy should precede the setting of reparations figures. Without such analyses, they argued, reparations might be pegged so much higher than Germany's capacity to pay that they might produce starvation. The issue was complicated by the fact that the Soviets were carting away everything they could lay their hands on under the guise of "war booty," which would not count as reparations. When protracted negotiations failed to make headway, Secretary of State Byrnes began proposing a scheme whereby each occupying power would extract what it chose from its zone. As most German manufacturing was located in the west, industrial goods would be traded for agricultural products from the Russian area. Molotov indicated that the Soviets had no objection to this plan "in principle."

The western boundary of Poland had a direct bearing on the reparations issue. At Yalta, [Winston] Churchill and [Franklin D.] Roosevelt had supported a Polish-German boundary at the Oder River but had rejected Stalin's proposal to set the border at the Oder–Western Neisse, which would have ceded to Poland an additional 8,100 square miles. Shortly before Potsdam, word had been received that the Soviets were unilaterally turning over lands as far as the Oder–Western Neisse to Poland and that this territory would provide no reparations. All this would reduce the German economic base and further burden it with the need to provide for millions of evicted people "bringing their mouths with them," as Churchill put it.

Conditions in Eastern Europe also produced disagreement. Although the United States and Great Britain had recognized the Polish provisional government, they refused to recognize the regimes imposed by the Soviets in Romania, Bulgaria, and Hungary on the grounds that they did not conform to the Declaration on Liberated Europe. "When these countries were established on a proper basis," Truman declared, "the United States would recognize them and not before." Anglo-American complaints that their representatives were being subjected to so many restrictions in these nations that they could not even find out what was going on were dismissed by Stalin as "all fairy tales."

After a morning session on July 25, Churchill, Foreign Minister [Anthony] Eden, and Labour leader Clement Attlee, who was a member of the delegation, left for London to await the results of Britain's national elections. To the surprise of Truman, Byrnes, and likely Stalin, Labour won. Three days later, Attlee returned as the new prime minister, with Ernest Bevin as foreign minister. Anyone who thought the Labour government would prove more accommodating to the Soviet Union was mistaken. Bevin's first words upon landing were, "I will not have Britain barged about." Truman and Byrnes, who were more inclined to compromise than the British, began negotiating with the Soviets privately.

THE AMERICAN PROPOSALS

On July 30, Byrnes offered Molotov three proposals that, he stressed, the United States regarded as a package—the acceptance of any one depended on the acceptance of all. First, he put forward his plan to have each power take reparations from its own zone in Germany, this time citing specific percentages of industrial goods that would be made available to the Soviets in return for agricultural products. He then stated that the United States was prepared to accept Polish administration of German territories east of the Oder–Western Neisse pending a final peace settlement. Finally, he proposed that recognition of the Soviet-sponsored regimes in Eastern Europe should be referred to the foreign ministers for settlement after elections were held in these nations. The key point here is that Byrnes and Truman already had made it clear that the United States no longer insisted on participating in such elections but would be content to send observers.

On the next morning, July 31, Byrnes met again with Molotov to discuss the American proposals. He told the foreign minister that the United States had gone as far as it could to satisfy Soviet demands. Unless the package was accepted in its entirety, he said, "the President and I would leave for the United States the next day." At a plenary session that afternoon, Byrnes formally submitted the American "package." Stalin grumbled a bit about tying the issues together, but his only specific criticism was that the percentages of industrial equipment that Russia was slated to receive from the western zones was too low. Over British objections that the percentages already were "liberal," Truman and Byrnes promptly accepted the higher figures that Molotov suggested, and the deal was done.

With regard to the Far East, Stalin repeated his pledge to join the war against Japan. Soviet armies would be ready about August 15, he said, but would not move until Sino[2]-Soviet negotiations over Manchuria were completed. This hedge did not disturb Truman because he knew that the atomic bombs would be ready before August 15, and the scheduled invasion of Japan was still months away. The president was rankled, however, by Molotov's proposal that the United States and its allies formally request Soviet entry. After nearly four years of fighting, he did not wish to be placed in the position of pleading for what was expected to be a brief contribution. He sidestepped the issue by having Byrnes suggest that the Soviets base their declaration of war on sections of the UN Charter.

EXAMINING TRUMAN'S BEHAVIOR

One aspect of Truman's behavior at Potsdam remains unclear. Midway through the conference, at the end of a session, the president walked over to Stalin, who was standing with the Soviet interpreter. With deliberate casualness, he told the Soviet leader that the United States had developed a "weapon" or "bomb" (it is unclear which word he used, let alone how it came out in translation) of unusual destructive force; he did not say it was atomic. With equal casualness, Stalin replied that he hoped it would be used to good effect against the Japanese. Truman thereupon left.

Because Truman previously had agreed with advisers and with Churchill that he should inform the Soviets about the atomic bombs, his failure to be specific has been criticized as a deliberate effort to mislead Stalin into thinking he was referring only to some powerful conventional weapon. A more likely explanation is that Truman fully expected Stalin to ask about the weapon—a perfectly natural reaction—and was prepared to answer in a general way. When the Soviet leader showed no interest, however, Truman must have been pleased because it meant there would be no embarrassing requests to be brought into partnership, which he was not prepared to grant. Truman probably thought Stalin knew the truth, anyway. Secretary of War Stimson had told FDR that Soviet spies most likely had penetrated the American atomic program, and it is improbable that he failed to so inform Truman.

Records of the Potsdam Conference belie the notion that Truman either grew "tougher" after learning of the atomic test or

2. Sino is another term for China.

no longer sought Soviet help against Japan. Quite the opposite was true. He accepted Molotov's proposals on reparations percentages, over British objection. He agreed to a Polish-German boundary farther west than FDR had been willing to concede at Yalta. (The part about waiting for the final peace settlement was a fig leaf: No one believed the Soviets later would permit the disputed area to be given back to the Germans.) Although he refused to recognize existing East European governments, his request merely to have observers present at subsequent elections signaled that he would go along with Polish-style arrangements without being sticky about compliance with the Declaration on Liberated Europe. And he had not changed his mind about Soviet entry into the Pacific war. "I've gotten what I came for," he wrote his wife from Potsdam; "Stalin goes to war with no strings on it. . . . I'll say that we'll end the war a year sooner now and think of the kids that won't be killed."

Secretary of State Byrnes later referred to the Potsdam Conference as "the success that failed." By that, he meant that the agreements reached there were sound enough, provided both sides had carried them out in good faith. At the time, Truman had reason to be pleased with what had been done, although his confidence in being able to "deal" with Stalin had been somewhat shaken. Several times during the conference, he had put forward a pet scheme of his to internationalize certain European waterways to reduce national rivalries. Stalin not only refused to discuss the plan but objected even to mentioning in the official report that Truman had brought it up. On the last day, the president made a final appeal: "Marshal Stalin, I have accepted a number of compromises during this conference to conform with your views, and I make a personal request now that you yield on this point." Without waiting for a translation, Stalin burst out, "Nyet," then in English, "No, I say no!" Flushing in anger, Truman turned to his aides and said, "I cannot understand that man."

Events moved quickly after the conference ended. The atomic bomb was dropped on Hiroshima [August 6] while Truman was still at sea, and Japan made its first peace overture shortly after he arrived in Washington. The behavior of the Soviets during these days was troublesome. Their declaration of war against Japan on August 8 obviously constituted an effort to get in on the kill because Stalin had said their forces would not be ready until later. This was understandable, but their delay in endorsing the proposed Allied reply to Japan's offer made it appear that they were trying to prolong the war. Every day the fighting continued, they were seizing more territory in Manchuria and strengthening their claim to assume a part in administering Japan, which Truman was determined to prevent.

The president remained optimistic in spite of these aggravations. Before and during Potsdam, he had referred to Stalin as a "horse trader." When selling, a horse trader first demands an absurdly high price without expecting it to be met. He then appears "reasonable" as he lowers the figure during subsequent negotiations, but he still hopes to get more than the horse is worth. Truman said as much of Stalin at Potsdam when an adviser expressed alarm at how much the Soviet leader was asking for. He replied that a good deal of what the Soviets were claiming was "bluff" and went on to explain what he thought their "real claims were confined to." He maintained that attitude at war's end. Well after Japan's surrender, he told an American official that "it was inevitable that we should have real difficulties but we should not take them too seriously." They could be resolved "amicably if we gave ourselves enough time." Unfortunately for humanity, his prediction proved untrue.

THE UNITED STATES DECIDES TO DROP THE ATOMIC BOMB

DONALD KAGAN

The development of the atomic bomb started in 1939, when the process of fusion was discovered. In 1942 the Manhattan Project began. Led by physicist J. Robert Oppenheimer in Los Alamos, New Mexico, it was an effort to design and build the first atomic bombs. On July 21, 1945, an atomic bomb was successfully tested in New Mexico. Four days later, President Harry S. Truman approved using atomic bombs on Japan. The first of these bombs fell on Hiroshima on August 6, while the second hit Nagasaki on August 9.

The decision to drop the atomic bomb was perhaps the most debated of Truman's presidency. Donald Kagan argues in the following essay that Japan would not have surrendered during World War II if the United States had not dropped the atomic bombs. According to Kagan, the military leaders of Japan were prepared to continue fighting and were supported in those efforts by the Japanese government. He writes that Truman could not seek anything other than the unconditional surrender of Japan and that it was the decision to drop the bombs that led to Emperor Hirohito's agreeing to surrender. Kagan is the Hillhouse Professor of History and Classics at Yale University and the author of *On the Origins of War and the Preservation of Peace*.

Donald Kagan, "Why America Dropped the Bomb," *Commentary*, September 1995, pp. 17, 20–22. Reproduced by permission of the publisher and the author.

On August 6, 1945 the American war plane *Enola Gay* dropped an atomic bomb on Hiroshima, killing between 70,000 and 100,000 Japanese. Three days later another atomic device was exploded over Nagasaki. Within a few days Japan surrendered, and the terrible struggle that we call World War II was over.

At the time, the American people cheered the bombings without restraint, and for the simplest of reasons. As the literary historian Paul Fussell, then a combat soldier expecting to take part in the anticipated invasion of Japan, would later recall:

> We learned to our astonishment that we would not be obliged in a few months to rush up the beaches near Tokyo assault-firing while being machine-gunned, mortared, and shelled, and for all the practiced phlegm of our tough facades we broke down and cried with relief and joy. We were going to live.

At that moment, few if any Americans doubted that the purpose of this first use of atomic bombs was to bring the war to the swiftest possible end, and thereby to avert American casualties.

THE RISE OF THE REVISIONISTS

But the moment was short-lived. As early as 1946, challenges to the dominant opinion appeared and soon multiplied. To a large extent, the early revisionists—prominent among them such figures as Norman Cousins, P.M.S. Blackett, Carl Marzani, and the historians William Appleman Williams and D.F. Fleming—were influenced by the emerging cold war, whose origins, for the most part, they attributed to American policy under President Truman. As one exemplar of the new revisionist movement put it:

> The bomb was dropped primarily for its effect not on Japan but on the Soviet Union. One, to force a Japanese surrender before the USSR came into the Far Eastern war, and two, to show under war conditions the power of the bomb. Only in this way could a policy of intimidation [of the Soviet Union] be successful.

Another phrased the same purpose in different words:

> The United States dropped the bomb to end the war against Japan and thereby stop the Russians in Asia, and to give them sober pause in Eastern Europe. . . .

JAPAN WOULD NOT HAVE SURRENDERED

[One] argument that the dropping of the bomb was unnecessary goes as follows. The Japanese had already been defeated, and it was only a brief matter of time before continued conventional bombing and shortages caused by the naval blockade would have made them see reason. They were, in fact, already sending out peace feelers in the hope of ending the war. If the Americans had been more forthcoming, willing to abandon their demand for unconditional surrender and to promise that Japan could retain its emperor, peace could have come without either an invasion *or* the use of the bomb.

This particular case rests in large part on a quite rational evaluation of the condition of Japan and its dismal military prospects in the spring of 1945, and on the evidence that Japanese officials were indeed discussing the possibility of a negotiated peace, using the Soviets as intermediaries. But neither of these lines of argument proves the point; nor do both of them taken together.

Even the most diehard military leaders of Japan knew perfectly well how grim their objective situation was. But this did not deter them from continuing the war, as the most reputable study of the Japanese side of the story makes clear. Although they did not expect a smashing and glorious triumph, they were confident of at least winning an operational victory "in the decisive battle for the homeland." Since *any* negotiated peace would be considered a surrender which would split the nation apart, Japan's militarists wanted to put it off as long as possible, and to enter negotiations only on the heels of a victory.

Some thought an American invasion could be repelled. Most hoped to inflict enough damage to make the invaders regroup. Others were even more determined; they "felt that it would be far better to die fighting in battle than to seek an ignominious survival by surrendering the nation and acknowledging defeat."

Premier Kantaro Suzuki supported the army's plan, and was content to prosecute the war with every means at his disposal— for that, after all, was "the way of the warrior and the path of the patriot." At a conference on June 8, 1945, in the presence of the emperor, the Japanese government formally affirmed its policy: "The nation would fight to the bitter end."

In spite of that, some Japanese officials did try to end the war by diplomatic negotiation before it was too late. Early efforts had been undertaken by minor military officials, who approached American Office of Strategic Services (OSS) officers in Switzerland in April; but they were given no support from Tokyo. In July, some members of the Japanese government thought they could enlist the help of the Soviet Union in negotiating a peace that would not require a surrender or the occupation of the home islands. It is hard to understand why they thought the USSR would want to help a state it disliked and whose territory it coveted, especially when Japanese prospects were at their nadir; but such indeed was their hope.

The officials sent their proposals to Naotake Sato, the Japanese ambassador in Moscow. Their messages, and Sato's responses, were intercepted and must have influenced American plans considerably.

Sato warned his interlocutors in Tokyo that there was no chance of Soviet cooperation. An entry in the diary of Secretary of the Navy James V. Forrestal for July 15, 1945, reports "the gist of [Sato's] final message . . . Japan was thoroughly and completely defeated and . . . the only course open was quick and definite action recognizing such fact." Sato repeated this advice more than once, but the response from Tokyo was that the war must continue.

THE NEED FOR UNCONDITIONAL SURRENDER

Revisionists and others have argued that the United States could have paved the way by dropping the demand for unconditional surrender, and especially that the U.S. should have indicated the emperor would be retained. But intercepts clearly revealed (according to Gerhard Weinberg in *A World at Arms*) that "the Japanese government would not accept the concept of unconditional surrender even if the institution of the imperial house were preserved." And then there were the intercepts of military messages, which led to the same conclusion—namely, as Edward J. Drea writes, that "the Japanese civil authorities might be considering peace, but Japan's military leaders, who American decision-makers believed had total control of the nation, were preparing for war to the knife."

The demand for unconditional surrender had in any case been asserted by [Franklin D.] Roosevelt and had become a national rallying cry. [Harry S.] Truman could not lightly abandon it, nor is there reason to think that he wanted to. Both he and Roosevelt had clear memories of World War I and how its unsatisfactory conclusion had helped bring on World War II. In the former conflict, the Germans had not surrendered unconditionally; their land had not been occupied; they had not been made to accept the fact of their defeat in battle. Demagogues like Hitler had made use of this opportunity to claim that Germany had not lost but had been "stabbed in the back" by internal traitors like the socialists and the Jews, a technique that made it easier to rouse the Germans for a second great effort. In 1944, Roosevelt said that "practically all Germans deny the fact that they surrendered during the last war, but this time they are going to know it. And so are the Japs."

In the event, Truman did allow the Japanese to keep their emperor. Why did he not announce that intention in advance, to make surrender easier? Some members of the administration thought he should do so, but most feared that any advance concession would be taken as a sign of weakness, and encourage the Japanese bitter-enders in their hope that they could win a more favorable peace by holding out. And there were also those who were opposed to any policy that would leave the emperor in place. These, as it happens, were among the more liberal members of the administration, men like Dean Acheson and Archibald MacLeish. Their opposition was grounded in the belief that, as MacLeish put it, "the throne [was] an anachronistic, feudal institution, perfectly suited to the manipulation and use of anachronistic, feudal-minded groups within the country." It is also worth pointing out, as did the State Department's Soviet expert, Charles Bohlen, that a concession with regard to the emperor, as well as negotiations in response to the so-called peace feelers on any basis other than unconditional surrender, might well have been seen by the Soviets as a violation of commitments made at Yalta and as an effort to end the war before the Soviet Union could enter it.

What if the U.S. had issued a public warning that it had the atomic bomb, and described its fearful qualities? Or warned the Japanese of the imminent entry of the Soviet Union into the fighting? Or, best of all, combined both warnings with a promise that Japan could keep its emperor? Again, there are no grounds for believing that any or all of these steps would have made a difference to the determined military clique that was making Japan's decisions.

Even after the atomic bomb had exploded at Hiroshima on August 6, the Japanese refused to yield. An American announcement clarified the nature of the weapon that had done the damage, and warned that Japan could expect more of the same if it did not surrender. Still, the military held to its policy of resistance and insisted on a delay until a response was received to the latest Japanese approach to the Soviet Union. The answer came on August 8, when the Soviets declared war and sent a large army against Japanese forces in Manchuria.

WHY JAPAN FINALLY SURRENDERED

The foolishness of looking to the Soviets was now inescapably clear, but still Japan's leaders took no steps to end the fighting. The Minister of War, General Korechika Anami, went so far as to deny that Hiroshima had been struck by an atomic bomb. Others insisted that the U.S. had used its only bomb there, or that world opinion would prevent the Americans from using any others they might have. Then on August 9 the second atomic bomb fell on Nagasaki, again doing terrible damage.

The Nagasaki bomb convinced even Anami that "the Americans appear to have 100 atomic bombs . . . they could drop three per day. The next target might well be Tokyo." Even so, a meeting of the Imperial Council that night failed to achieve a consensus to accept defeat. Anami himself insisted that Japan continue to fight. If the Japanese people "went into the decisive

In an effort to force Japan's surrender, the United States dropped an atomic bomb on Hiroshima, destroying over 60 percent of the city.

battle in the homeland determined to display the full measure of patriotism . . . Japan would be able to avert the crisis facing her." The chief of the army general staff, Yoshijiro Umezu, expressed his confidence in the military's "ability to deal a smashing blow to the enemy," and added that in view of the sacrifices made by the many men who had gladly died for the emperor, "it would be inexcusable to surrender unconditionally." Admiral Soemu Toyoda, chief of the navy's general staff, argued that Japan could now use its full air power, heretofore held in reserve in the homeland. Like Anami, he did not guarantee victory, but asserted that "we do not believe that we will be possibly defeated."

These were the views of Japan's top military leaders *after* the explosion of two atomic bombs and the Soviet attack on Manchuria.

Premier Suzuki and the others who were by now favoring peace knew all this was madness. The Allies would never accept the military's conditions—restrictions on the extent of Japanese disarmament, on the occupation of Japan, and on trials of Japanese leaders for war crimes—and the continuation of warfare would be a disaster for the Japanese people. To break the deadlock he took the extraordinary step of asking the emperor to make the decision. (Normally no proposal was put to the emperor until it had achieved the unanimous approval of the Imperial Council.) At 2 A.M. on August 10, Emperor Hirohito responded to the premier's request by giving his sanction to the acceptance of the Allied terms. The Japanese reply included the proviso that the emperor be retained.

There was still disagreement within the American government on this subject. Public opinion was very hostile to the retention of the emperor, and in particular, as Gerhard Weinberg has written, "the articulate organizations of the American Left" resisted any concessions and "urged the dropping of additional atomic bombs instead." At last, the U.S. devised compromise language that accepted the imperial system by implication, while providing that the Japanese people could establish their own form of government.

Although the Japanese leaders found this acceptable, that was not the end of the matter. Opponents of peace tried to reverse the decision by a *coup d'état*. They might have succeeded had General Anami supported them, but he was unwilling to defy the emperor's orders. He solved his dilemma by committing suicide, and the plot failed. Had it succeeded, the war would have continued to a bloody end, with Japan under the brutal rule of a fanatical military clique. Some idea of the thinking of this faction is provided by an intercept of an August 15 message to Tokyo from the commander of Japan's army in China:

> Such a disgrace as the surrender of several million troops without fighting is not paralleled in the world's military history, and it is absolutely impossible to submit to the unconditional surrender of a million picked troops in perfectly healthy shape. . . .

It was the emperor, then, who was decisive in causing Japan to surrender. What caused him to act in so remarkable a way? He was moved by the bomb—and by the Soviet declaration of war. (That declaration, scheduled for August 15, was itself hastened by the use of the bomb, and moved up to August 8.) But statements by the emperor and premier show clearly that they viewed the Soviet invasion as only another wartime setback. It was the bomb that changed the situation entirely.

CHRONOLOGY

1920

January 2: In the "Palmer Raids," Attorney General A. Mitchell Palmer sends federal agents to round up and deport thousands of suspected Communists, although most have not committed any crimes.

January 16: The Eighteenth Amendment, which bans the manufacture, sale, and transport of intoxicating liquors in the United States, takes effect; this marks the beginning of Prohibition.

May 5: Nicola Sacco and Bartolomeo Vanzetti are arrested in Massachusetts on murder charges.

August 26: The Nineteenth Amendment, which gives American women the right to vote, is ratified.

November 2: Warren G. Harding is elected president.

F. Scott Fitzgerald's *This Side of Paradise* and Sinclair Lewis's *Main Street* are published.

1921

March 4: Harding is sworn in as president.

May 19: Congress cuts foreign immigration by 97 percent.

July 14: Sacco and Vanzetti are convicted of murder.

Rudolph Valentino stars in *The Sheik*; Charlie Chaplin stars in *The Kid*.

1922

May 30: The Lincoln Memorial is dedicated.

T.S. Eliot's *The Waste Land*, Lewis's *Babbitt*, Fitzgerald's *The Beautiful and the Damned*, and Claude McKay's *Harlem Shadows* are published.

1923

March 23: Henry R. Luce and Briton Hadden publish the first issue of *Time* magazine.

August 2: President Harding dies of a heart attack and is succeeded by Calvin Coolidge.

December 6: Calvin Coolidge gives the first official presidential message on radio.

1924

June 30: Following a congressional investigation, former Interior Secretary Albert B. Fall and others are indicted for their role in the Teapot Dome scandal.

November 4: Calvin Coolidge wins the presidential election.

Clarence Darrow successfully defends Nathan Leopold and Richard Loeb, who had admitted to kidnapping and murdering fourteen-year-old Bobby Franks, convincing the jury to find them mentally ill and saving them from the death penalty.

1925

January 5: In Wyoming, Nellie Tayloe Ross becomes the first female governor in the United States when she completes her deceased husband's term.

July 10–21: John T. Scopes is put on trial and convicted in Dayton, Tennessee, for teaching evolution.

July 26: William Jennings Bryan, the famed lecturer and political leader who was an associate prosecutor in the Scopes trial, dies.

August 8: More than thirty thousand members of the Ku Klux Klan march in Washington, D.C.

Fitzgerald publishes *The Great Gatsby*.

1926

May 9: Admiral Richard Byrd and Floyd Bennett fly to the South Pole.

August 6: Gertrude Enderle swims across the English Channel, the first woman to do so.

August 23: Rudolph Valentino dies.

September 23: Gene Tunney defeats Jack Dempsey in a heavyweight fight.

Ernest Hemingway publishes *The Sun Also Rises*; Langston Hughes publishes *The Weary Blues*.

1927

February 23: Congress creates the Federal Communications Commission to regulate the radio industry.

May 16: The first Oscars ceremony is held.

May 20–21: In a 33½-hour flight, Charles A. Lindbergh becomes the first person to successfully fly solo across the Atlantic, from New York to Paris.

August 23: Sacco and Vanzetti are executed.

September 22: Tunney defeats Dempsey in a rematch in a fight known as "The Battle of the Long Count."

September 27: Babe Ruth hits his sixtieth home run, setting a record that would stand until 1961.

October 6: The first "talkie," *The Jazz Singer*, premieres.

Sinclair Lewis publishes *Elmer Gantry*.

1928

November 6: Herbert Hoover is elected president.

November 18: The first cartoon with sound, *Steamboat Willie*, is released.

McKay publishes *Home to Harlem*.

1929

February 14: Seven of Al Capone's rivals, all members of George "Bugs" Moran's gang, are killed in the St. Valentine's Day Massacre.

October 24: Thirteen million shares of stock change hands, leading to sharp drops in stock prices, on "Black Thursday."

October 29: On "Black Tuesday," Wall Street suffers the worst day in its history; 16 million shares are sold and investors lose $14 billion.

Albert B. Fall is convicted for his role in Teapot Dome. Hemingway's *A Farewell to Arms* and William Faulkner's *The Sound and the Fury* are published.

1930

June: Hoover signs the Smoot-Hawley Tariff Act, which raises U.S. custom duties by an average of 20 percent.

October: Hoover forms the President's Emergency Committee for Employment.

1931

May 1: Hoover dedicates what is then the world's tallest building, the Empire State Building.

Charlie Chaplin stars in *City Lights*.

1932

March 1: Lindbergh's twenty-month-old son is kidnapped.

June: More than 20,000 veterans and their families march on Washington, D.C., demanding that they be paid their World War I bonuses; in response, Hoover calls on General Douglas MacArthur to drive the marchers out of the capital.

July 1: Justice Department establishes the U.S. Bureau of Investigation, which in 1935 is renamed the Federal Bureau of Investigation.

July 21: Hoover signs the Emergency Relief and Construction Act.

November 8: Franklin Delano Roosevelt defeats Hoover in the presidential election.

1933

January 30: Adolf Hitler becomes Germany's chancellor.

March 4: Roosevelt delivers his inaugural address, beginning the first hundred days of the New Deal.

March 9: Congress passes the Emergency Banking Relief Act.

March 12: Roosevelt delivers his first Fireside Chat.

March 31: The Civilian Conservation Corps, which provides 250,000 jobs for men between the ages of eighteen and twenty-five, is established.

May 12: Congress passes the Agricultural Adjustment Act and establishes the Federal Emergency Relief Administration.

May 18: Congress creates the Tennessee Valley Authority, which establishes flood control, builds dams, and generates and sells electricity.

May 27: Congress passes the Federal Securities Act.

June 6: The Securities and Exchange Commission is created.

June 16: Congress establishes the National Industrial Recovery Act; the Federal Deposit Insurance Corporation is created.

December 5: Prohibition is repealed.

1934

August 19: Hitler becomes führer of Germany.

During the summer, hundreds of thousands of residents of Oklahoma, Texas, Arkansas, and other Dust Bowl states migrate, largely to California and the Pacific Northwest. Fitzgerald's *Tender Is the Night* and Langston Hughes's *The Ways of White Folks* are published.

1935

May 6: Roosevelt creates the Works Progress Administration.

June 2: Babe Ruth retires with 714 home runs.

July 5: Congress establishes the National Labor Relations Act, or Wagner Act.

August 13: The first Neutrality Act, which prohibits loans to belligerent parties but encourages noninvolvement in foreign affairs, is passed.

August 14: Congress passes the Social Security Act.

November 9: Labor leaders create the Committee for Industrial Organization.

1936

January 13: The Supreme Court declares the Agricultural Adjustment Act unconstitutional.

April 3: Bruno Hauptmann is executed for the kidnapping and murder of Charles A. Lindbergh Jr., the aviator's son.

August: Jesse Owens wins four gold medals in the Summer Olympics, held in Berlin.

November 3: Roosevelt is reelected president.

December 28: General Motors employees begin a sit-down strike at a body plant in Cleveland, which lasts forty-four days.

1937

February 5: Roosevelt submits a proposal to increase the number of Supreme Court justices, an idea labeled "court-packing" by his opponents.

May 1: Roosevelt signs the second Neutrality Act, which prohibits arms and loans to belligerent nations.

May 6: The zeppelin *Hindenburg* crashes.

July 22: Roosevelt abandons his Supreme Court proposal.

The first feature-length cartoon, *Snow White and the Seven Dwarfs*, is released. John Steinbeck publishes *Of Mice and Men*; Zora Neale Hurston publishes *Their Eyes Were Watching God*.

1938

June 22: Joe Louis defeats Max Schmeling in a heavyweight bout.

June 25: Congress passes the Fair Labor Standards Act, which limits work hours and establishes a national minimum wage.

1939

April 30: New York Yankee first baseman Lou Gehrig sits out a game, ending his 2,130 consecutive game streak. He is later diagnosed with amyotrophic lateral sclerosis and dies on June 2, 1941.

May 27: The *St. Louis*, a ship carrying almost a thousand Jewish refugees who are fleeing from the Nazis, arrives in Cuba, and all but twenty-two are refused admittance to Cuba and the United States, with the rest sent back to Europe.

August 23: Hitler and Soviet leader Joseph Stalin sign a non-aggression pact.

September 1: Germany attacks Poland, setting off World War II.

September 3: England, France, New Zealand, and Australia declare war on Germany.

September 5: Roosevelt declares America's neutrality.

November 4: Roosevelt signs a revised version of the Neutrality Act that lifts the arms embargo.

John Steinbeck publishes *The Grapes of Wrath*. The film versions of *The Wizard of Oz* and *Gone with the Wind* are released.

1940

May 10: Germany invades Belgium, France, Luxembourg, and the Netherlands, while Winston Churchill becomes Great Britain's prime minister.

June 11: Italy declares war on England and France.

June 13: Roosevelt signs a $1.3 billion defense bill.

June 14: Paris falls to Germany.

June 22: France surrenders to Germany.

July 10: The Battle of Britain begins as the German Luftwaffe drops thousands of bombs on English cities.

September 5: The America First Committee is officially launched.

September 15: The Battle of Britain ends, though blitzing of London continues into May 1941.

September 27: Japan joins the Axis.

November 5: Roosevelt is reelected president for an unprecedented third term.

December 17: Roosevelt submits a lend-lease proposal to Congress. The proposal calls for the United States to send supplies to Great Britain and any other nation facing Nazi aggression.

December 21: F. Scott Fitzgerald dies.

Hemingway publishes *For Whom the Bell Tolls*.

1941

January 6: Roosevelt delivers his Four Freedoms speech.

March 11: The Lend-Lease Act becomes law in the United States, and the nation begins to supply war materials to the Allies.

May 10–11: Nazi bombers damage Westminster Abbey, Big Ben, and the House of Commons.

May 15: New York Yankee Joe DiMaggio begins his fifty-six game hitting streak.

June 22: Germany invades the Soviet Union.

July 24–26: The United States stops trading with Japan.

August 9–12: Roosevelt and Churchill meet off the coast of Newfoundland, Canada, and write the Atlantic Charter, under which the Allied nations promise to support the right of nations to choose how they wish to be governed.

September 1: Nazis order all Jews under their control to wear yellow stars.

October 17: Hideki Tojo becomes Japan's prime minister.

December 7: Japan bombs Pearl Harbor and declares war on the United States and Great Britain.

December 8: The United States and Britain declare war on Japan.

December 11: Germany and Italy declare war on the United States.

Ted Williams hits .406 for the Boston Red Sox.

1942

January 20: Nazi officials meet to plan the "Final Solution," which was their effort to kill all of Europe's Jews.

January 26: American troops arrive in Great Britain.

February 19: Executive Order 9066 orders the internment of all Japanese Americans.

April: Japanese Americans living in the United States are sent to relocation centers.

April 9: American troops surrender to Japanese on the Bataan Peninsula, Philippines.

May 15: The Women's Army Corps is created.

May 16: After Corregidor falls to the Japanese, all American forces in the Philippines surrender.

June 4–6: The United States cripples the Japanese fleet in the Battle of Midway.

June 24: General Dwight D. Eisenhower takes command of all American troops in Europe.

September 14: German troops lay siege to the Soviet city of Stalingrad, but are met with stiff resistance when they reach the center of the city eight days later.

November 8: The United States invades North Africa. *Casablanca* is released.

1943

January 27: United States launches its first bombing attack on Germany.
February 2: Germans suffer major defeat at Stalingrad.
May 13: German and Italian troops surrender in North Africa.
July 25–26: Italian dictator Benito Mussolini is arrested and his Fascist government falls.
September 8: Italy surrenders.
October 13: Italy declares war on Germany.

1944

January 16: Eisenhower is named supreme commander of Allied forces in Europe.
January 27: Soviets end a nine-hundred-day siege by defeating the Germans at Leningrad.
June 6 (D day): Allies launch the formal liberation of Western Europe by landing on the beaches of Normandy, France.
June 15: United States bombs Tokyo.
August 21–29: Allied representatives meet in Washington, D.C., to discuss forming the United Nations.
August 25: Allies liberate Paris.
October 23–26: An American fleet annihilates a Japanese naval fleet in the Battle of Leyte Gulf, the largest naval battle of the war.
November 6: Roosevelt is elected to a fourth term.
December 16–27: The Battle of the Bulge, the war's last major German offensive, is fought in Ardennes.

1945

January 26: Soviet troops liberate the Auschwitz concentration camp.
February 4–11: Roosevelt, Churchill, and Joseph Stalin meet at Yalta and agree to divide Germany into separate zones that would be controlled by Allied forces.
February 13–14: Allies firebomb and destroy the German city of Dresden.
March 16: In a battle that costs four thousand American lives, American forces take the island of Iwo Jima.

April 12: Roosevelt dies in Warm Springs, Georgia, and is succeeded by Harry Truman; the Allies liberate the Bergen-
Belsen and Buchenwald concentration camps.

April 23: The Soviets enter Berlin.

April 28: Mussolini is captured and hung.

April 29: American troops liberate the Dachau concentration
camp.

April 30: Soviets reach the Reichstag (parliament building) in
Berlin; Hitler commits suicide in his bunker.

May 7: Germany surrenders to the Allies.

May 8: V-E (Victory in Europe) Day celebrates the conclusion of
the European war.

July 1: American, British, and French troops occupy Berlin.

July 16: The first atomic bomb test is conducted in New Mexico.

July 17–August 2: Truman, Churchill, and Stalin meet at Potsdam to demand Japan's unconditional surrender and plan
for peace in Europe.

August 6: Americans drop an atomic bomb on Hiroshima,
Japan.

August 8: The Soviet Union declares war on Japan.

August 9: Americans drop an atomic bomb on Nagasaki, Japan.

August 14: Japan surrenders unconditionally.

August 15: V-J (Victory over Japan) Day celebrates Japan's surrender.

September 2: World War II officially ends when Japan signs final surrender terms on the American battleship *Missouri*.

October 24: The United Nations is created.

FOR FURTHER RESEARCH

OVERVIEWS OF THE ERA

Sean Dennis Cashman, *America in the Twenties and Thirties: The Olympian Age of Franklin Delano Roosevelt*. New York: New York University Press, 1989.

Robert A. Divine, ed., *The Age of Insecurity: America, 1920–1945*. Reading, MA: Addison-Wesley, 1968.

Herman E. Krooss, *Executive Opinion: What Business Leaders Said and Thought on Economic Issues, 1920s–1960s*. Garden City, NY: Doubleday, 1970.

Isabel Leighton, ed., *The Aspirin Age, 1919–1941*. New York: Simon and Schuster, 1949.

Michael E. Parrish, *Anxious Decades: America in Prosperity and Depression, 1920–1941*. New York: W.W. Norton, 1992.

Cabell Phillips, *From the Crash to the Blitz: 1929–1939*. New York: Fordham University Press, 2000.

William Preston Jr., *Aliens and Dissenters: Federal Suppression of Radicals, 1903–1933*. Urbana: University of Illinois Press, 1994.

THE 1920S

Frederick Lewis Allen, *Only Yesterday: An Informal History of the 1920s*. New York: John Wiley and Sons, 1997.

Herbert Asbury, *The Great Illusion: An Informal History of Prohibition*. New York: Greenwood Press, 1950.

Fon W. Boardman Jr., *America and the Jazz Age: A History of the 1920s*. New York: Henry Z. Walck, 1968.

Dorothy M. Brown, *Setting a Course: American Women in the 1920s*. Boston: Twayne, 1987.

Paul K. Conkin, *When All the Gods Trembled: Darwinism, Scopes, and American Intellectuals*. Lanham, MD: Rowman and Littlefield, 1998.

Sarah Jane Deutsch, *From Ballots to Breadlines: American Women, 1920–1940*. New York: Oxford University Press, 1994.

Lynn Dumenil, *The Modern Temper: American Culture and Society in the 1920s*. New York: Hill and Wang, 1995.

Robert H. Ferrell, *The Presidency of Calvin Coolidge*. Lawrence: University Press of Kansas, 1998.

Felix Frankfurter, *The Case of Sacco and Vanzetti: A Critical Analysis for Lawyers and Laymen*. Boston: Little, Brown, 1927.

David J. Goldberg, *Discontented America: The United States in the 1920s*. Baltimore: Johns Hopkins University Press, 1999.

John Kobler, *Ardent Spirits: The Rise and Fall of Prohibition*. New York: G.P. Putnam's Sons, 1973.

Charles A. Lindbergh, *We*. New York: G.P. Putnam's Sons, 1955.

Bettina Miller, ed., *From Flappers to Flivers*. Glendale, WI: Reminisce Books, 1995.

Ethan Mordden, *That Jazz!: An Idiosyncratic Social History of the American Twenties*. New York: G.P. Putnam's Sons, 1978.

Leonard Mosley, *Lindbergh: A Biography*. Garden City, NY: Doubleday, 1976.

George E. Mowry, ed., *The Twenties: Fords, Flappers, and Fanatics*. Englewood Cliffs, NJ: Prentice-Hall, 1963.

Robert K. Murray, *The Harding Era: Warren G. Harding and His Administration*. Minneapolis: University of Minnesota Press, 1969.

———, *Red Scare: A Study in National Hysteria, 1919–1920*. Minneapolis: University of Minnesota Press, 1955.

Burl Noggle, *Teapot Dome: Oil and Politics in the 1920s*. Baton Rouge: Louisiana State University Press, 1962.

Arnold S. Rice, *The Ku Klux Klan in American Politics*. Washington, DC: Public Affairs Press, 1962.

John T. Scopes and James Presley, *Center of the Storm: Memoirs of John T. Scopes*. New York: Holt, Rinehart, and Winston, 1967.

Andrew Sinclair, *Prohibition: The Era of Excess*. Boston: Atlantic, 1962.

THE STOCK MARKET CRASH AND THE GREAT DEPRESSION

John A. Garraty, *The Great Depression*. San Diego: Harcourt Brace Jovanovich, 1986.

James Goodman, *Stories of Scottsboro*. New York: Vintage Books, 1995.

Thomas E. Hall and J. David Ferguson, *The Great Depression: An International Disaster of Perverse Economic Policies*. Ann Arbor: University of Michigan Press, 1998.

William K. Klingaman, *1929: The Year of the Great Crash*. New York: Harper and Row, 1989.

Donald J. Lisio, *The President and Protest: Hoover, Conspiracy, and the Bonus Riot*. Columbia: University of Missouri Press, 1974.

Brad D. Lookingbill, *Dust Bowl, USA: Depression America and the Ecological Imagination, 1929–1941*. Athens: Ohio University Press, 2001.

Ann Marie Low, *Dust Bowl Diary*. Lincoln: University of Nebraska Press, 1984.

Gypsy Moon, *Done and Been: Steel Rail Chronicles of American Hobos*. Bloomington: Indiana University Press, 1996.

Albert U. Romasco, *The Poverty of Abundance: Hoover, the Nation, the Depression*. New York: Oxford University Press, 1965.

Gene Smith, *The Shattered Dream: Herbert Hoover and the Great Depression*. New York: Morrow, 1970.

Harvey Swados, ed., *The American Writer and the Great Depression*. Indianapolis: Bobbs-Merrill, 1966.

Studs Terkel, *Hard Times: An Oral History of the Great Depression*. New York: Pantheon Books, 1970.

Gordon Thomas and Max Morgan-Witts, *The Day the Bubble Burst*. Garden City, NY: Doubleday, 1979.

T.H. Watkins, *The Great Depression: America in the 1930s*. Boston: Little, Brown, 1993.

ROOSEVELT'S PRESIDENCY AND THE NEW DEAL

Russell D. Buhite and David W. Levy, eds., *FDR's Fireside Chats*. Norman: University of Oklahoma Press, 1992.

Robert Dallek, *Franklin D. Roosevelt and American Foreign Policy, 1932–1945*. New York: Oxford University Press, 1981.

Kenneth S. Davis, *FDR, into the Storm 1937–1940: A History*. New York: Random House, 1993.

———, *FDR, the New Deal Years, 1933–1937*. New York: Random House, 1986.

Joseph P. Lash, *Dealers and Dreamers: A New Look at the New Deal*. New York: Doubleday, 1988.

Katie Louchheim, ed., *The Making of the New Deal: The Insiders Speak*. Cambridge, MA: Harvard University Press, 1983.

Raymond Moley, *After Seven Years*. Lincoln: University of Nebraska Press, 1971.

Edgar Eugene Robinson, *The Roosevelt Leadership, 1933–1945*. Philadelphia: J.B. Lippincott, 1955.

WORLD WAR II

Thomas B. Allen and Norman Polmar, *Code-Name Downfall: The Secret Plan to Invade Japan and Why Truman Dropped the Bomb*. New York: Simon and Schuster, 1995.

Leonard Baker, *Roosevelt and Pearl Harbor*. New York: Macmillan, 1970.

Hanson W. Baldwin, *Great Mistakes of the War*. New York: Harper and Brothers, 1949.

Alan Brinkley, *The End of Reform: New Deal Liberalism in Recession and War*. New York: Alfred A. Knopf, 1995.

Wayne S. Cole, *America First: The Battle Against Intervention, 1940–1941*. Madison: University of Wisconsin Press, 1953.

Roger Daniels, *Prisoners Without Trial: Japanese Americans in World War II*. New York: Hill and Wang, 1993.

Robert A. Divine, *The Illusion of Neutrality*. Chicago: University of Chicago Press, 1962.

Justus D. Doenecke, ed., *In Danger Undaunted: The Anti-Interventionist Movement of 1940–1941 as Revealed in the Papers of the America First Committee*. Stanford, CA: Hoover Institution Press, 1990.

Robert H. Ferrell, *Harry S. Truman and the Modern American Presidency*. Boston: Little, Brown, 1983.

Deborah Gesensway and Mindy Roseman, *Beyond Words: Images from America's Concentration Camps*. Ithaca, NY: Cornell University Press, 1987.

John Keegan, *The Second World War*. New York: Viking, 1989.

Warren F. Kimball, *The Most Unsordid Act: Lend-Lease, 1939–1941*. Baltimore: Johns Hopkins Press, 1969.

Robert James Maddox, *The United States and World War II*. Boulder, CO: Westview Press, 1992.

———, *Weapons for Victory: The Hiroshima Decision, Fifty Years Later*. Columbia: University of Missouri Press, 1995.

Arthur D. Morse, *While Six Million Died: A Chronicle of American Apathy*. New York: Ace, 1967.

Geoffrey Perrett, *Days of Sadness, Years of Triumph: The American People 1939–1945*. New York: Coward, McCann, and Geoghegan, 1973.

Richard Rhodes, *The Making of the Atomic Bomb*. New York: Simon and Schuster, 1986.

Jack Stenbuck, ed., *Typewriter Battalion: Dramatic Frontline Dispatches from World War II*. New York: William Morrow, 1995.

James L. Stokesbury, *A Short History of World War II*. New York: William Morrow, 1980.

A.J.P. Taylor, *The Origins of the Second World War*. New York: Atheneum, 1961.

Nancy Baker Wise and Christy Wise, *A Mouthful of Rivets: Women at Work in World War II*. San Francisco: Jossey-Bass, 1994.

David S. Wyman, *The Abandonment of the Jews: America and the Holocaust, 1941–1945*. New York: Pantheon Books, 1984.

SPORTS AND CULTURE

William J. Baker, *Jesse Owens: An American Life*. New York: Free Press, 1986.

Humphrey Carpenter, *Geniuses Together: American Writers in Paris in the 1920s*. London: Unwin Hyman, 1987.

Mervyn Cooke, *The Chronicle of Jazz*. New York: Abbeville Press, 1998.

Malcolm Cowley and Robert Cowley, *Fitzgerald and the Jazz Age*. New York: Scribner, 1966.

John Dewey, *Philosophy of Education*. Paterson, NJ: Littlefield, Adams, 1958.

Thomas Doherty, *Projections of War: Hollywood, American Culture, and World War II*. New York: Columbia University Press, 1993.

George H. Douglas, *The Early Days of Radio Broadcasting*. Jefferson, NC: McFarland, 1987.

Jack C. Ellis, *A History of Film*. Boston: Allyn and Bacon, 1995.

Ted Gioia, *The History of Jazz*. New York: Oxford University Press, 1997.

William Goldhurst, *F. Scott Fitzgerald and His Contemporaries*. Cleveland: World Publishing, 1963.

Clayton R. Koppes and Gregory D. Black, *Hollywood Goes to War: How Politics, Profits, and Propaganda Shaped World War II Movies*. New York: Free Press, 1987.

William McPheron, *John Steinbeck: From Salinas to Stockholm*. Stanford, CA: Stanford University Libraries, 2000.

Babe Ruth, as told to Bob Considine, *The Babe Ruth Story*. New York: E.P. Dutton, 1963.

Leo Trachtenberg, *The Wonder Team: The True Story of the Incomparable New York Yankees*. Bowling Green, OH: Bowling Green State University Popular Press, 1995.

INDEX